Rewards and Reform

Rewards and Reform

Creating Educational Incentives That Work

Susan H. Fuhrman

Jennifer A. O'Day

Editors

Consortium for Policy Research in Education

and the

Pew Forum on Education Reform

Jossey-Bass Publishers • San Francisco

Substantial discounts on bulk quantities of Jossey-Bass books are available to corporations, professional associations, and other organizations. For details and discount information, contact the special sales department at Jossey-Bass Inc., Publishers (415) 433–1740; Fax (800) 605–2665.

For sales outside the United States, please contact your local Simon & Schuster International office.

 Manufactured in the United States of America on Lyons Falls Pathfinder Tradebook. This paper is acid-free and 100 percent totally chlorine-free.

Library of Congress Cataloging-in-Publication Data

Rewards and reform : creating educational incentives that work / Susan
  H. Fuhrman, Jennifer A. O'Day, editors. — 1st ed.
     p.   cm. — (The Jossey-Bass education series)
  Includes bibliographical references and index.
  ISBN 0–7879–0237–3
  1. Motivation in education—United States.   2. Educational change—
United States.   3. School management and organization—United
States.   4. Education—Standards—United States.   5. Education—
United States—Aims and objectives.   I. Fuhrman, Susan.
II. O'Day, Jennifer A., date.   III. Series.
LB1065.R49 1996
370.15'4—dc20

                                                                    96–3862
                                                                       CIP

FIRST EDITION
HB Printing   10 9 8 7 6 5 4 3 2 1

The Jossey-Bass Education Series

Contents

Preface

This book is an edited volume intended to broaden thinking about incentives in education. It incorporates the perspectives of various disciplines and sectors, addresses incentives targeted at various stakeholders and participants in education, and considers a variety of incentive approaches beyond the monetary rewards commonly referred to in incentive discussions. The intended audience includes policy makers at the national, state, and district levels; teacher educators and other education professionals; reform advocates; and professors of education policy and administration.

At least forty-five states claim to be engaged in setting challenging standards for student learning and coordinating key policies around the standards. The Clinton administration has made this approach, systemic reform, the cornerstone of its Goals 2000 and Elementary and Secondary Education Act (ESEA) programs.

Underlying systemic reform is a belief that a well-conceived and publicly supported system of standards and related reforms speak to some of the most fundamental, intrinsic motivations of everyone involved in the educational enterprise. Standards-based reforms address our desire to promote learning and to see evidence of progress. Because common expectations for student learning should represent societal agreement on important schooling outcomes, standards could bring more meaning and reinforcement to classroom work. In addition, assessments linked to the standards could model expected performance for the students, supply welcome feedback to teachers, and provide a means for legitimate accountability based on school and system improvement toward clear outcome expectations. Criteria for success would be apparent and collectively endorsed; success would therefore be more easily identified and celebrated. Over time, as more and more citizens share the standards and as what it takes to make progress toward them becomes clearer, the motivation to achieve them would grow.

However, although a mature standards-based system could motivate participants as described, we are a long way from such a system today. What can be done now to improve motivation for all concerned to move in the direction of more ambitious teaching and learning? What kinds of policy incentives could be set in place, and what sorts of principles should guide their design and implementation?

Of course, many suggestions and incentive initiatives are already out in the field. For example, some suggest that student employment opportunities and college admission decisions could be linked more closely to school performance. To encourage teachers to take more responsibility for student learning, we could bolster the professional nature of teaching. Approaches might include workplace redesigns that speak to teachers' needs for autonomy and participation; reforms in preservice education and in professional development to give teachers the opportunities and skills to function as collaborative, continuous learners; and professional self-regulatory mechanisms for teacher and school evaluation. Other possibilities include recognition for teaching excellence through mechanisms such as the National Board for Professional Teaching Standards and compensation systems designed to reward knowledge and skill acquisition rather than random credit accumulation.

For schools and systems, incentive design should extend beyond monetary rewards for improvement although those might be part of the package. Many have urged the removal of disincentives to change, like finance formulas, program regulations, or union contract provisions that lock schools into certain staffing ratios and organizational patterns. For example, states could revise formulas based on classroom or teacher units that pose barriers to more flexible class sizes and scheduling. Accounting systems that clarify and permit public understanding of school resource use might be considered, as might governance changes such as choice and charter schools that alter the relationships between providers and consumers.

The purposes of this book are to shed light on the underlying issues surrounding incentives and reform, to develop an agenda for future research, and, where possible, to suggest policy implications. Although the book aims at expanding consideration of incentives in a number of new directions, the chapters are unified by common purposes and a set of common themes, many of which are discussed in the opening chapter.

Overview of the Contents

The book is divided into three parts. Part One, "Incentives and Student Performance," includes chapters by Arthur G. Powell and David K. Cohen. Part Two, "Motivation and School Context," includes chapters by Susan Albers Mohrman and Edward E. Lawler III and Linda Darling-Hammond. Part Three, "Going to Scale," includes chapters by Brian Rowan, Allan Odden, Richard J. Murnane and Frank Levy, and Richard F. Elmore.

Chapter One, "Introduction: Incentives and School Improvement," by Jennifer O'Day, gives an overview of the key issues and themes that cut across the authors' diverse contributions. These include the relationship between incentives for students and incentives for teachers, the complexities of individual motivation and intrinsic and extrinsic rewards, the school as a motivational context, and the need for a systemic approach to incentives development.

In Chapter Two, "Motivating Students to Learn: An American Dilemma," Arthur G. Powell maps out the broad territory of student motivation and incentives with a particular emphasis on cultural factors. He begins by arguing that motivation to learn is a unique American dilemma because of the unique American commitments to universal secondary and mass postsecondary schooling, and to decentralized local control as the primary education governance mechanism. He maintains that compulsory schooling has produced a system where participation for as long as possible is valued more than demonstrable achievement and that localism guarantees that there is no clearly understood conception about what students should know and thus be motivated to learn. Compounding the problem is a lack of community support. Powell argues that businesses do not provide schools or students with information on what curricula, grades, scores, or references are required for various kinds of entry-level jobs, and cognitive achievement is not widely valued in American society.

Powell asserts that the answer to the problem of student motivation is to create incentives that are really important in the long run, such as access to valued vocations and valued higher education institutions. He points out that this system was once in place, from 1900 to 1941, in the form of the College Entrance Examination Board, which controlled admission to the most desirable

American colleges. But after the war, democratizing influences led to college selection based on talent rather than preparation, and the College Board's system of common standards collapsed. An exception is the Advanced Placement program, a systemic approach but only for the most able students. Powell argues that AP represents the closest current American approximation of high-stakes, externally assessed, curriculum-driven achievement examinations. Powell concludes by arguing that powerful incentives and disincentives are generated by additional contexts—particularly by the quality of school communities, the quality of families, and how the two interact. He asserts that schools can create incentives to learn by, every day, visibly celebrating and exemplifying the benefits of some focused conception of learning and by developing a limited core curriculum and communicating clearly what it is.

In Chapter Three, David K. Cohen focuses on three broad themes. One is that despite many efforts to institute performance reward schemes there is relatively little reliable knowledge about their operation and effects. He argues that while we know enough to rule out simplistic and punitive schemes we do not know enough to inform choices among more complex and sophisticated alternatives. This creates several problems for the design of schemes that might be both educationally sound and likely to work, which he explores in the chapter. Cohen's second theme is that performance rewards alone cannot solve the problems of weak school performance. Even the best designed scheme would require critical additional elements—including assistance for some failing schools, and measures to reform others that might have to include closing schools or re-assigning staff—to improve performance in the schools that need the most assistance. While such measures would be difficult and expensive, much of the appeal of performance rewards lies in the idea that they would be a relatively simple and cheap solution to a complex and difficult problem. Cohens's third theme is that though performance rewards would require unprecedented clarity about measures of performance and criteria of success, these are matters about which U.S. citizens deeply disagree. Public schools embody many different hopes and purposes and have been the site of many compromises over fundamental social issues; Thus they have accumulated many diverse and often competing purposes. Performance rewards would require that such complex and contrary purposes be replaced with clear criteria of success, but it would not be surprising if such efforts were accompanied by more disputes.

In Chapter Four, "Motivation for School Reform," Susan Albers Mohrman and Edward E. Lawler III examine basic models of employee motivation and the high-involvement organizational approaches that have been found to create conditions where employees are motivated to participate in organizational improvement. They begin with a discussion of expectancy theory, which posits that motivation is a function of two personally held expectations: (1) the extent to which a person believes that his or her effort will lead to success and (2) the extent to which he or she believes that achieving the intended performance will lead to important personal outcomes. They go on to argue that two factors shape expectancies: (1) experiences that have led to success or failure and (2) the organization and its processes and structures. Although organizations cannot change an employee's experiences, Mohrman and Lawler maintain that it is possible to establish new organizational conditions that will enable new expectations to be formed. These conditions include goal-setting, the design of work, and rewards.

To create organizational designs where motivating conditions are in place, Mohrman and Lawler advocate systemwide change and high-involvement management. This framework entails increasing the presence of four key organizational resources: (1) information about performance, strategy, mission, and goals; (2) knowledge and skills that enable employees to understand and contribute to organizational performance; (3) power to make decisions; and (4) rewards. Mohrman and Lawler go on to describe three different organizational design features that can be employed to ensure that these resources are available to all employees: (1) parallel suggestion involvement, which involves employees in solving problems, generating ideas, and making recommendations; (2) job involvement, which entails designing work in ways that will motivate high levels of performance; and (3) organizational involvement, which focuses all employees on the success of the entire organization.

In Chapter Five, "Restructuring Schools for High Performance," Linda Darling-Hammond uses the lens of "high-involvement" management to examine how several extraordinarily successful schools in New York City operate. Darling-Hammond includes a case study of the Central Park East Secondary School to illustrate characteristics of the high-performance schools she describes. The analysis is organized around four aspects of organizational functioning that are commonly identified as central to high-involvement workplaces: the decentralization and reconfiguration of power, knowledge, information, and rewards.

The analysis illustrates how decentralization of these organizational resources and enhanced teacher participation allow schools to redesign education in ways that are significantly more successful for students. In particular, Darling-Hammond links the organization and availability of these features to the intrinsic and extrinsic incentives they provide for both students and teachers. She notes the importance of a small, caring, and supportive school environment, student choice, and involvement of both students and teachers in the design of learning experiences that reflect high standards to the success of these schools.

From the organizational theory perspective, Brian Rowan examines the promises and pitfalls of the current standards-setting movement by speculating about the effects of educational standards on teachers in Chapter Six, "Standards as Incentives for Instructional Reform." His analysis is centered on two questions: (1) What factors control the instructional performances of teachers? and (2) Is there any reason to expect that new educational standards can shape these factors in ways that promote desired instructional practices?

In answer to the first question, Rowan argues that three global factors affect the performance of employees in all kinds of organizations, including schools: (1) an employee's motivation to perform a job, (2) the job-relevant skills or abilities that the employee brings to the job, and (3) the situation in which the employee performs the job. In answer to the second question, Rowan describes a set of conditions that he believes must be present if standards-based management is to have an impact on teaching performance. He maintains that standards must (1) have value to teachers either personally or through consequences for students, pay, cultural controls, or the congruence of values; (2) be based on an empirically valid theory of employee performance that should be systemic and take in the complex processes by which motivation, ability, and situational constraints interact to produce teaching outcomes; and (3) overcome various problems of measurement since employees seek to score well on measured criteria even if these criteria are not valid. Rowan concludes with a discussion of whether or not it is possible to create a coherent system of educational standards in the United States given the nation's tradition of decentralized educational governance and diverse educational preferences.

In Chapter Seven, "Incentives, School Organization, and Teacher Compensation," Allan Odden provides a historical overview of teacher compensation systems and analyzes the attempts throughout the twentieth century to change teacher pay. He argues that these attempts have nearly all failed because they treated compensation as a set of practices that were relatively independent of the larger educational context, and organizations and compensation are inextricably linked. Odden recognizes that the compensation structure cannot be the lead instrument for organizational change. Nonetheless, he contends, compensation can be designed as an incentive that reinforces the goals, norms, values, human resources policies, and workers' roles in any organizational change that a system could adopt.

He maintains that current education reforms, and higher-performing school organizations, require individuals who have an array of curriculum and instructional skills far beyond those attained for initial licensure, and that they also require individuals with skills to engage in a variety of nonteaching functional and managerial tasks in schools. He argues that these goals could be reinforced with a salary schedule that provided pay increases on the basis of skills, knowledge, and expertise—as well as bonuses for school and within-school team performance improvements—rather than years of experience and educational units. Although Odden admits that developing such a system would be problematic, he argues that it is appropriate to consider the formal, extrinsic incentive in the education system—compensation—and to reconstitute it so that it reinforces the broader changes in education.

In Chapter Eight, "Teaching to New Standards," Richard J. Murnane and Frank Levy give a detailed account of Vermont's efforts to reform its educational system through the implementation of a portfolio assessment system. They describe the promises and pitfalls of implementing the new system and conclude with lessons they are able to draw out of the Vermont experience. Murnane and Levy argue that any state seeking to monitor the success of schools in teaching students critical skills needs to (1) develop an assessment strategy that is consistent with teachers' sense of effective teaching and learning, (2) couple new assessment strategies with other change designed to improve teaching performance, and (3) give adequate time before demanding results.

In Chapter Nine, "Getting to Scale with Successful Educational Practices," Richard F. Elmore argues that attempts to fundamentally change the stable patterns in the core of schooling are usually unsuccessful on anything more than a small scale. As evidence for his argument, Elmore points to the progressive era and the curriculum reform efforts of the 1950s and 1960s. He contends that though both of these education reform movements had powerful ideas that found their way into tangible materials and practice in a few settings, they failed to achieve widespread change. Elmore attributes this failure to the following: (1) the inadequacy of professional development to help teachers integrate the new ideas into their classrooms, (2) concentrating the reform efforts in single schools with no concrete plans for replication, and (3) insulating the reform movement from public discourse and scrutiny. He also notes the underlying American belief that ambitious teaching is a personal trait rather than a set of learned professional competencies.

To overcome the problems of bringing successful educational practices to scale, Elmore offers four strategies for reform: (1) develop strong external normative structures for practice that set professional and social expectations for what good teaching practice is; (2) develop organizational structures that intensify and focus intrinsic motivation to engage in challenging practice; (3) create intentional processes for reproduction of success; and (4) create structures that promote learning of new practices and incentive systems that support them.

Chapter Ten, "Conclusion: Building a Better System of Incentives," by Susan Fuhrman, serves to weave together the common threads that span the various contributions to this volume. It draws out of the chapters the implications for both policy and practice and discusses the need for further research on incentives.

It is our hope that the chapters in this book will advance understanding about these issues and provide insight into the complexity of getting people motivated for reform.

Acknowledgments

Rewards and Reform: Creating Educational Incentives That Work grew out of a Policy Forum cosponsored by the Consortium for Policy Research in Education (CPRE) and the Pew Forum on Education Reform.[1] Participants included those with expertise in other public and private sector activities as well as individuals from the fields of education policy, practice, and research.

CPRE unites five of the nation's leading research institutions in an exciting venture to improve student learning through research on education policy and finance. Members of CPRE are the University of Pennsylvania, the University of Wisconsin–Madison, Harvard University, Stanford University, and the University of Michigan. CPRE is part of a nationwide, U.S. Department of Education–supported network of university-based research and development centers.

The Pew Forum on Education Reform comprises some of the leaders of American education who share an interest in education reform. The Forum considers how state and national education policy systems should be structured so that they stimulate, focus, and support the professional creativity and commitment of local educators to provide high-quality instruction to all students. The Forum is supported by the Pew Charitable Trusts.

The authors gratefully acknowledge the advice and critiques they received from one another, as well as from all the forum participants: William Clune, Thomas Corcoran, William Firestone, Margaret Goertz, Christine Gutierrez, Kati Haycock, David Hornbeck, Eugenia Kemble, Milbrey McLaughlin, Jens Ludwig, Richard Mills, Thomas Payzant, Claire Pelton, Bella Rosenberg, Alan Ruby, Robert Schwartz, Brett Scoll, Albert Shanker, Marshall Smith, and Janis Somerville. Helen Ladd provided helpful comments when she served as a discussant on some of the papers at the 1995 annual meeting of the American Educational Research Association. We would also like to thank James Fox and Duc-Le To, our Office of Educational Research and Improvement (OERI) program officers at the U.S. Department of Education, and all the CPRE management committee members who commented on the papers. Special thanks go to Theresa Luhm, who patiently worked with all the authors, handled the logistics, and compiled the volume with the help of CPRE's wonderful secretary, Robb Sewell, as well as to Ralph Levine, the administrator of the Pew Forum.

Susan H. Fuhrman   *Philadelphia, Penn.*
Jennifer A. O'Day   *Stanford, Calif.*
                                                March 1996

Note

1. The chapters draw from research funded by a number of sponsors, including the Office of Educational Research and Improvement, the U.S. Department of Education, the National Science Foundation, the Carnegie Corporation, the Pew Charitable Trusts, and the MacArthur Foundation. The opinions are those of the authors and do not represent the views of the sponsors, the Pew Forum, CPRE, or any of its member institutions.

The Editors

Susan Fuhrman is the Dean of the Graduate School of Education at the University of Pennsylvania and Director of the Consortium for Policy Research in Education (CPRE). Previously, she was a professor of Education Policy at Rutgers, The State University of New Jersey. CPRE, a consortium of Rutgers University, Harvard University, the University of Michigan, Stanford University, and the University of Wisconsin–Madison, conducts research on state and local education policies and finance. CPRE is funded by the Office of Educational Research and Improvement of the U.S. Department of Education.

Fuhrman is the author of numerous articles, research reports, and monographs on education policy and finance. She is the editor of two books on systemic reform, *Designing Coherent Education Policy: Improving the System*, published in 1993 by Jossey-Bass, and *The Governance of Curriculum*, published in 1994 by ASCD. She has served on numerous task forces and commissions, including the National Academy of Sciences' Committee on a National Educational Support System for Teachers and Schools, the Standards Task Force of the National Council on Educational Standards and Testing, and the New Jersey Task Force on Educational Assessment and Monitoring. Between 1986 and 1992, she served on the school board in Westfield, New Jersey. Her research interests include state policy design, accountability, deregulation, and intergovernmental relationships.

Jennifer O'Day is the Associate Director of the Pew Forum on Education Reform, an ongoing body of education leaders, researchers, practitioners, and advocates who share an interest in improving American schools. The Forum's mission is to explore how state and national policy can be structured to help stimulate, focus, and support the professional creativity and commitment of local educators and communities to provide high-quality instruction to all students.

O'Day has carried out research and analysis in the areas of systemic reform, educational equity, and capacity-building strategies. She has served on several national advisory groups, including the Stanford Working Group on Federal Education Programs for Limited English Proficient Students and the congressionally mandated Independent Review Panel for the evaluation of Title I and other federal education programs. Her current research interests include teacher and system learning, student assessment, and the education of linguistic minority students.

The Contributors

David K. Cohen is John Dewey Collegiate Professor and Professor of Public Policy at the University of Michigan. Dr. Cohen's research interests include educational policy, the relations between policy and instruction, and the nature of teaching practice. His past work has included studies of the effects of schooling, various efforts to reform teaching, the evaluation of educational experiments and large-scale intervention programs, and the relations between research and policy. Prior to his appointment to the University of Michigan, he was John A. Hannah Distinguished Professor of Education and Social Policy at Michigan State University (1986–1993) and, before that, Professor of Education and Social Policy at the Harvard Graduate School of Education. He was Chairman of Harvard Graduate School of Education's Programs in Administration, Planning, and Social Policy in 1982–1983 and 1983–1984. In 1976–1977, he was a visiting professor at the Institution for Social and Policy Studies of Yale University, and he was a part-time research associate for several years thereafter. He received his Ph.D. from the University of Rochester in 1961.

Linda Darling-Hammond is currently William F. Russell Professor of Education at Teachers College, Columbia University, and Co-Director of the National Center for Restructuring Education, Schools, and Teaching (NCREST). She is engaged in research, teaching, and policy work on issues of school restructuring, teacher education reform, and the enhancement of educational equity. She is author or editor of six books, including the *Review of Research in Education, Volumes 19 & 20, The New Handbook of Teacher Evaluation, Professional Development Schools: Schools for Developing a Profession, A License to Teach: Redesigning Teacher Education and Assessment for 21st Century Schools,* and *Authentic Assessment in Action.* In addition, she has authored more than 100 journal articles, book chapters, and monographs on educational policy issues.

Richard F. Elmore is Professor of Education and Chairman of Programs in Administration, Planning, and Social Policy at the Graduate School of Education, Harvard University. He is also a Senior Research Fellow of the Consortium for Policy Research in Education. His research focuses on state–local relations in education policy, school organization, and educational choice. He teaches regularly in programs for public sector executives and holds several government advisory positions. He holds degrees in political science from Whitman College and the Claremont Graduate School and a doctorate in educational policy from the Graduate School of Education at Harvard University.

Edward E. Lawler III is Professor of Research in the Graduate School of Business Administration at the University of Southern California and Director of the Center for Effective Organizations (CEO). He is the author or coauthor of twenty-two books, including *The Ultimate Advantage* (Jossey-Bass, 1992).

Frank Levy is Daniel Rose Professor of Urban Economics in MIT's Department of Urban Studies and Planning. He has written extensively in the areas of income inequality, living standards, and the economics of education. His last book, *Dollars and Dreams,* is a standard reference on the development of U.S. income distribution.

Susan Albers Mohrman is Senior Research Scientist at the Center for Effective Organizations at the University of Southern California. Her research is in the areas of organizational change and design, high-involvement organizations, teams, and other forms of lateral organization. For the past three years, she has been involved in a study of school-based management through the School of Education at the University of Southern California. She is an editor of *School-Based Management: Organizing for High Performance* (with Priscilla Wohlstetter) and a coauthor of *Designing Team-Based Organizations* (with Susan G. Cohen and Allan M. Mohrman, Jr.) and *Creating High Performance Organizations: Practices and Results of Employee Involvement and Total Quality Management in Fortune 1000 Companies* (with Edward E. Lawler III and Gerald E. Ledford, Jr.).

Richard J. Murnane, an economist, is a Professor of Education at the Harvard Graduate School of Education and a member of the National Academy of Education. Murnane has written widely about the relationship between education and the economy, about pub-lic–private school comparisons and the effects of family choice in education, and about teacher labor markets. His latest book, pub-lished by Harvard University Press, is entitled *Who Will Teach? Policies That Matter.* In 1996, the Free Press will publish his and Frank Levy's new book, which deals with the effects that changes in the economy have had on the skills new labor force entrants need to get good jobs and the changes in schooling that are needed to pro-vide all graduates with the requisite skills.

Allan Odden is Professor of Educational Administration in the School of Education, and Co-Director of the Finance Center of the Consortium for Policy Research in Education (CPRE) in the Wis-consin Center for Education Research, all at the University of Wis-consin–Madison. He is the Director of the CPRE Teacher Compensation Project. Odden's specialties are education policy, school finance, teacher compensation, and education policy imple-mentation. He was president of the American Education Finance Association in 1979–1980. His most recent books include *Educa-tional Leadership for America's Schools* (1995, with Eleanor Odden), *Rethinking School Finance: An Agenda for the 1990s* (1992), *School Finance: A Policy Perspective* (1992, with Lawrence O. Picus), and *Education Policy Implementation* (1991).

Arthur G. Powell is senior assistant to the Annenberg Institute for School Reform at Brown University. Prior to that he was director of the Commission on Educational Issues of the National Associa-tion of Independent Schools and associate dean of The Harvard Graduate School of Education. He received his A.B. (Amherst) and Ph.D. (Harvard) degrees in History of American Civilization. Among his books are *The Uncertain Profession* (1980) and (with E. Farrar and D. Cohen) *The Shopping Mall High School* (1985). His examination of the American prep school tradition was published in 1996.

Brian Rowan is a Professor of Education and Associate Dean for Research in the School of Education at the University of Michigan.

He received his B.A. (1972) from Rutgers University in sociology and his Ph.D. (1978) from Stanford University in sociology. Rowan's research focuses on the application of organization theory to the analysis of schooling, paying special attention to the nature of teachers' work, the organization and management of instruction, and the analysis of school effectiveness. Prior to joining the faculty at the University of Michigan, Rowan was a faculty member in education and sociology at Michigan State University and a senior research director at Far West Laboratory for Educational Research and Development. He has served on the editorial boards of the *American Educational Research Journal, Educational Administration Quarterly, Educational Evaluation and Policy Analysis, Educational Researcher,* and *Teachers College Record.*

Rewards and Reform

Chapter One

Introduction: Incentives and School Improvement

Jennifer A. O'Day

"It used to be in school you wrote something once, turned it in, and got an A, B, or C. With my students, the real learning occurs when the kids are asked to rewrite, revise, rethink. It's an incredible change! And it's very demanding. I struggle with that—the workload it generates. When I'm conferencing, it's so exhausting!" With these words, Maria Lopez, a California middle school teacher, expresses both her commitment and her frustration as she moves toward the type of teaching envisioned by the standards-based reforms of recent years. The changes Maria describes and demonstrates in her classroom are fundamental, running to the core of her professional work. They involve her understanding of subject matter, her conception of practice, and her relationships with her students and even her fellow teachers. The changes are not easy ones to make. They require first that she see the need for change and a possibility for doing things differently. They require both a willingness and an opportunity to see these things. They also require new knowledge and skills, action to develop the needed competencies, and a willingness to take that action.

Whence comes such willingness? What motivates teachers like Maria or others—students, teachers, administrators, even parents and other community members—to put in the hard work required to substantially improve student learning? Can reformers and policy makers create incentives to motivate, support, and maintain a commitment to such change? Will different actors respond to different

1

incentives differently, and what might this mean for attempts to move the whole system forward?

The selections in this volume address these and other questions in their exploration of issues concerning incentives for instructional reform. The authors take a variety of cuts at the issues. Whereas some take up incentives for students, others look at teachers, and still others consider multiple stakeholders in a school or state. Some focus on the improvement at the school site, and others address broader policy issues that may support site-based improvement. Some chapters are concerned with specific policy initiatives like performance awards, skill-based compensation, or statewide performance assessment. Others focus on the interplay of incentives in organizations and systems and on broad-based strategies for reform. The tone of the chapters varies as well as the content. Several authors adopt a more cautious tone, admonishing policy makers to beware of the potential pitfalls and negative consequences of various incentive strategies; others appear to be advocating particular directions or solutions.

Despite these differences in perspective or focus, however, all the authors are concerned with a common problem: how can incentives be developed to move instruction and student achievement toward much more ambitious standards, and to do so for the vast majority of American students? Not surprising, several common themes cut across some or all of the chapters. In the remainder of this introduction, I discuss four sets of these cross-cutting themes as they are developed in the chapters that follow. In the conclusion, Susan Fuhrman revisits some of the themes and their implications for policy and research.

The Joint Production of Learning and Incentives for Students

The first theme in these chapters is one that takes on particular importance as policy makers look to business and industry for incentives to increase educational productivity. Defining student learning as the outcome and teachers as the workers, various incentives schemes have been promoted to reward teachers for increasing student achievement. Other incentive schemes may encourage teachers to improve practice on the assumption that such improvement will automatically and directly lead to higher student achievement. The authors in this volume would seem to urge caution in such simplistic assumptions, however.

For any discussion of incentives in education reform, they say, must be based in the distinctive nature of teaching and learning in classrooms. More specifically, it must be based on an understanding that learning is jointly produced by teachers and students. Indeed, although most of the chapters in this volume focus on incentives for educators, several authors remind us that, in the final analysis, students are the chief agent of their own learning. As Art Powell observes in his chapter on student incentives, "Teachers don't learn students, students learn themselves."

What this means for teachers, says David Cohen, is that they do, in fact, depend on students for their professional success. "[Teachers'] art and craft are useless until students embrace the purposes of instruction as their own and seek them with their own art and craft" (p. 90). Student consent is thus a crucial element in the teaching–learning dynamic. In addition, teachers' dependence on students means that the teaching process is inherently uncertain. Teachers cannot predict the outcome of their own endeavors because students, not they, are the primary architects of those outcomes. This uncertainty is exacerbated when the learning goals are more complex and challenging, both because they then require greater effort on the part of students and because the educational technology for such challenging teaching is as yet limited.

The dependence of teachers on students and the uncertainty it engenders are no esoteric matters. They have deep implications for the design of incentives for education reform. The chief implication is this: if reformers want to improve student achievement, they cannot rely on a one-sided strategy of providing incentives to teachers. They must pay attention to student motivation and incentives at the same time as they try to foster improvements in teaching practice.

Providing avenues for student choice is one way to ensure greater student consent and to thus reduce uncertainty in teaching. Choice is a theme in several of the papers in this volume. Powell, for example, sees the element of choice as a major factor in the success of the Advanced Placement program in high schools. Students voluntarily select into the program, choose which courses they want to take, choose whether they want to take the external assessment at the end of the coursework, and so forth. The AP program has grown both because the opportunity for choice is motivating for students and because this sort of volunteerism is a political credible model in the current social and political climate.

Linda Darling-Hammond, in her discussion of the high-performing high schools in New York City, also emphasizes the motivating effects of choice on students. That students choose to attend these alternative schools and that they also have considerable choice within the curriculum means they have already given initial consent to the learning process. This freedom of choice helps create greater bonds between teachers and students, she says, reduces the uncertainty in the teaching and learning process, and allows teachers in these schools to be more adventurous educationally.

For their part, teachers also seem to be motivated by opportunities for choice. Teachers choose to teach in the AP program and in New York's alternative high schools just as students choose to participate in those endeavors. In addition, both Powell and Elmore note that many of the reform-oriented professional associations and activities depend on voluntary participation by teachers. For teachers, as for students, consent is a necessary condition to their putting in the time and effort to learn and change in the directions of the reforms.

As important as choice may be, however, these authors do not see it as a solution in itself. Darling-Hammond, for example, stresses that it is the *combination* of student choice, high expectations, and considerable support for student achievement that account for the success of these schools. Meanwhile, Powell notes the differential effect of choice on different students. He argues that free elective curricular systems provide incentives for those students who are clear on their educational goals and are committed to pursuing them. But too much choice may actually be a disincentive for the majority of young people who are not so self-directed. Elmore sees a similar pattern for teachers and argues that exclusive reliance on voluntary associations of reform-minded teachers has worked against the broad dissemination of curriculum and instructional reforms of the past.

Thus, while choice may be the mantra of many current-day policy makers and economists, these authors see it as useful primarily in combination with other avenues for providing incentives. Some of the avenues for student incentives explored in these pages include external assessments tied to valued outcomes in higher education and employment (Powell and Cohen), school-based graduation portfolios (Darling-Hammond), selectivity in student enrollment, and social rewards and personalized relationships with peers and teachers. A system of such incentives would motivate students through a combination of valued intrinsic and extrinsic incentives to learn. They would also reduce the uncertainty for teachers and relieve them of sole responsibility for motivating students.

The Complexities of Individual Motivation

A second set of themes in this volume centers on the complex nature of individual motivation and its implications for educational incentives. Indeed, the very idea behind the incentives discussed in these chapters is to *motivate* people—be they students, teachers, administrators, or parents—to put in the effort required to improve student learning. The underlying assumption is that motivation is a key element in human performance, an assumption made explicit by Rowan in his chapter on standards.

Based on the theoretical and empirical literature on employee performance, Rowan presents a model in which performance is influenced by three central factors: employee motivation to perform the job, the job-relevant skills and abilities the employee brings to the job, and the situation in which the employee performs the job. Since the purpose of this volume is to explore issues of incentives for improved performance, the chapters focus on the first of these factors, motivation. However, it should be noted, as does Rowan, that most scholars assume interactive relationships among the three factors, and most of the authors here deal with the other factors, competence and situation, particularly as they affect motivation.

Mohrman and Lawler take a close analytical look at the nature of human motivation using the lens of expectancy theory. According to this theoretical perspective, an individual's motivation to perform a task is a function of his or her expectation of success and the value he or she places on the anticipated outcome of that success. Although not always accurate, these two expectancies drive human behavior. It is not surprising, therefore, that these two themes—valued outcomes and expected success—run throughout the chapters of this volume.

Valued Outcomes

"Incentives have to operate on individual values; that is, what the individual values determines to some degree what the institution can elicit with incentives" (Elmore, p. 313). Values thus become central to any discussion of incentives.

Individuals may value outcomes that are either intrinsic or extrinsic to the task in question. Positive intrinsic outcomes may take the form of personal satisfaction with a job well done, a belief that one has contributed to a task that is important in some larger sense, personal enjoyment or intellectual stimulation from the activity, and so forth. Intrinsic value may also be attached to some aspect closely connected to the work. For example, teachers and students may gain rewards from the social relationships they develop with their peers in the course of their activities, or students may value the individual attention and caring of their teachers.

The authors in this volume find intrinsic value ascribed to the work to have particularly strong motivational effects. Linda Darling-Hammond, for example, says that teachers in the high-performing schools she has studied "continually describe the intrinsic rewards that derive from their increased success with students as the most powerful factor that keeps them engaged in the intensive work of transforming their pedagogy and reforming their school organization." Cohen describes such internal rewards as "central to human improvement." And Mohrman and Lawler say that "well designed work promotes psychological states associated with intrinsic satisfaction."

As important as intrinsic rewards may be, however, none of the authors in this volume would suggest that they are enough to inspire the substantial changes envisioned by the reforms, or at least to do so for the vast majority of teachers and students. Elmore argues, for example, that even in peak times, education reform strategies have never mobilized more than about one-fourth of the total population of teachers to change instruction. Because these strategies rely on intrinsic rewards, he suggests that this 25 percent may represent the proportion of teachers who have sufficient intrinsic motivation to undertake the grueling work required to move to ambitious and challenging practice. Even among those so motivated, it is likely that a combination of intrinsic and extrinsic rewards may be important for eliciting or sustaining effort.

Mohrman and Lawler provide some explanation for the limitation of intrinsic motivation. According to expectancy theory, a task or performance may involve various outcomes, some intrinsic, some extrinsic. Some of these outcomes will be valued positively by the individual and others valued negatively. In deciding whether to take on a task or how much effort to expend on it, the individual balances out the positive and negative values of the expected outcomes. Thus, a teacher may value high achievement for her students and may expect substantial personal satisfaction from such an accomplishment. However, she may also expect considerable personal costs in terms of added effort and time away from family or other personally enjoyable activities.

Linda Darling-Hammond notes the specific tradeoffs mentioned by teachers in her schools. These teachers report giving up valued personal autonomy and subjecting themselves to review and potentially negative criticism in order to gain collegial feedback and greater success for their students, both of which are valued outcomes for these teachers. They also may be willing to put in additional time for tutorials and parent meetings in order to gain the benefits of smaller class size and lighter pupil loads.

Teachers may also weigh the benefits they attach to various outcomes for students, taking account of the multiple goals of schooling. Thus, in deciding the amount of homework to assign, a teacher may balance value attached to academic objectives against the value of students' social and other development. Students, of course, will make similar judgments, but from a different perspective and set of values.

Because individuals differ greatly in what they value and in how they might evaluate such tradeoffs, reliance on intrinsic motivation to learn and to teach in ambitious ways is likely to be insufficient. Hence, the role of extrinsic rewards. Cohen argues that external rewards and punishments are essential "to help us both to decide what is most important out of all we need and want and to influence others' decisions." (p. 97) Extrinsic incentives for teachers may include such things as compensation, working conditions, and professional prestige. For students, they might range from symbolic awards and praise to access to future educational or employment opportunities.

Powell argues that extrinsic incentives are particularly important for American students, most of whom are in school not to learn but because of the force of law, habit, or desire to be with peers. Moreover, Powell contends that the sharp distinction between intrinsic and extrinsic incentives made by many theorists is oversimplistic. Extrinsic incentives can motivate students to work hard and learn, but in the process, the learning itself may motivate them to continue and learn more. In this line of reasoning, "intrinsic motivation for many if not most students is the desired product of extrinsic motivation" (p. 42). Though Darling-Hammond clearly places greatest emphasis on intrinsic incentives and rewards, she advances a similar argument when she says that "extrinsic incentives, including time and financial support for teacher learning, and teacher time available to students, support the attainment of intrinsic rewards" (p. 179). Similarly, Murnane and Levy note that although Vermont teachers engaged in Camp Portfolio came mainly for the chance to talk with colleagues and improve their skills, the $500 stipend provided additional incentive to participate. Indeed, each of the authors in this volume would seem to agree that a combination of intrinsic and extrinsic incentives is important for both students and teachers.

Despite the logical importance of extrinsic incentives to learn, they are rare in American education. The authors in this volume observe that American education has few external incentives that support challenging learning, indeed, few incentives targeted at the core of schooling at all. For example, the single salary structure for teachers, observes Odden, provides little incentive for teachers to develop the new knowledge and competencies required by the current reform goals. And unlike other nations, the United States has no external examination system to tie school learning for students to opportunities in employment or higher education.

Neither the causes nor the solutions to this situation lie solely within schools and school systems, however. Rather, they are deeply rooted in the broader American history and culture. Odden, for example, traces the development of the single salary schedule to social dissatisfaction with the overt discrimination in salaries and to increasing bureaucratization. Powell argues that American localism is at the heart of much of the problem, resulting in the lack of a widely understood conception of what students should know and teachers should teach. Locally constructed grades based on variable curricula and widely disparate expectations are of little use to either employers or institutions of higher education and so provide little motivation for students to work hard and learn. In addition, both he and Cohen note the deep ambivalence of Americans about intellectual work; that is, Americans tend to value persistence and job-related skills over intellectual endeavor, and innate talent over effort. Combined with the abundance of college slots, this means that neither employers nor nonelite colleges pay close attention to the results of school learning. There are few incentives for students to work hard or for teachers to push high intellectual accomplishment when attainment rather than achievement may be the determining factor in students' eventual success.

Lack of incentives for achievement is not the only cultural factor working against students' intellectual accomplishment. At the same time, students are enmeshed in a web of competing incentives, chief among which is what Powell calls the "intoxicating youth culture," geared toward material consumption and undemanding pleasures. Not only does youth culture take time away from learning, he says, it engenders habits of passivity and immediate gratification, which run directly counter to the goals of high intellectual endeavor.

To really foster student achievement, then, will require attention to cultural norms and values both inside and outside school and will necessitate the involvement of more stakeholders than just teachers and students alone. Parents, businesses, higher education institutions, and others will need to be involved. Gaining this kind of involvement and commitment is a hefty challenge for reformers to take on. Yet some are engaged in just such efforts. Faculty at the schools of which Darling-Hammond writes work with parents toward common understanding of goals so that values pursued at school may be reinforced at home as well. On a larger scale, Murnane and Levy report that more than 200 employers have joined the reform effort in Vermont by committing themselves to use the statewide student portfolios in hiring decisions. This latter example is of course both experimental and highly unusual. Nonetheless, it may be a step in the direction of changing cultural norms and should be watched carefully for effects on student motivation and achievement.

Expected Success

Motivation to perform a given task depends not only on whether that performance will result in valued outcomes but also on the individual's belief that he or she can, in fact, accomplish the task. Mohrman and Lawler identify three factors that influence this effort-to-performance expectancy: the individual's belief that he or she has the requisite skills and knowledge, a clear understanding of the goals and nature of the desired performance, and the situational support (for example, resources). I focus here on the individual's perceived competence; goal clarification and situational support I discuss further in the next section.

Three themes emerge from these authors' treatment of the effort-to-performance expectancy. First, all the authors in this volume acknowledge that the challenging student standards associated with the reforms require greater competence on the part of teachers as well as of students. Teachers must know their subject matter deeply, must expand their repertoire of instructional strategies, must develop habits of mind conducive to continual improvement, and must be able to communicate and collaborate with colleagues and others. Since, as Rowan points out, successful performance depends in part on the knowledge and skills an individual brings to a task, the implication is that to improve student learning in the directions desired, reformers must also improve the competence of teachers and other educators.

The importance of teacher competence goes beyond this simple relationship, however. For if an individual has the requisite skills, he or she will be more likely to expect a successful performance and thus be more motivated to undertake the task in the first place. This indirect impact of competence on performance, through its influence on motivation, is the second theme of these chapters. And the combination of direct and indirect impact serves to underscore the value of investing in high-quality professional development.

In addition, because of the dual impact of teacher competence, it may make sense for policy makers to place some of that
investment in additional incentives to encourage teachers to pursue further learning. Of course, some teachers will do so on their
own because they value the reform goals and have the required
resources. But for many, extrinsic incentives, such as the pay-
for-skill compensation schemes suggested by Odden or the stipends and release time for professional development described by
Darling-Hammond, are likely to be significant initial motivators.

A third theme with respect to the effort-to-performance expectation is that efforts to increase teacher competence must be
understood in the broader social and cultural context. For teachers
to seriously believe they can foster high levels of student achievement on challenging content, they must believe both that students
are able to learn the material and that they (teachers) are able to
teach it—or, at least, that they can learn to teach it. Several authors,
however, note cultural norms that work against such confidence.

One of these is the widely held American belief that student
achievement is more a function of individual talent than it is of
effort. Powell documents the rise of this belief and its embodiment
in norm-referenced standardized tests. He argues that the emphasis on talent over effort serves to undercut student motivation to
learn and excel in school. Cohen concurs and adds that such belief
undercuts teacher motivation as well. Teachers, particularly teachers of disadvantaged students, will be unlikely to put in the extra
effort to teach, or to learn to teach, in challenging new ways if they
believe that some students are simply doomed to low achievement
by their genes or family circumstances—that is, if they believe that
student background, rather than schools and teachers, is responsible for student success.

Elmore addresses the counterpart of this belief as applied to
teachers. He focuses not on whether teachers believe students can
learn, but whether they believe they can learn to teach in more
challenging and engaging ways. Elmore's analysis of the progressive education movement of the 1920s and 1930s and the curricular reforms of the 1950s and 1960s suggest that a long-standing
problem in education reform is the prevailing American belief that
"successful teaching is an individual trait rather than a set of
learned professional competencies" (p. 314). To the extent that
teachers hold such a belief, they will be less inclined to put in the

time or effort to gain additional competence because they will not
have the expectation of success in doing so. Extrinsic incentives
like those mentioned earlier may provide needed motivation for
some to invest the time and effort. Moreover, successful experience
in such efforts could change expectancies for future success and
could even eventually alter underlying limiting beliefs. In addition,
these authors suggest that attention to increasing skills and knowledge of teachers and students must be combined with attention to
developing cultural norms that stress the value of continual improvement and of effort over talent.

School as a Motivational Context

A third set of issues addressed in these chapters concerns the
design of schools to promote motivation. In Mohrman and
Lawler's terms, these are schools that "create strong expectancies
for being able to perform successfully and where valued outcomes
result" (p. 125). Whereas Chapters 4 and 5 focus specifically on the
school context, several other chapters address issues of school organization in the context of a broader discussion. Three cross-cutting
themes emerge.

The first of these is the importance of school purpose. In the
broad sense, this is the "purposeful school community" of which
Powell writes: "a place that projects to students in endless ways the
value of learning and of decency." To create such an environment,
Powell argues, schools should establish a limited curriculum and
communicate clearly what it is, giving students the opportunity to
engage with others about a common educational task. Reflecting
a similar emphasis on clarity of purpose, Mohrman and Lawler
describe goal-setting as the "linchpin of organizational motivation."
Goal-setting helps clearly define performance objectives both for
students and for teachers, thus creating greater expectation for success. Rowan discusses the same phenomenon in terms of output
standards, which are believed to improve performance through
increasing employee motivation.

Moving from the theoretical to the concrete, Linda Darling-
Hammond's chapter on high-performing schools in New York City
notes that each school has articulated a set of educational ideals to
guide all organizational decisions. Curriculum goals and student

standards help concretize performance objectives further, and "highly visible shared exhibitions of student work and performance make it clear what the school values and how students are doing." Through such mechanisms, the school community defines both a general mission and specific performance objectives against which individuals are able to measure their progress.

A second organizational theme raised by several authors is the motivating power of a personalized, caring school community for students. According to Darling-Hammond, students in her sample of schools "voice over and over again how important it is to them to be cared for" (p. 183). Teachers' personalized attention and support create trust and a willingness on the part of students to expend effort on tasks valued by teachers. Powell agrees and adds that a close relationship between teachers and students creates opportunities for students to observe the positive consequence of learning for others. Teachers thus become role models through whom students come to value the intrinsic rewards of learning.

A caring environment does more than demonstrate the value of learning, however. It also fosters student motivation by increasing the likelihood of their success. Darling-Hammond notes the rich feedback provided students on their performance. This feedback, which helps guide students to successful completion of the learning task, is a manifestation of the high level of professional accountability for student learning that teachers in these schools accept. Such a caring environment is particularly important for students who have few other sources of support and who might well fall through the cracks in a less personalized, more bureaucratic school setting.

Personalization benefits teachers as well. Because students are more likely to put in effort on learning and because teachers come to know students and their needs better, the uncertainty in the teaching–learning situation decreases, and the likelihood of successful teaching performance increases. Teachers thus also become more motivated and may even be more creative in setting their goals and designing their instructional strategies than they might otherwise be.

A final organizational theme developed through these chapters is that teacher motivation will be stronger where teachers have the organizational resources and authority to create the expectation of success. Mohrman and Lawler identify four types of organizational resources relevant to teacher motivation: information, knowledge, power, and rewards. Since the impact of these resources on motivation is developed in depth both in their chapter and in Chapter 5, I will not belabor it here. Suffice it to say that the general argument runs as follows: when teachers (and students) have input into the goals of the school, when they have authority to design learning environments to more effectively meet those goals, when they have access to pertinent information about students and student performance, when they have opportunities to develop the requisite knowledge and skills to design and implement effective instructional strategies, and when they are rewarded for their efforts, professional motivation and participation in improvement efforts are likely to be high. Teachers will, in short, value outcomes they have had a voice in setting and will have higher expectancy for success if they can control the teaching and learning situation.

One obvious conclusion from these discussions, therefore, is that the school context may be the most powerful motivational tool available to reformers. With respect to systemwide change, however, a caution may be in order. As Elmore points out, there are impressive examples of high-performing schools developed in earlier reform efforts. But moving from a few such successful schools to a broad-based strategy is no easy task and requires processes both inside and outside the school unit. Here enters the need for the policy initiatives and scaling-up strategies that are the focus of the other chapters in this volume.

A Systemic Approach to Incentives

Although the policy implications of these chapters is the focus of the book's conclusion, one central policy theme seems worth mentioning here as well. This is that a multifaceted, integrated approach to incentives, rather than the current piecemeal and incremental one, is essential for the kinds of systemwide improvements sought by today's standards-based reforms. Three aspects of this general theme stand out.

First, incentives to support reform must be multifaceted, incorporating a variety of both intrinsic and extrinsic rewards, primarily for students and teachers but also for other participants in the educational process. The reasons for this flow from the preceding discussion on motivation. A multifaceted approach is warranted because learning is jointly produced by teachers and students, because different people value different outcomes, and because even individuals must weigh the various values they ascribe to the multiple outcomes of any undertaking. Because of this complexity and variety, no single approach can possibly fill the bill.

Second, incentives need to be integrated and mutually reinforcing because they interact both with one another and with other policy initiatives. Darling-Hammond's analysis of New York's high-performing high schools demonstrates the power of incentives to influence performance when they reinforce one another and the goals of the organization. By contrast, several authors comment on the limited effect of incentives when they are not part of an integrated system. For example, Odden points out that a single salary schedule does not motivate the necessary development of teacher capacity because the rewards are disconnected from the reform objectives. Similarly, Rowan argues that a partial, nonsystemic approach to standard-setting will not only fail to produce the desired effects on teaching performance, but may actually reduce motivation for teachers who experience failures as a result. Misaligned standards (when coupled with accountability and incentives structures), he conjectures, could have other negative consequences as well, such as low morale, resistance, or even cheating. Cohen underscores the possibility of negative consequences when potential conflicts in incentives or between incentives and cultural norms are ignored, when resources needed to attain the valued rewards are vastly unequal, or when incentives and accountability for teachers are not accompanied by similar mechanisms for students.

Finally, incentives should be systemic in that they take effect at both the individual and the organizational level. The influence of the organizational context (both positive and negative) on motivation of its members provides ample reason why this is the case, and many of the authors touch on ways in which policies might strengthen or support the motivational power of the school environment.

In addition to the preceding characteristics of an incentive system, two other observations are in order with respect to the policy themes in these chapters. One of these is the importance of *quality* in all aspects of the performance goals and the measures used to assess them. Rowan, for example, argues that if standards are to have value for teachers, they must be based on an empirically valid theory of employee performance. In addition, both he and Cohen stress the need to overcome problems in measurement if incentives are to have any hope of being effective. Elmore then stresses that the reforms and the incentives that support them must embody an explicit theory about how human beings learn to do things differently.

This brings us to the final theme for this chapter: for incentives to be effective, in both the long term and the short term, they must be targeted not only on improving student performance per se but also on increasing capacity throughout the system to enable that performance. Thus learning—for teachers, administrators, and the system as a whole—must be an explicit goal of the incentive system. It is to contribute to that learning that the authors of this volume have directed their efforts.

Part One

Incentives and Student Performance

Chapter Two

Motivating Students to Learn: An American Dilemma

Arthur G. Powell

Students as Workers: Educational Prerequisite, American Conundrum

One of the more comforting characteristics of modern health care, at least until recently, is that active patient participation has rarely been essential to getting desired results. Most patients covet the role of painless passivity. Swallowing an antibiotic to cure a simple infection requires little effort but usually works. A patient under anaesthesia is hardly a participant in his or her own appendectomy. These often unpleasant services, frequently agreed to by recipients with reluctance and anxiety, are satisfactorily rendered when professionals do virtually all the work.

But the wellness movement increasingly demands that people take more responsibility for their own health. We must stop smoking and start exercising, and these behavioral changes are ones only we can make. Sometimes physicians can help, through blunt talk about the consequences of inaction, and sometimes pills can come again to our rescue by weakening well-established habits despite our docility. But we often find it hard to change behavior even when the reasons for doing so are excellent and well understood. AIDS is one of the most easily prevented of horrible afflictions, yet the number of those infected grows despite the pervasiveness of AIDS education.

Many service–provider relations, in short, work smoothly when the professional expert does most of the work. Yet when clients must participate actively for their own benefit, their commitment to do so often wavers. A satisfactory outcome becomes less certain.

Consider school learning from this perspective. The most obvious point is that virtually all school learning requires substantial active work by students. The more complex the learning, the more demanding the work. Teachers never learn students. Students learn themselves. There is no pill to swallow to achieve desired learning outcomes—or at least not yet. (One assumes that the coming years will bring pharmacological research products bearing at least indirectly on student willingness to learn, such as lengthened attention-span or memory-enhancement drugs.)

Educators of all philosophical persuasions agree that serious learning demands serious student mental exertion. Traditionalists who value knowledge transmission, acquisition, and retention know that student effort is indispensable to these goals, and often believe that learning the value of effort is a worthy goal in itself. More intellectual objectives, such as the understanding and active use of knowledge long after formal study is completed, or the acquisition of various lifelong habits of mind, require even more mental exertion. Student willingness to do this is probably the most fundamental prerequisite in the educational process.

All teachers, especially in middle and high school, know how difficult it is to achieve this objective with most students. School learning, mainly academic and cognitive in intended content above the lower grades, can be complex, difficult, and time consuming (Perkins, 1992, p. 160). It can be, at least at first, neither especially interesting nor much fun. Even young students who excel at math or history rarely choose to do math problems or read history books in their spare time. Most students do not come to school mainly to learn. Their presence owes more to law, habit, peer relations, and the absence of anything better to do than the active seeking out of a valued service.

Opportunities for students to learn are available in great abundance in most American schools. But opportunities to learn algebra or explore the world of *Native Son* do not guarantee that students will seize them. If the will to engage the material is not present, learning will not occur. The opportunities will sit there unused—the envy of students all over the world, and especially the developing world, who marvel at what American youth take for granted but reject.

So it is no news that many students put in little effort. Some actively resist school learning and drop out either physically or mentally. Others go through the motions to receive high school diplomas or college acceptances but display bloodless, passive, and cynical minimalism toward their studies. The large continuum from total to partial student disengagement from learning is abetted by different kinds of classroom treaties or bargains with their teachers, as school-based ethnographic research abundantly documents (Cusick, 1983; McNeil, 1985; Powell, Farrar, and Cohen, 1985; Sedlak, Wheeler, Pullin, and Cusick, 1986).

Unsurprisingly, educators, researchers, and policy makers from widely varying perspectives have focused new attention on why and how students become willing to exert themselves to learn. What drives or energizes them to put in the time and effort that school learning requires? What pulls them in the reverse direction—to avoid learning and devote energy to other activities? Teachers and psychologists typically label this issue *motivation,* while economists and policy makers more frequently speak of *incentives.* Most youth lack neither motivation nor incentives in their nonschool lives. The problem is motivation to learn in school.

In this essay, I sketch the broad territory of student motivation and incentives, as well as the possibilities of policy initiatives to increase them. I develop four connected themes, which I summarize in this section and elaborate on in the remaining ones.

The first theme is that motivation to learn is an American dilemma because of unique American commitments to universal secondary and mass postsecondary schooling, and to decentralized local control as the primary means of education governance. A crucial consequence has been to place important constraints on students' motivation to learn. America offers fewer incentives for students to learn than most other industrialized societies and many developing ones. Further, American youth culture competes significantly with schools. Thus, American society has made an unprecedented commitment to mass schooling, but it provides relatively weak incentives to learn and relatively strong disincentives not to.

The second theme is that Americans have coped with the problem of student motivation by regarding it mainly as a problem to be solved by individual teachers inside classrooms. The job of motivating students is part of a teacher's regular job description. This enormous burden is in addition to the task of instruction itself.

How teachers might motivate students has focused on within-classroom procedures like discipline, pedagogy, curriculum, and assessment. Although the line between motivating and instructing is thin, the ability to motivate—to get students to behave, to work hard, to take an active role in their learning, to lure or cajole or coerce them to engage material—is an enormously valued American teacher skill. Being a good teacher often means being able to motivate students to work. Being an acceptable teacher often means being able to negotiate an orderly classroom in the face of unmotivated and resistant students.

Because American teachers are expected to play the most pivotal role in motivating students, and because decentralization is so characteristic of our educational system, it is not surprising that very different approaches to the problem exist. They have fought pitched battles or, more often, have uneasily coexisted. Although it is convenient and not wholly inaccurate to characterize the main warring camps as *intrinsic* and *extrinsic* approaches to student motivation, the reality is more complex. The two positions overlap at countless points. Almost every sensible educator has embraced elements of both. One especially instructive point in common is that both approaches, to have much success, require far more skilled teachers than present teacher education and professional development arrangements provide.

The third theme follows from this last point. Since the early 1980s, many Americans have become profoundly frustrated with student passivity and disengagement. The frustration is clearly linked to new problems of international economic competitiveness and inner city educational collapse. More robust policy interventions seem necessary. Dissatisfied with the limited effects of decentralizing motivation to classroom teachers, they have advocated instead the establishment of extrinsic incentives with far-reaching economic and social consequences for individual students.

The word *incentives* is used to suggest that such social rewards may produce greater attitude change in students, and thus more effort and academic achievement, than teacher-produced motivation. Policy ideas like high-stakes examinations that assess world-class national or state educational standards, for example, deliberately reject the teacher-based motivation tradition. Most American youth, the argument goes, do not work hard in school because intellectual effort and achievement bring no significant recognition or worthwhile rewards. This applies both to school-to-postsecondary and school-to-work transitions. Until cultural signals change, academic passivity is perfectly rational.

None of this argument denies the motivating power of a few remarkable teachers on a few students, or the fact that some students are motivated by their families, by their own fiery curiosity or ambition, or by the accidents and good fortunes of life. Students are turned on to learning all the time. The issue is how policy might encourage far more of them to be so engaged.

These *top-down* prescriptions, as they are often called, have themselves been attacked. The push for more systemic incentive systems has usefully created a variety of counterproposals that defend, if sometimes with modifications, the traditional American commitment to localism. One approach vigorously contends that education is not decentralized enough. Liberating individual schools and teachers from top-down constraints will actually increase student motivation by increasing the motivation of teachers. The answer to weak student incentives is more democratic localism, not less.

The fourth theme is that Americans have underutilized a powerful store of student incentives: the context of students' lives. Context means schools and families—an experiential world larger than teachers, curriculums, and classrooms, but smaller than national culture, national policy, or state policy. Context in this sense calls special attention to the motivational powers of a school—but only if a school is a purposeful educational community.

A final conundrum, lurking throughout the discussion, is whether sufficient incentives exist among the American people to support increasing incentives for students to learn. If most parents are basically satisfied with their children's education, if academic achievement and the effort needed to attain it are not valued for themselves or for what they lead to, current arrangements are unlikely to change. Furthermore, there is always the curious possibility that raising the stakes—increasing the incentives—might actually work.

But that outcome would increase the pool of candidates for good jobs and good college places in a country worried about the supply of good jobs and good college places. There would be more competition, and groups currently favored might suffer. Alternatively, raising the stakes might increase the punishments for those who do not achieve. It might increase inequality. Given these uncertainties, and the potential alliance against incentives between those who seek social continuity and those who seek social change, the constituency for new incentive policies is not self-evident.

Incentives in a Universal, Compulsory, Decentralized System

In the early 1990s, about 85 percent of American late adolescents graduated from high school each year, and about two-thirds of them immediately entered postsecondary education. About 60 percent of the entire age cohort enrolled in some sort of college right after high school. For more than four decades, high school completion and some education beyond high school has increasingly become an expected and normal part of growing up American. Some 2,100 four-year institutions grant at least a bachelor's degree, and 1,400 two-year institutions grant associate degrees. They are supplemented by 6,500 postsecondary technical and vocational institutes. These 10,000 private and public institutions devoted to the cause of postsecondary participation have helped expand it more in America than anywhere else in the world.

Although secondary education in Japan and Western Europe has recently become a near-universal student experience, the uniquely American commitment to maximize educational opportunity is still apparent. For example, about 33 percent of the French late adolescent age cohort and 30 percent of the similar (West) German cohort pass the baccalaureate and Abitur examinations required to enter universities in those countries. About 36 percent of the Japanese adolescent age cohort enters higher education. Only about 2 percent of the Chinese age cohort does. These lower participation rates than in the United States reflect cultural traditions about social stratification and mobility as well as the scarcity of places in the upper reaches of a country's educational system (Eckstein and Noah, 1993, p. 174).

Since the beginning of the century, Americans have invested heavily in expanding secondary school capacity and increasing the compulsory attendance age to sixteen. And since the 1950s, they have made a similar investment in higher education. With the exception of a few years when the postwar baby boom descended on a somewhat surprised and unready higher education sector, American higher education has always had more places than candidates. When higher education expanded to meet the postwar demand, becoming postsecondary education in the process, the more familiar situation of oversupply was restored. A product of nineteenth-century entrepreneurial zeal, based both on religious conviction and local boosterism, colleges were born (and often died) without much regard for whether a market existed for them. Excess capacity was the typical lot of American higher education.

Americans' desire to school the entire population through mid-adolescence by law, to prevent by persuasion dropping out until at least high school completion, and to expand postsecondary education so extensively that oversupply was endemic had many different causes. At least three bear brief mention. First, the unprecedented responsibility of forging large numbers of immigrants into a politically viable nation was one driving motive whose nobility, complexity, and general success is usually underrated.

Second, universal and compulsory schooling became a national crusade because its appeal crossed political boundaries. A more conservative mentality has wished to keep youth off the streets, out of trouble, acculturated to mainstream values, and equipped with concrete life skills. A more liberal mentality has seen schooling as a new frontier offering social mobility and equality of opportunity, especially in the twentieth century when the old geographical frontier was closed. It also has hoped (as Lawrence Cremin once put it) to democratize education without vulgarizing it and to create genuine social democracy by means of education.

Third, the enormously large education profession benefits directly from retaining consumers of its products for as long as possible. Education became one of America's biggest industries. Adult jobs depend at all levels on student retention. This expansive and expensive commitment, made possible only by a new and confident country with abundant resources to keep youth out of the workforce while building schools and colleges for all to attend, has had several consequences for student motivation to learn.

One consequence is amplified by an additional characteristic of American education. Because substantial national control is constitutionally prohibited and active state involvement has often been minimal, education governance remains highly local and decentralized. All components of schooling have been responsive to the preferences and financial resources of school districts, and even to individual schools within the same district. The most extreme examples of localism occur within postsecondary education, where astonishing discrepancies in mission and entry requirements exist among the 10,000 functioning institutions. Many of these institutions have no admission requirements at all. Even the absence of a high school diploma is not an insuperable barrier to college attendance. Nor for that matter is lack of the basic literacy traditionally associated with elementary school.

The meaning of good education and educational standards, therefore, varies widely across the United States. Localism guarantees there is no clearly understood conception about what students, especially adolescents, should know and thus be motivated to learn. Democratic localism complicates (or enriches) the motivation issue by adding to it the question of motivation to learn what. Beyond basic literacy, there has been no widespread American consensus about what learning is of most worth or even that a consensus is desirable.

Are book learning, academic learning, and intellectual learning more valuable than they are worthless or dangerous? Thinking about effective motivation inextricably depends on what vision of learning is being advocated in individual school districts, schools, and classrooms. Inculcation of orderly behavior or the times tables, for example, suggests different motivational techniques than promoting a grasp of the Civil War, an understanding of Newtonian mechanics, or an enthusiasm for Mozart.

Localism also guarantees that there are no consistent consequences for different levels of school effort or achievement. Students who do virtually nothing in school may continue on to their first-choice postsecondary destinations, whereas other students who perform at high levels may be rejected by all the colleges to which they apply. Algebra I and even physics may seem relatively clear domains, but they often mean very different things in different classrooms. Localism reduces the possibility of broad social communication or signals to students about the relation between school achievement and life consequences. Motivation to learn becomes highly dependent on local context and the accidents of personal experience or residence.

Further, the mix of universalism, compulsion (or the expectation of continued attendance), and localism has produced a system where participation for as long as possible is valued more than demonstrable achievement or learning at any stage within the system. Since the American goal is selecting-in or inclusiveness rather than selecting-out, it could hardly have been otherwise.

This shapes the impact of postsecondary education on high school motivation to learn. With no need to select-out, because places at the next educational stage are not scarce but abundant, Americans have not needed (with minor exceptions) national selecting-out mechanisms such as government-supported achievement examinations. Instead, Americans pride themselves on never erecting final educational barriers to success, on the society's willingness to give everyone second, third, and fourth chances, and on the resulting presumption that any failure is self-inflicted. The scarcity of schooling places that motivates students to achieve in other countries has not been an incentive in America because of an abundance of places. In contrast, one-third of French baccalauréate candidates fail the exam (Eckstein and Noah, 1993, p. 174).

Self-advancement has depended more on satisfactory school attendance (measured usually by time spent and credits accumulated) than by measured academic achievement. The relative ease with which one can negotiate an American high school diploma and postsecondary attendance without significant effort helps schools and colleges retain students. Why should admissions requirements demand serious achievement when most colleges survive by luring students in rather than by erecting barriers to keep them out? For the past generation, "enrollment management" in postsecondary education has focused on recruitment and marketing, not selection and standards. These priorities do not especially support motivation to learn.

It is true that, since the 1950s, a small number of private colleges and central campus state universities have been selective in admissions because of a surplus of qualified applicants. Academic effort and performance is mobilized by student motivation to attend these institutions. But this situation is atypical and recent. It existed virtually nowhere in the country in 1940. Even the tiny band of elite institutions like Harvard were elite on economic rather than meritocratic grounds until after World War II. Only then could they say that they had more qualified applicants than places.

The more selective institutions have influenced the motivation of only a relatively small number of students. Ironically, the ways many of them dealt with their recent ability to be choosy may have made motivation to learn more problematic for most American youth. Elite colleges, because of understandable democratic and self-interested motives to attract capable students regardless of social or economic background, pioneered in the development of aptitude tests to play decisive roles in admissions decisions. In the 1940s, these supplanted curriculum-driven achievement examinations as a factor in student selection. Emphasizing aptitude over achievement was assumed to be the fairest way to procure the ablest student body. Aptitude—often a thinly veiled euphemism for native cognitive capacity—did not depend on what a student had studied. Emphasizing aptitude would not confer unfair advantages on average students who had received excellent preparation in good schools and would not penalize talented students who had attended poor schools.

But an important and unanticipated result of this meritocratic emphasis on talent rather than learning is that motivation to learn became less important than the motivation to demonstrate talent. Native "God-given" ability has seemed more important to scholastic success than effort or persistence in the face of difficulty. The Scholastic Aptitude Test is but one of many aptitude tests that helped shape the idea of motivation in America. Either one was innately good at something, in which case practice might make one somewhat better, or one was not good at something, in which case practice would never allow one to catch up to one's betters (Valentine, 1987; Conant, 1970, pp. 128–138, 417–432).

The tension between effort and innate ability is clear from an international perspective. Compared with Japan, for example, "American children view learning mathematics as a process of rapid insight rather than lengthy struggle" (Stevenson and Stigler, 1992, pp. 105, 94–112). If the insight is not rapid, the cultural presumption is that math learning is impossible, and the motivation to learn withers away. When the American occupation of Japan ended following World War II, the Japanese abandoned the aptitude tests that Americans had imposed on their college admission process and restored achievement tests (Eckstein and Noah, 1993, p. 206). The same critique is made by contemporary American motivational psychology. It argues that motivation to engage in challenging learning tends to increase when effort rather than ability is emphasized. The professional terminology is different—the psychologist Carol Dweck (1986) speaks of "entity theory" instead of ability, and "incremental theory" instead of effort—but the point is similar (Maehr and Midgley, 1991, p. 402; Ames, 1992).

But the rise of norm-referenced tests in place of criterion-referenced tests has only reinforced the emphasis on ability. The point of a norm-referenced test is to pick winners and losers in order to help institutional selection. A criterion-referenced test, in which theoretically all students can succeed or fail, has far less value as a selection device. Even if students persist to learn more math, their place in the norm-referenced pecking order may not change. And so motivation to learn math may fall.

The relation between schools, college admissions, and student motivation is complex because admissions requirements usually exist amid a web of school–college institutional linkages. Colleges may often have weak reasons and procedures to motivate students to learn in schools, but they have powerful incentives to motivate students to become interested in attending their institutions. They develop ever more sophisticated marketing materials and cultivate personal relations with college guidance counselors.

High schools, especially suburban public, elite urban, and independent schools, in turn, have powerful incentives to present themselves and their students to colleges in the best possible light. Transcripts, test score results, school or teacher recommendations, and student essays may not always represent substantial student achievement. But most colleges at least take transcripts and their contents into account in the admissions process. Students know, for example, that completion of a college preparatory curriculum with a minimum grade point average is indispensable for acceptance at typical middle-range, four-year institutions. They are motivated at minimum to produce these results.

But for students who plan to enter the workforce directly after high school, institutional linkages to business and industry analogous to these are virtually nonexistent. Business provides schools or students with no information on what curricula, grades, scores, or references are required for various kinds of entry-level jobs. Business seeks no such data from applicants because it cannot usefully interpret information produced by a decentralized system where comparability is absent and because it has no tradition of working directly with schools.

Public school counselors typically spend little time on college counseling compared with independent school counselors. They spend even less time on school-to-work transitions. If they have personal relations with some college admissions offices, no comparable relations exist with business. The key school people with connections to business are often teachers in vocational programs who have established their own placement networks over the years.

The yawning gap between school and business creates another problem of student motivation since no signals exist that achievement is especially important to getting a job or getting ahead. Various studies indicate that the amount and quality of education is indeed related to business productivity and employee compensation, but curiously neither high school students nor businesses seem to know this.

The problem is deeply embedded in American history. For most adult Americans in this century, achieving a desirable lifestyle has not necessarily required superior educational performance in high school. How well one did in school did not much affect how well one did in life. Possessing a high school diploma did and does have real consequences. But the diploma has usually been obtainable by persisting in school—by regular attendance and decent behavior. Americans and American business have valued persistence. It is a proxy for responsible behavior with clear workplace implications.

So mere completion of high school has been credential enough for American business. It has not trusted and valued how well students have done in school, it has not trusted school to make serious judgments about students, and it has bypassed school in hiring decisions. This lack of linkage contrasts profoundly with countries like France (where special baccalaureate examinations exist to govern access to vocations), or Germany (where an examination-based apprenticeship system governs and sustains the idea that education and vocational success are interdependent), or Japan (where schools and many industries are so closely linked that schools actually choose which students get the best jobs) (Rosenbaum and Kariya, 1989; Rosenbaum, 1989; National Center on the Educational Quality of the Workforce, 1995a; National Center on the Educational Quality of the Workforce, 1995b).

The relative weakness of incentives to learn provided by either school-to-postsecondary or school-to-work transitions is the most discussed of incentive problems and the area where policy recommendations are most numerous. But an additional problem may be more fundamental. American society also offers disincentives to learn and, indeed, active competition to the idea of learning. The economist John H. Bishop (1994, p. 26) has concluded that American schools may not be as inefficient as many critics have believed. "Maybe they are highly adaptive to a dysfunctional incentive environment." Perhaps, as Stevenson and Stigler (1992, p. 206) put it, "the most intractable obstacle to improving public education is American society itself." This problem is more awkward to address.

One side of the problem is the tradition of American anti-intellectualism and suspicion of academic learning. "To a degree unknown in the United States," Rosenbaum and Kariya report (1989, p. 1344), "Japanese employers are concerned that new employees have basic academic skills, and they prefer to hire students with higher academic achievement." A recent survey of American business (National Center on the Educational Quality of the Workforce, 1995a, p. 12) confirms that characteristics of entry-level job applicants associated with school achievement (years completed, grades, school reputation, teacher recommendations) were least valued by employers. Foreign observers (Judge, Lemosse, Paine, and Sedlack, 1994, pp. 123, 140–147, 250) and astute home-grown historians (Hofstadter, 1962) have consistently pointed to the American preference for social or student-centered educational goals rather than academic or intellectual ones. Americans emphasize the heart over the head.

Another side of the same problem is the vigorous competition schools and learning face daily in America. The explosive mixture of unprecedented youth affluence and modern communications technology has produced an intoxicating youth culture that competes directly for the loyalty of the young. The options of American youth for undemanding pleasures are probably unrivaled in the history of the world. The tremendous purchasing power of American youth has created industry after industry that directly challenge schools by offering youth easy and thrilling pleasure (sometimes violent and barbaric pleasure) without effort.

Instead of motivation to learn, students are taught by the youth business to acquire lifetime habits of material consumption. One cable television executive explained his company's decision to enter the preschool market by admitting "if we start getting kids to watch us at this age, we have them for life" (Carter, 1994, p. 1). James B. Conant (1959, p. 45) wrote at the end of the 1950s that "It is an uneven contest when the choice between easy and tough [school] programs is left to students with convertibles, plenty of money, and community approval for spending most of their evenings in social activities." The contest is far less even today.

The great advantage of youth culture over school learning is that the former's rewards are immediate, pleasurable, and accessible without effort. The issue of incentives to participate in youth culture does not really arise; motivation is largely intrinsic. Motivation to learn is more complex. Some students of the subject believe that motivation to learn is a habit that itself must be learned. "Everything in and around us, including our minds and our feelings, competes for our motivation. . . . motivation to learn must find a place along with motivation to play, motivation to be a good friend, and all the other motivations that exist and are born in the developing lives of children" (Wlodkowski and Jaynes, 1991, pp. 8–11). In American society, children as they grow older encounter many compelling distractions—legal and illegal—that act as disincentives to learn in school. Youth culture distracts not only by taking time from learning, but by undercutting the very methods and characteristics of learning. Passivity is more valued than activity, immediate gratification more than persistence, and simplicity more than complexity (Chance, 1992, p. 206).

Student motivation to learn, in sum, has a cultural dimension that must be understood by policy makers who wish to increase it. Cognitive achievement or mastery, whether narrowly academic (scoring well on tests, getting high grades) or broadly intellectual (engaging voluntarily in the world of ideas), is not widely valued in America. Stevenson and Stigler (1992, pp. 54, 69, 93, 124–125) put the matter succinctly. Asian parents "regard doing well in school as the single most important task facing their children," whereas American parents "balance academic achievement" with other goals like self-esteem, social skills, and extracurricular activities. Japanese parents take pride in presenting children with their own personal desks as a tangible sign of their main job during the elementary and high school years.

Teachers as Motivators

The relatively weak social incentives that surround and support American teachers make ability to motivate a crucial classroom skill. Maintaining order is a first prerequisite, one of many skills characterized by the solitary rather than shared motivational assignment given teachers. (In Japan, by contrast, student leaders even in elementary schools take some responsibility for order and discipline, on the assumption that such responsibility is theirs more than the teacher's.) In a universal, compulsory, and decentralized system, the burden of getting students to behave and be courteous—much less persuading them to engage in learning without resistance—can be enormous. The relative absence of this burden is the main reason private schools can attract teachers despite lower salaries. Students' willingness to learn—and thus the possibility that teachers can teach—is a crucial positive condition of teachers' work.

The great difficulty of motivating students in lonely isolation is certainly one reason teachers rely so much on extrinsic motivators to help them get through the day. The behaviorist tradition in modern American educational psychology, as shaped early in the century by Edward L. Thorndike, emphasizes the potency of concrete rewards and punishments in producing short-term behavior. Behaviorism and universal school attendance grew up together, and it was only natural that harassed teachers with enormous student loads looked then and now for easy ways to keep students orderly and engaged in some task resembling learning.

Gold stars, tokens, candy, stickers, honor rolls, special treats like field trips, praise, corporal punishment (now infrequent), public censure like standing in the corner, and (above all) tests, grades, and class rank are among the familiar extrinsic motivators teachers routinely use. These rewards and punishments are "outside the task" in the parlance of motivational psychology. Behavior that teachers seek but students find difficult or uninteresting is induced by providing students with something they desire. In a country largely bereft of socially powerful incentives to learn, teacher-generated extrinsic motivators have a long history of success in achieving desired short-term behavior, especially involving compliance and discipline. Although many of these extrinsic motivators are associated with elementary schooling, grades, class rank, and extracurricular eligibility assume greater importance in high school.

Few educators and fewer psychologists of motivation condone the exclusive use of such extrinsic motivators. If all school activity is engaged in only to gain a reward or avoid a punishment that has nothing to do with the activity—if it is literally outside the activity—it is hard to imagine that the activity would subsequently be pursued in the absence of the extrinsic reward or punishment. Yet genuine learning means—whatever else it may mean—retention, understanding, and active use of what has been studied after classes or courses (and their rewards and punishments) are over. An exclusive and obsessive diet of immediate rewards or punishments at best is likely to have little positive effect on motivation to learn. At worst, such a diet can have a profoundly negative effect.

Most educators have no problem with modest teacher use of extrinsic incentives. It is a nonissue. Robert Slavin (1991, p. 89) typically acknowledges that most students are "unlikely to exert the sustained, systematic effort needed to truly master a subject without some kind of reward, such as praise, grades, or recognition." He cannot imagine highly motivated scientists, singers, or inventors who receive no rewards for their labors.

But a classic position within the history of student motivation in America, and one powerfully represented in the contemporary school reform movement, is actively hostile to almost all conceptions of extrinsic motivation. It asserts that only intrinsic motivation—satisfaction or pleasure derived from the task itself rather than from what external rewards success in it may bring—creates lasting learning, engagement, or interest. Motivational psychologists and their allies who take this position argue that rewards have exactly the opposite result from their intention. They reduce motivation to learn. Rewards actually punish (Deci, Vallerand, Pelletier, and Ryan, 1991, p. 335; Kohn, 1993).

The intrinsic motivation camp follows directly in the tradition of child-centered progressive education as associated with the work of John Dewey. It has gained new vigor from the sheer visibility of the motivation to learn issue (which plays to its strengths), from the *constructivist* movement within many scholarly disciplines, and from significant changes in the field of motivational psychology within the past quarter century.

Constructivism in part reflects the relativism and suspicion of authority characteristic of American cultural and intellectual life in the past generation. When applied to school learning, it suggests that knowledge is never transmitted to the young (much less poured in) if it is meant to be lasting and authentic as distinct from fleeting and coerced. Instead, students learn by actively making or constructing knowledge and meaning for themselves. In a sense, knowledge is uniquely customized as their own. In student-centered learning, students integrate personal experiences, interests, and needs—intrinsic qualities—with domains of knowledge that others have provisionally constructed over the centuries. Motivation increases because students have more control over their own learning.

Classic progressive child-centered education, as usually practiced, was often rightly regarded as hostile to the life of the mind. Contemporary versions like constructivism care deeply about intellectual engagement and interests. Relevance is but a starting point. Intellectual objectives such as "teaching for understanding" and "using one's mind well" imply pedagogies where students are lured from prosaic personal interests into the more complex and mind-opening world of human experience. If these intrinsic forces can be cultivated, proponents argue that motivation to learn will rise along with the chance that teaching will have lasting effects. Student-centered but also prointellectual efforts have emerged from such varied sources as the Coalition of Essential Schools, a small school in East Harlem, and research centers at Stanford, Rutgers, and Michigan State (Sizer, 1984; Sizer, 1992; Meier, 1995; Cohen, McLaughlin, and Talbert, 1993).

Contemporary motivational psychology overwhelmingly supports a pedagogical emphasis on intrinsic rather than extrinsic motivation. If motivational psychology in America began with the study of animal behavior, it has become preoccupied with issues of human cognition. Self-perception, as Bernard Weiner (1990) has put it, is now the key determinant of prior or future success and failure—and hence of motivation. The emphasis on intrinsic motivation is driven by the very different effects on self-perception two conditions can have—either being in control of events or being controlled by them.

The "self-determination" research and theory of Edward Deci and his colleagues (1991) is a good example of how this emphasis on self leads motivational psychologists directly to intrinsic motivation. Human beings, Deci suggests, have three basic and inherent psychological needs: competence, relatedness, and autonomy (or self-determination). These are "motivational universals"—that is, motivation to learn will be maximized in social contexts that allow these needs to be satisfied. Since people "need" to be self-determined, not controlled, it is more effective to encourage learning by stressing intrinsic rather than extrinsic motivators. All extrinsic motivation is controlling though Deci and his colleagues admit that some kinds of extrinsic motivation are less controlling than others.

The self-determination versus control distinction is fundamental in motivational psychology's defense of intrinsic motivation. The issue goes beyond fears of manipulation or brainwashing. The psychological argument is that any sense of being controlled denies a human need. Thus, it is normal and human for the self to reject extrinsic motivation *and to become less interested in tasks rewarded by extrinsic motivators.* Such rewards actually punish in the sense of diminishing the desire to learn. Deci (1991, pp. 333–334) argues that praising students for "what they 'should' have done or what you told them to do is likely to lead to their feeling controlled, which in turn would reduce intrinsic motivation and strengthen their nonautonomous forms of extrinsic motivation."

The most troubling aspect of the revival of intrinsic interests is not the basic goal itself: every competent teacher wishes students to become interested in learning for the pleasures and satisfactions of learning itself. But at least three obstacles stand out. First, remarkably few new proposals to implement an intrinsic approach to student motivation have been made. The present agenda would largely have been familiar to progressive educators in the 1930s. Examples include the following suggestions.

Identify individual student interests and build on them. Make curriculum relevant to student's lives. Make learning interesting, meaningful, and challenging. Give students more choices about what they should study. Emphasize creativity. Encourage them to work actively at learning by discovery, constructing ideas, asking questions, teaching peers. Make sure they understand the personal utility of whatever they are asked to do. Acknowledge their feelings when they find a task uninteresting. Give positive feedback in an uncontrolling manner. Allow everyone to feel success. Make education learner centered. Focus not only on understanding but on deep understanding. Abolish grades and all extrinsic incentives (Kohn, 1993; Ames, 1992, p. 263; Dweck, 1986, p. 1045; Deci, Vallerand, Pelletier, and Ryan, 1991, pp. 333–342; Perkins, 1992, pp. 164–166).

The second obstacle follows from the first. These motivation-generating tasks are very difficult for teachers to accomplish, even the most gifted teachers (Kohn, pp. 216–218). One study interviewed teachers who were unusually skilled with students at risk of dropping out. Since the students were not "voracious for academic content," the teachers appealed to their "lifeworld" concerns. "This meant getting to know the students and their lifeworlds more closely than might appeal to many other teachers." The study confirmed the magnitude of developing motivation among many American students. The work involved was extraordinarily difficult—especially if taken seriously. Interesting lessons adapted to individual needs take more work to prepare and to teach. Attacks on extrinsic incentives were unfair to teachers and students who needed them to survive (Duckworth and Lind, 1989, p. 26).

It is instructive that the major centers of progressive education activity before World War II, such as the participants in the famous Eight Year Study of the Progressive Education Association, were typically privileged private and public schools whose students were already highly motivated to learn but bored by the low level of intellectual challenge available in regular schools. The traditional market for progressive child-centered education was notable for the intrinsic and extrinsic incentives it already possessed, not for the incentives it lacked. An exclusive emphasis on intrinsic incentives avoids not only issues of teacher quality and the teacher education knowledge base. It also avoids the issue of how much easier progressive ideas are to implement when students come to school eager to learn.

This is the third problem with intrinsic incentives. Too many proponents see them not only as desired ends, but as the only acceptable means. All else is hurtful to students. But students sometimes lack skills to obtain intrinsic rewards. If they cannot read, they cannot obtain the intrinsic rewards available through reading. So it is important to teach them to read regardless if reading interests them (Chance, 1992, p. 206).

A teacher completing a classroom research study comparing intrinsic and extrinsic teaching techniques (Hilker, 1993) thought that the psychologists' bias toward the intrinsic was wrongheaded. It conflicted with the combination of intrinsic and extrinsic interests that routinely characterized adults with obvious passions for this or for that subject. Besides, she opposed schools that provided students with opportunities to learn only what was interesting to them. It was as if schools had no responsibility to stand for important learning goals regardless of student preferences or of teachers' capacities to make learning enjoyable.

Even thoughtful motivational psychologists like Deci (1991, pp. 328–330) do not close the door entirely on the value of some kinds of extrinsic motivation. He arranges extrinsic motivation into a continuum of student incentives ranging from the receipt of teacher praise, at one extreme, to a situation where behavior (called "integrated regulation") expresses entirely and authentically who an individual is and what is valued by and regarded as important to that individual. The latter sounds rather like an individual who has come to transform what had been external and required to something internal and desired. Deci even gives "being creative" as an example. Who could ask for anything more from extrinsic incentives? But he never quite admits that extrinsic motivation can become truly intrinsic. Instead, he repeats the dictum that "Intrinsic motivation is characterized by interest in the activity itself, whereas integrated regulation is characterized by the activity's being personally important for a valued outcome."

Reviving Extrinsic Motivation

Many reformers have recently argued that teacher and classroom-centered approaches to motivation, especially those that emphasize intrinsic motives almost exclusively, cannot generate the powerful incentives American students need to learn more. However revitalized, they regard the Deweyan tradition as relevant only to a few teachers and a few students. What is needed instead, in their view, is more invasive social policy that influences youth behavior widely and predictably. Schools need the outside support of more public (though not necessarily governmental) incentives to work and learn. This novel American support for public incentives responds to fears about our capacity to compete in a brain-based world economy, to international test score comparisons, and to awareness of international incentive systems of which we have been largely ignorant. It also responds to the need to address equity issues in new ways, and finally to a sense that schools cannot solve all social problems without tangible supports from the rest of society.

Supports, in this instance, means incentives to learn in addition to incentives teachers themselves attempt to produce. The so-called top-down versus bottom-up debate created by the rise of a more systemic approach to extrinsic incentives rivals in ferocity, and has partly shoved aside, the older debate between child-centered and subject-centered educators.

The starkest of extrinsic incentives—the kind that seem unalloyed bribes—are usually responses to the most desperate circumstances. The dropout problem, especially in inner cities, has spawned monetary and other material incentive programs because the consequences of dropping out in these communities are so dreadful. The rewards of these programs come from outside teachers and schools.

Almost all such programs give students money, or its equivalent in coupons for fast-food or merchandise discounts, in return for staying in school or getting passing grades. Paying students to attend school and pass may seem a telling example of the collapse of belief in learning, but the principle is as American as apple pie. "The reality is that parents don't work for free, why should kids?" opined a Newton, Massachusetts, high school junior who put together a coupon book worth $250 in pizzas and movie tickets for students in his school who made the honor roll (*Education Week,* 1995, p. 3).

Far more elaborate but similar programs exist. Nuclear Fuel Services of Erwin, Tennessee, gives "Goal Cards" to local students in grades 1–12 who get straight A's over a marking period, and "Achiever Cards" to those with nothing lower than a B, perfect attendance, and a pattern of improvement. The cards contain the student's photo ID and the principal's signature, and entitle holders to discounts on area merchandise for six weeks (Seoane and Smirk, 1991).

Other programs bypass coupons and pay hard cash. At the low end is Newt Gingrich's "Learning by Earning" program. It pays students $2 for reading a book and answering questions about it. He tells participants, "We want you to work at learning how to read so well that someday you can earn a very good living" (Seelye, 1995, p. B9). Seventh-grade and above Cleveland students have been able to accumulate money in college-scholarship-in-escrow accounts according to the grades they receive in core academic subjects through high school (for example, $20 for a B). One of the most prominent dropout prevention programs, the I Have a Dream Foundation established by businessman Eugene Lang, provides significant guaranteed college scholarship assistance to those who finish high school (Goldman, 1989; Punsalan, 1993; Richmond, 1990).

Direct bribe programs are somewhat marginal and even embarrassing to most extrinsic incentive enthusiasts. Although school attendance and effort may be hard work for some students, the implication that it is onerous work that should be financially compensated teaches offensive lessons that most educators do not want students to learn. That learning is inherently different from enjoyable activity is not an especially attractive lesson.

But several qualities about these programs are worth noticing. First, they are more popular and more numerous than is often believed. Second, anecdotal and sometimes systematic evaluation as reported by the National Dropout Prevention Center (Seoane and Smirk, 1991) suggests they are reasonably successful on their own terms. Participants tend to get higher grades and stay in school longer. Third, one reason they work is that no punishments are meted out to those who choose not to participate. There are no obvious losers, and therefore no constituencies to offend.

Indeed, relatively few extrinsic incentive programs attach high-stakes punishments for student noncompliance. Perhaps the best known of these are Texas competency-based graduation tests, the Texas "no pass, no play" rule, and the efforts of a few states to push school attendance upward by denying driver's licenses to dropouts. Programs that carry immediate—but not long-term—punishments are always controversial and contested. The long-term economic punishment for high school dropouts (and increasingly for those who do not complete postsecondary education) is enormous compared to a delayed driver's license, but few students at risk think long term. Finally, the vast majority of direct bribe programs are supported not by government agencies or school systems but by private enterprise. Most taxpayers are unwilling to use public revenues to entice students to participate in educational institutions that already constitute a significant tax burden.

High-Stakes Incentives

In contrast, the main thrust of the extrinsic incentives movement addresses student transitions from school-to-college and school-to-work, higher standards of academic achievement, and assessment to determine whether standards are met that give access to desired colleges or jobs. Almost all proposals to create "high-stakes" incentives designed to change student behavior deal with how these themes interact. And almost all of them start with similar diagnoses of the problem.

Marc Tucker, for example, notes that "no country in the world that has achieved high educational performance did so without high and explicit standards and without attaching to those standards explicit rewards for students who attain them" (O'Neil, 1992, p. 20). Eckstein and Noah (1993, p. 23) conclude, after exhaustive study of international examination systems, that "with the notable exception of the United States and Sweden, it is difficult to name a modernized or modernizing nation that does not rely on a national system of examinations to certify completion of secondary education, to allocate opportunities for further education or training, or to regulate hiring." And John Bishop (1992, p. 16) asserts "we are the only industrialized country in the world that does not have a system providing externally graded competency assessment keyed to the secondary school curriculum."

The logic of the argument seems clear enough. Create incentives that are really important in the long run—not gold stars or teacher praise or even grades, but access to valued vocations and valued higher education institutions. Make these desired rewards dependent on quality academic performance. Assess performance by examinations that are respected for fairness and competence by most Americans. The result would be systemic support for the work of good teachers. Social policy would support teachers. No longer would they struggle to motivate students alone.

Further, the argument rejects the traditional dichotomy between extrinsic and intrinsic incentives. Proponents wish to use extrinsic incentives, such as high-stakes external examinations, to motivate students to work hard and learn. They believe that learning itself, in quality educational settings, will motivate students to learn more. They believe that intrinsic motivation, for many if not most students, is the most desired product of extrinsic motivation.

The skill of reading opens the door to the joy of reading. Exposure to science, by means of a high-stakes science examination requirement, forces a young woman to confront material that her culture says is too hard, too boring, and too unfeminine. Required exposure disciplined by credible assessment emancipates students from ignorance. It allows them to think for themselves about domains that the larger culture, especially pop culture, hides from them.

The system that these reformers wish to put into place—goals highly valued by students, access to them by meritocratic academic performance, achievement judged by examinations whose results have wide public legitimacy—has an important but not well-known history in this country (Powell, 1993). From 1900 to 1941, admission to many of the most desirable American colleges was determined by just such a system, which was anchored by the annual essay examinations administered by the College Entrance Examination Board. The College Board is a nongovernmental association of colleges and schools originally organized to create common college admissions requirements in place of different and confusing requirements. Although only a small number of usually privileged American youth experienced the system, it was a homegrown analogy to what many extrinsic incentive reformers propose today in imitation of other countries. In 1940, more than 37,000 College Board examinations were taken in 36 subjects at 318 test centers nationwide.

By 1900, strong incentives existed for some students to seek admission to desired colleges. At the same time, those colleges had equally strong incentives to admit well-prepared students. Faced with applicants from very diverse secondary school backgrounds, they wanted assurances that admitted students could do college-level work. They also wanted to make sure that their own idiosyncratic admissions requirements would not turn students away. College supply exceeded student demand at the same time many colleges were attempting to upgrade student preparation.

In these circumstances, common entrance examinations of a certain sort seemed desirable. The College Board program linked student (and family) incentives to academic effort and performance. If the college of one's choice was a college that used the College Board examinations, the way to gain admission was to pass those examinations. Academic achievement had desirable, predictable, and clear consequences.

The key to the system was a credible mechanism to assess high school academic performance. For four decades, the essay exams of the College Board maintained that credibility. Their content was credible because of the central role leading scholars (as well as a few leading teachers) played in their construction. American parents and teachers were more inclined in the early decades of the century to defer to academic scholars on what constituted preparation for college. Much consensus existed on basic domains of knowledge, but not so much as to avoid vigorous battles within subjects.

Indeed, curriculum debate was dominated not by older fights about the place of classical languages and mathematics, but by fights within genuinely new school subjects like modern and American history, modern languages and literatures, and science. Even the methods of the College Board examinations broke sharply from the traditions of the previous generation. Written essays permitted the display of thought rather than oral recitation or rote recall. Language translations required students to make sense of passages they had never seen before. Science had a laboratory component.

Further, the examinations were purposefully designed to help colleges select-in rather than select-out. Instead of identifying the "best" from a pool of qualified applicants, the examinations selected-in all those who indicated potential to do successful college work. The scoring was criterion referenced, not norm referenced. Everyone had a chance to meet whatever a particular college's passing grade was. Thus, average students could hope to pass them through intensive preparation. There was no sense that only bright students could succeed on the College Boards or that hard work had no pay-off. Schools and teachers usually took more pride in the percentage of their students who succeeded on the Boards than in the tiny number who did exceedingly well. The exams rewarded effort.

The three-hour examinations were also externally set and externally graded. A student's teachers neither created nor scored them. They were developed by committees of examiners, consisting of college and school teachers, and graded by hundreds of readers who gathered annually for a week at Columbia University. External assessment enormously improved the credibility of the scoring. Although the charge of subjectivity was never absent from essay scoring, the charge of favoritism could not be fairly made.

What is perhaps most intriguing about this incentive system is its collapse in early 1942. The incentives for colleges to maintain it rapidly weakened during the 1930s, and other social changes overwhelmed many of its assumptions. The elite colleges and universities who had maintained the College Board system gradually sought more academically talented students and gradually realized that these could be found inside any American high school if only the right techniques were employed and sufficient financial aid was available. Why continue to emphasize examinations that ordinary students could pass with effort if other tests could be devised that identified genuine ability? Why continue procedures for selecting-in when at least a few colleges began to have the luxury of using admissions practices to select-out?

Moreover, the credibility of the old College Boards began to erode. Proponents of scientific test construction attacked the essays as neither reliable, valid, nor cost effective. Debates about the fairness of any curriculum-driven examination arose. Suppose students attended inferior schools that could not prepare for the exams? Wasn't an emphasis on aptitude rather than on learning or effort more equitable?

When unprecedented numbers of Americans wanted to attend college after World War II, and more versions of postsecondary education were created, the legitimacy of any single standard of academic preparation for college collapsed. It conflicted with student preferences, organized lobbies, and institutional self-interest. Who could agree on one standard of school performance in a nation where most students wanted a college degree? If no agreement could be secured, except perhaps the most minimal, then no standard or examination to meet it could be constructed. Systemic extrinsic incentives would evaporate.

Such was the general rationale for the rise of aptitude tests like the SAT, which effectively replaced the old College Boards. But one effect of this, as we have seen, was to contribute to the growing American belief that ability not effort was what led to success. The demise of the old College Boards removed a powerful incentive for average students to work hard. At the same time, incentives to work hard actually increased for students aspiring to desired colleges when those institutions became selective.

It was because of these additional incentives for ambitious students that the Advanced Placement examination program became somewhat redirected from its original mid 1950s goals to unanticipated objectives in later decades. Advanced Placement was a series of high school courses taught at a college level and accepted for college credit by many institutions. It was designed to make school-to-college transitions more financially and educationally rational. AP intended to eliminate the common practice of forcing able students to repeat and pay for as college freshmen what they had just finished studying in high school (Valentine, 1987, pp. 79–100).

But AP has grown not primarily because students were motivated to avoid repeating courses or to avoid paying part of college tuition. Most AP students have stayed in college for the full four tuition-paying years, and relaxed college requirements instituted in the 1960s made moot the course repetition problem. AP became the centerpiece of the late-century college acceptance incentive system, a partial successor to the old College Boards, because it was challenging and because it was thought to improve one's college admissions chances. And even though AP superficially resembled the old College Boards in the sense of curriculum-driven achievement tests with a heavy essay component, AP gave far more attention to the politically sensitive issues of technical validity and reliability. Unlike the old College Boards, AP has retained credibility among educators and the public.

Advanced Placement examinations, though entirely voluntary and administered by the nonprofit, nongovernmental College Board, represent the closest current American approximation of high-stakes, externally assessed, curriculum-driven achievement examinations. The main problem AP poses for incentives policy is that only a tiny number of high school students participate. AP exams help only a few students gain admission to a few colleges, are more difficult and time consuming than similar courses, and charge a modest fee. In some ways, they are like the various prizes available to students, such as the Westinghouse science talent search. They provide real incentives, but only to a few. The basic problem of an AP-type model is that its appeal as an incentive is presently confined to a limited population. But at a time when government seems somewhat suspect, the voluntary and nongovernmental character of AP make it one of the most politically credible models on which to build more systemic extrinsic incentive policies—incentives carrying important, life-changing consequences.

Nevertheless, mechanisms like AP are of limited policy use unless both the givers of rewards (colleges, employers) and the seekers of rewards (students, parents) believe that serious academic achievement is necessary to get those rewards. Bishop demonstrates that Canadian students from provinces with externally assessed, curriculum-driven, end-of-high-school examinations score higher on math–science assessments taken when they are age thirteen. But he does not demonstrate why knowing this fact will cause other provinces, universities, employers, or students to demand that these examinations be adopted in their own jurisdictions (Bishop, 1994; Bishop, 1995).

Indeed, national-type examinations (including both the old College Boards and AP) did not arise anywhere from a desire to raise national standards. Much more specific and practical reasons were at work. Internationally, these included widening meritocratic opportunities via education, checking patronage and corruption, recruiting for occupations that required specific knowledge, and fairly allocating scarce places. In America, the objectives of regularizing college admission requirements and the transition from school to college were originally paramount. The existence of high-stakes examinations everywhere owes little to a concerted desire to raise standards. It is not clear that public support for such examinations would exist if the goal was simply standard raising (Eckstein and Noah, 1993, pp. 2–17).

Perhaps this is why Bishop emphasizes good information or "signals" as crucial incentive-building strategy. He wants to persuade students *and* employers that student achievement is in everyone's self-interest. One kind of signal is that academic achievement matters in real life. Years and quality of schooling lead to both increased economic productivity and increased earnings. Systemic incentive policy should therefore emphasize the communication of important information to students *and* employers about the consequences of achievement and the lack of it (Bishop, 1993; Bishop, 1994).

Signaling also means communicating clear and credible measures of academic achievement. One reason students do not work hard or learn much to get a B grade in most fields is exactly the same reason an employer or university admissions officer pays little attention to a B. Because such grades are locally constructed, they are usually meaningless as comparative indicators. They are usually useless as any indicator unless the admissions officer happens to know personally the grading practices of individual teachers.

AP scores help solve the comparability problem, but the single number AP grade (from 1 to 5) signals little information to anyone about what a student knows and can do following a year's close encounter with a domain of study. Still, AP is a clear improvement over grades, class rank, and aptitude scores as a credible measure of work effort and school achievement. The more that colleges and employers value and use AP-like examinations, the more rewards there will be for students who seriously address the materials that these examinations address. (Other tests like the College Board Achievement Tests are not curriculum driven and much less credible as evidence of hard work in school.)

Policy Directions for High-Stakes Incentives

A policy strategy more basic and more difficult than signaling information is the expansion of AP-like assessment programs. Why merely communicate that external assessment is valuable? Why not extend it systemically through decisions by policy makers? Why not, for example, link student incentives with systemic reform by having state universities and four-year state colleges require that all entering freshmen minimally receive a passing score (that is, a 3 score) on one Advanced Placement examination and a 2 score on a second AP examination? One examination could be drawn, at the student's choice, from the science–math–computer science area, the other from the humanities–arts–social sciences area.

It is clear from the expansion of AP enrollments nationally that this is not an unreasonable burden for students bound for four-year institutions. It would have, at the least, a salutary effect on both student and teacher work effort. And it would not aggravate tracking. Greater incentives would exist for college-bound students of different abilities to experience at least some of the same curriculum. And greater pressure would be exerted on schools to make challenging courses available to students below the top group. Many independent schools containing mixed-ability college-bound students teach AP American history and AP English to all students.

Current AP examinations are primarily interesting as an example of external assessment rather than as a program to be slavishly imitated. It is probably crucial to have many kinds of examinations with many degrees of difficulty, as European countries have learned. One of the most instructive features of the old American College Boards is that they were not too difficult. Because average students could pass them through effort in order to achieve their goal of college admission, average students took them seriously. High-stakes standards that effectively select-out (or punish) most of the population may be appropriate for advanced fields like medical board certification but are self-defeating when the intention is to raise effort and achievement across the entire school-age population.

Many organizations or consortia besides the College Board might develop their own examination systems. The strength of voluntarism in the United States—as evidenced by the influence of the College Board, Advanced Placement (administered by the Board but in many respects quite apart from it), and professional organizations like the National Council of Teachers of Mathematics—suggests that such groups may have as much influence on future achievement examinations as will state governments. There is no reason important businesses could not work together to create external examinations more suited for their job requirements. If business really values particular entry workforce skills, it could in collaboration with schools develop suitable external examinations just as other countries have developed examinations for entry to occupations. The fundamental question is the depth of business incentives to create incentives for students to learn in school.

This is not to suggest that examinations are the only solution to the school-to-work transition problem. Other strategies could help close the current gap between schools and employers. In the aftermath of Vietnam, it has become unthinkable to suggest a revival of compulsory military service for those not bound for postsecondary education. Yet many remember, especially in the relatively peaceful years after Korea and before the Vietnam buildup, the profoundly positive transformation of vocational purpose and self-esteem that the armed services caused in students who had found no incentives to learn in school.

More realistically, scholars like James Rosenbaum (1989, pp. 14–15) emphasize not only signaling mechanisms but the establishment of relationships between schools and businesses more like those between schools and colleges (if not quite like the remarkably close relationships Japanese businesses have with schools). "Schools can improve incentives for work-bound students by having strong ties with employer recruiters as they do with college recruiters, by providing information and counseling for work-bound students as they do for college-bound students, and by writing recommendations for work-bound students as they do for college-bound students." He emphasizes that grades can be made more meaningful without creating new examinations by reporting effort and achievement grades, and reporting them clearly. Businesses, in turn, should tell school counselors about job openings and hiring criteria, trust counselors' recommendations, and make hiring decisions while youth are still in school.

Reformers who dislike Advanced Placement for whatever reasons might similarly collaborate to create different or more intellectually ambitious external examination systems. The Coalition of Essential Schools, for example, has advanced for more than a decade a set of reasonably clear principles aimed at students' learning to use their minds well. Some of these principles are different enough from Advanced Placement to permit building exciting new curricula whose credibility could be established by external assessment. The nature of the external assessment would itself be innovative.

An example might be a ninth-grade interdisciplinary English–Social Studies–Arts course, focusing on a few essential questions, in which active student work and collaborative learning changed the teacher's role from sage to coach, and in which student work was assessed and feedback given by portfolios and exhibitions. This would constitute an interesting alternative to AP, one firmly grounded in the progressive tradition of intrinsic motivation.

But to signal to students, parents, colleges, and employers that such a course in fact promotes mental exertion and serious achievement, the credibility provided by a competent external assessment is almost indispensable. Otherwise, reform remains confined to a few true believers, brings to bear few extrinsic incentives to support teachers in very difficult ventures, and continues to place all the responsibility for success on teachers and students themselves.

Why are such straightforward policy initiatives rarely tried? Why does the oldest and most famous state-level example of external assessment—the examinations conducted by the New York State Board of Regents—support fewer student incentives to learn today than it did a generation ago? Regents scores used to determine scholarship assistance and much else within New York State. Today, most selective colleges and employers have no interest in Regents scores at all (Bishop, 1995, p. 13).

And why do the most innovative state initiatives, such as Kentucky's educational reform legislation, put high-stakes performance incentives on schools but not on individual students? Elsewhere, state mandates on students are usually minimal. They define as high school standards what educators admit are ordinary expectations for eighth graders. Why are Americans reluctant to adopt public incentive policies that may affect students adversely?

One reason is principled democratic objections to excessive

top-down intrusiveness, by government or any powerful agency above the schools, in the most value-laden of subjects—the education of children. This objection becomes sharpened when government is perceived as representing educational values different from one's own. The principled argument against government involvement sometimes reinforces and sometimes conflicts with practical self-interest. Issues like school prayer, sex education, outcomes-based education, and critical thinking often set off bitter battles between local communities and more distant governance structures.

A second reason is faith that teachers and students in individual schools, if unshackled from the chains of policy imposed from above, can motivate students to learn without extrinsic supports. The Coalition of Essential Schools, for example, supports principles of school-based decision making that have the effect of nearly rejecting out of hand the very kind of ninth-grade curriculum just imagined. The Coalition has so far created no alternatives to AP examinations because the idea of external student assessment, especially of curriculum created outside individual schools, may undercut the educational energy and creativity of local control.

A third reason is that no social consensus exists that more external examination programs are necessary. It is not clear whether business really wants student skills beyond basic literacy, the work ethic, and the habit of obedience. It is not clear how much higher education (or high schools) are willing to trade off in return for greater student effort and achievement. Many educational jobs depend on remediating what earlier levels of schooling fail to accomplish. The economic pain of winning the Cold War has been great—and greatly resisted. Yet that was a war nearly every American wanted to win. The war against ignorance and educational passivity has fewer soldiers enlisted in the cause.

It is not clear why the middle class would want more ambitious courses in high school when their absence does not prevent access to higher education and their presence would increase the time demands on youth already overburdened with extracurricular activities and part-time employment. Besides, any move from voluntarism to requirements in high school life would inevitably produce more high scorers and more college competition. One possible benefit might result if "merit" was restored as a criterion for financial aid along with need. An economic as well as admissions pay-off might increase incentives to learn in middle-income families too rich to qualify for financial aid but too poor to afford college without life-changing debt. Merit-based financial aid, in fact, is increasing as moderately selective colleges attempt to keep a critical mass of able students (McPherson and Shapiro, 1994).

It is hard to see why equity advocates, with some exceptions, should have any more sympathy for high-stakes external assessments than do the better-off middle classes. They tend to regard extrinsic incentives as opportunity door-slammers, not door-openers. The rewards that doing well can confer are less obvious than the punishments that failure will ensure. Signaling poor and minority students about the rewards of education seems especially crucial. It is not clear that incentives for them to work hard at academics can be achieved by any sort of coercion.

School Context as Motivation

If the standards movement has suffered some setbacks from the opposition just discussed, and if teachers working alone in classrooms have not produced widespread student motivation to learn, what other promising directions present themselves? Framing the issue in this way may exaggerate the tensions between the intrinsic and extrinsic camps and underestimate national progress in the last decade. Bishop (1995) suggests a decidedly optimistic view of the future of voluntary and state-created external achievement examinations. He sees gradual movement in that direction without much of a federal role, growth in the percentage of youth enrolling in more demanding courses, and a reduction of achievement score gaps within and outside the United States.

At the same time, teachers have received recent major support from the creation of the National Board for Professional Teaching Standards, the efforts of the Holmes Group of major schools of education to focus energy on teacher education, the increased seriousness of research on pedagogy, and the usefulness of curriculum frameworks from subject-matter organizations. It is not entirely inconceivable that the American contempt for education methods courses may one day be somewhat reduced, just as similar contempt for medical school learning was rather suddenly reduced only a century ago (Judge, Lemosse, Paine, and Sedlak, 1994, pp. 148–154).

Yet an examination of student incentives seems incomplete if it considers only teachers' motivational strategies and macro or social motivational strategies. The gold star, discount coupon book, and interest-based relevant project may all have a place. So may the dreams of being on the honor roll, winning a merit-based scholarship, qualifying for the Marines, or becoming a CEO. But students live within educational incentive zones that are larger than what they experience in classrooms and smaller than the economic or cultural rewards available in the distant future.

Powerful incentives and disincentives are generated by these additional contexts—particularly by the quality of school communities, the quality of families, and how the two interact. These intermediary agencies are what is meant by context. Although this discussion concentrates on schools, families are equally important in creating incentives to learn. Since school achievement and working hard at learning are lower priorities for most American parents than parents in many other industrial societies, schools are immediately faced with a major context problem. Stevenson and Stigler (1992, pp. 68–69, 84) conclude that a "notable characteristic of the lives of American children is a striking discontinuity between home and school." In very few American elementary schools do children carry back and forth from home each day the little notebooks that Japanese children carry, in which parents ask questions and verify that children have done homework, and teachers raise questions and give feedback.

How then do American schools create *atmospheres* where motivation to learn becomes contagious? Everyone knows that some schools are boring places that by their nature reinforce aversion to learning in even the most committed, whereas other schools project an atmosphere where learning is infectious. Context motivates in different ways. Three matters seem especially central for incentives: what kind of educational community a school is, what kind of student body composes it, and how personalized is the atmosphere.

One way schools create incentives to learn is to, each day, visibly celebrate and exemplify the benefits of some focused conception of learning. A purposeful school community projects to students in endless ways the values of learning and of decency. In so doing, it sharply defines its role as not merely a part of society (which it inevitably is), but also as standing outside society to challenge antieducation forces. A school must consistently stand for an educational purpose and bear constant witness to that purpose. It cannot hope that a few teachers will carry the educational flag alone.

Schools must wake up to the fact that they are the last line of defense against powerful negative forces that spend enormous sums to create incentives in youth to consume pleasure and disincentives to exert mental effort. Immigrants who have not been mesmerized by the pleasures of passive consumption usually work harder in schools and colleges than do native-born Americans. They still see school as a unique opportunity to learn and get ahead. They do not take school for granted as another entitlement. Youth pop culture has not yet won them over.

How do purposeful schools support incentives to learn? It helps if a school can agree on a limited curriculum and communicate clearly what it is. In certain contexts, less can be more. A limited curriculum reduces choice but puts students and teachers in a common situation where much of the academic conversation addresses questions and problems that all must confront together. Situations where learners are forced to talk with one another about the same issues increase conversation and, given some luck, increase interest in the topic and future incentives to learn.

This is one of those curious areas where the old idea of a required experience for all and the newer idea of collaborative learning intersect. In both, the opportunities for students to engage with one another about a common educational task are increased. Students can help generate interests and incentives in other students—just as students learn to ride bikes by watching their peers rather than by following their fathers' advice.

Free elective systems of the sort that characterize most elite colleges create incentives for students already committed to particular fields to pursue them in depth. But they create disincentives to the majority of youth who do not have established interests and do not know how to make wise choices. In the absence of academic press by adults, students simply seek out popular teachers and popular courses. The abdication by adults of responsibility for defining general education is a serious disincentive for students to engage in learning. Wise policy addressed to all American youth should reduce curriculum choice.

A related theme is that a school's community—its teachers, administrators, but especially its students and families—determines its possibilities and limits. School is all these people. Recognizing this heightens the attention and respect owed students and families. They wield enormous educational power. Students and families are not the raw material on which schools work. They are as much school as are teachers.

Students and families are crucial causes of whatever incentives to learn exist in a school. Who the students and families are affect everyone's incentives. This is why public school choice is perhaps the fastest growing systemic reform in the United States. Incentives to learn are shaped in part by peers. If one's peers believe effort and learning are valuable, even students resistant to the idea tend to conform. Thus, thoughtful parents want their children to attend schools with students who, for whatever intrinsic or extrinsic reason, will engage in learning. The issue of private school choice is still ideologically and constitutionally contentious. But the people's wish for choice within public schools seems so well established that opponents are either on the defensive or in full-scale retreat.

Public choice options rarely have meritocratic admissions criteria. Families interested in incentives to learn do not care much about schools where admission is determined by tested evidence of high scholastic aptitude. They simply want parent and student commitment to learning—to work hard, do one's best, play by the rules. The admission standard of commitment—rather than academic capacity—perfectly expresses the idea that the best way to promote incentives to learn in an individual is to place him or her in a school where incentives to learn is the pervasive norm.

A third theme is personalization, a term that includes but is not synonymous with individualization of instruction. In personalized schools, students are helped to acquire incentives to learn because they see up-close and in different settings teachers who live rewarding lives based in part on what they teach. This is usually called modeling. Students acquire an interest because they observe that a teacher has that interest and, further, that the interest is highly pleasurable and educative over a long period. There is no better intrinsic incentive to learn than direct observation of the positive consequences of that learning in someone else. All good teachers should be intellectual role models.

Personalization also helps create incentives to learn in a quite different sense. As dual-career, single-parent, and wholly dysfunctional households have all increased, fewer adults know young people well. There is insufficient connective tissue among watchful, concerned adults and youth. So young people often fall through the cracks. They become invisible to grownups, influenced mainly by peers. In these circumstances, the role of teacher as caring adult assumes greater consequences. These consequences extend beyond the topic of motivation to learn but certainly include that topic.

Shocked by an adult who cares, a student pays that adult back by engaging in a learning activity that otherwise he or she might reject. The caring is the incentive in this instance, whereas the modeling is the incentive in the first example. Personalization has different dimensions. But all of them usually depend on reduced teacher loads so that teachers, in fact, can know something about individual students (Marks, 1994, p. B1; Darling-Hammond, 1996).

Personalization, in short, requires changes in teacher–student relationships, which, in turn, depend on structural changes in schools. For teachers to know students well, they cannot have too many of them. They must have opportunities to know them in unscheduled contexts outside class periods. Teachers and students should probably spend less time in regular classes. One reason Japanese elementary schools can enforce a work ethic is that students have more recess time—more time out of class—than American students. If learning requires effort, there must be breaks from that effort. If knowing students well means having time to talk to them, time must be made.

Thus, school context can motivate although these three context dimensions have rarely been the main concern of motivational psychologists or labor economists. Good schools are essential parts of any systemic approach to student incentives, as are good classroom teaching and extrinsic rewards that lure students toward learning for its own sake. Since each approach has problems of support in the society, there seems little alternative but to pursue them all simultaneously. But if systemic reform can accomplish anything in the field of student incentives, it must first be to convince the citizenry that learning requires student incentives, and that incentives in America are dangerously weak.

References

Ames, C. "Classrooms: Goals, Structures, and Student Motivation." *Journal of Educational Psychology,* 1992, *84* (3), 261–271.

Bishop, J. H. *A Strategy for Achieving Excellence in Secondary Education: The Role of State Government.* Working Paper 91–24. Ithaca, N.Y.: Center for Advanced Human Resource Studies, 1991.

Bishop, J. H. "Why U.S. Students Need Incentives to Learn." *Educational Leadership,* 1992, *49* (6), 15–18.

Bishop, J. H. *Incentives to Study and the Organization of Secondary Education.* Working Paper 93–08. Ithaca, N.Y.: Center for Advanced Human Resource Studies, 1993.

Bishop, J. H. *The Impact of Curriculum-Based Examinations on Learning in Canadian Secondary Schools.* Working Paper 94–30. Ithaca, N.Y.: Center for Advanced Human Resource Studies, 1994.

Bishop, J. H. *Improving Education: How Large Are the Benefits? How Can It Be Done Effectively?* Draft Working Paper 95. Ithaca, N.Y.: Center for Advanced Human Resource Studies, 1995.

Carter, B. "A Cable Challenge for PBS as King of the Preschool Hill." *New York Times,* March 21, 1994, p. 1.

Chance, P. "The Rewards of Learning." *Phi Delta Kappan,* 1992, *74* (3), 200–207.

Cohen, D. K., McLaughlin, M. W., and Talbert, J. (eds.). *Teaching for Understanding. Challenges for Policy and Practice.* San Francisco: Jossey-Bass, 1993.

Conant, J. B. *The American High School Today.* New York: McGraw-Hill, 1959.

Conant, J. B. *My Several Lives. Memoirs of a Social Inventor.* New York, Evanston, and London: Harper & Row, 1970.

Cusick, P. A. *The Egalitarian Ideal and the American High School: Studies of Three Schools.* New York and London: Longman, 1983.

Darling-Hammond, L. "Beyond Bureaucracy: Restructuring Schools for High Performance." In Fuhrman, S. H. and O'Day, J. (eds.): *Rewards and Reform.* San Francisco: Jossey-Bass, 1996.

Deci, E. L., Vallerand, R. J., Pelletier, L. G., and Ryan, R. M. "Motivation and Education: The Self-Determination Perspective." *Educational Psychologist,* 1991, *26* (3–4), 325–346.

Duckworth, K. and Lind, K. *Curricular Goals and Motivating Strategies With Non-College-Bound Students in Science and Social Studies.* Paper presented at the American Educational Research Association, March 1989.

Dweck, C. S. "Motivational Processes Affecting Learning." *American Psychologist*, 1986, *41* (10), 1040–1048.

Eckstein, M. A. and Noah, H. J. *Secondary School Examinations. International Perspectives on Policies and Practice.* New Haven and London: Yale University Press, 1993.

"For Honor or Money." *Education Week*, March 8, 1995, p. 3.

Goldman, J. P. "Learn to Earn! Growing Number of Schools Offer Cash, Prizes to Spur Students." *The School Administrator*, 1989, *11* (46), 12–14.

Hilker, J. B. *Toward Creating the Intrinsically Motivating Classroom: Can Students' Motivational Orientations Be Changed?* ERIC Document 359166, 1993.

Hofstadter, R. *Anti-Intellectualism in American Life.* New York: Vintage Books, 1962.

Judge, H., Lemosse, M., Paine, L., and Sedlak, M. *The University and the Teachers. France, the United States, England. Oxford Studies in Comparative Education,* Vol. 4, No. 1–2. Wallingford, Oxfordshire: Triangle Books, 1994.

Kohn, A. *Punished by Rewards. The Trouble with Gold Stars, Incentive Plans, A's, Praise, and Other Bribes.* Boston and New York: Houghton Mifflin, 1993.

Maehr, M. L. and Midgley, C. "Enhancing Student Motivation: A Schoolwide Approach." *Educational Psychologist*, 1991, *26* (3–4), 399–427.

Marks, P. "Turning Around Troubled Students, Intensively." *New York Times*, April 14, 1994, p. B1.

McNeil, L. M. *Contradictions of Control.* Boston and London: Routledge and Kegan Paul, 1985.

McPherson, M. S. and Schapiro, M. O. *Merit Aid: Students, Institutions, and Society.* CPRE Research Report Series Report #30. New Brunswick, N.J.: Consortium for Policy Research in Education, 1994.

Meier, D. *The Power of Their Ideas. Lessons for America From a Small School in Harlem.* Boston: Beacon Press, 1995.

National Center on the Educational Quality of the Workforce. *First Findings. The EQW National Employer Survey.* Philadelphia: National Center on the Educational Quality of the Workforce, 1995a.

National Center on the Educational Quality of the Workforce. *The Other Shoe: Education's Contributions to the Productivity of Establishments.* Philadelphia: National Center on the Educational Quality of the Workforce, 1995b.

O'Neil, J. "On Education and the Economy: A Conversation with Marc Tucker." *Educational Leadership*, 1992, *49* (6), 19–22.

Perkins, D. *Smart Schools. Better Thinking and Learning for Every Child.* New York: The Free Press, 1992.

Powell, A. G., Farrar, E., and Cohen, D. K. *The Shopping Mall High School.* Boston: Houghton Mifflin, 1985.

Powell, A. G. "Student Incentives and Academic Standards: Independent Schools as a Coherent System." In Fuhrman, S. H. (ed.): *Designing Coherent Educational Policy.* San Francisco: Jossey-Bass, 1993.

Punsalan, C. M. "Gotta Have It. Pepsi Challenges Students to Stay in School." *Vocational Education Journal,* 1993, *68* (4), 28–31.

Richmond, G. "The Student Incentive Plan: Mitigating the Legacy of Poverty." *Phi Delta Kappan,* 1990, *72* (3), 227–229.

Rosenbaum, J. E. *Empowering Schools and Teachers: A New Link to Jobs for the Non-College Bound. Background Paper No. 4.* Commission on Workforce Quality and Labor Market Efficiency. Washington, D.C.: U.S. Department of Labor, 1989.

Rosenbaum, J. E. and Kariya, T. "From High School to Work: Market and Institutional Mechanisms in Japan." *American Journal of Sociology,* 1989, *94* (6), 1334–1365.

Sedlak, M. W., Wheeler, C. W., Pullin, D. C., and Cusick, P. A. *Selling Students Short. Classroom Bargains and Academic Reform in the American High School.* New York and London: Teachers College Press, 1986.

Seelye, K. Q. "Urging Students to Read with a Little Cash." *New York Times,* March 2, 1995, p. B9.

Seoane, M. and Smirk, J. *Incentives and Education. A Series of Solutions and Strategies. No. 4,* Clemson, S.C.: National Dropout Prevention Center, 1991.

Sizer, T. R. *Horace's Compromise.* Boston: Houghton Mifflin, 1984.

Sizer, T. R. *Horace's School.* Boston and New York: Houghton Mifflin, 1992.

Slavin, R. E. "Group Rewards Make Groupwork Work." *Educational Leadership,* 1991, *48* (5), 89–91.

Stevenson, H. W. and Stigler, J. W. *The Learning Gap. Why Our Schools Are Failing and What We Can Learn from Japanese and Chinese Education.* New York: Summit Books, 1992.

Valentine, J. A. *The College Board and the School Curriculum.* New York: College Entrance Examination Board, 1987.

Weiner, B. "History of Motivational Research in Education." *Journal of Educational Psychology,* 1990, *82* (4), 616–622.

Wlodkowski, R. J. and Jaynes, J. H. *Eager to Learn. Helping Children Become Motivated and Love Learning.* San Francisco: Jossey-Bass, 1991.

Chapter Three

Rewarding Teachers for Student Performance[1]

David K. Cohen

Introduction

If professionals were perfect they would always consult carefully with clients and accurately determine the best course of action. If clients were perfect they would find the professionals they preferred, they would consult carefully to decide a course of action, and they would always work hard to do what had been decided.

But professionals and clients are not perfect. They often are unsure what to do. When they are sure they often turn out to be incorrect. And even when sure and correct they often fail to apply themselves to the solutions. There are many failures in professional practice.

The social organization of practice offers ways to manage such failures. In medicine, until recently in the United States, most doctors and patients found each other in markets. Dissatisfied patients could change physicians if they lived where practitioners were plentiful and price was not a problem. Physicians could refer or refuse cases that they found too difficult or otherwise unsuitable. Failures in practice could be remedied by choice.

But markets also fail. Many people have little or no health care, and many others who have care get only a low-grade version. They usually have little effective choice with which to remedy failures of professionalism. Some commentators argue that markets for health care create as many failures as they solve, and call for universal provision under some sort of public sponsorship or subsidy.

Elementary and secondary schools operate under one version

of public sponsorship. Education is provided by state and local authorities, and all students are included without reference to their families' ability to pay. Indeed, students are compelled by law to attend school, and most schools are not only sponsored but actually operated by state agencies. Teachers and students are assigned to each other by administrative decision. There are elements of choice around the fringes—families can use residential choice to select schools, or they can pay for private education that satisfies state criteria—but most teachers and students have only modest choice at best. It is difficult for most students to find schools or teachers different from those assigned, and it is no easier for most teachers to find students different from those assigned. These limits on choice increase as family incomes decrease.

By definition one finds few market failures under this regime, but that still leaves plenty of room for failures of professionalism. Though there is some evidence that school performance has either improved or held steady as more and more disadvantaged students entered and stayed on in school since the early twentieth century, critics and reformers have increasingly argued that test scores are too low or are declining. They argue that public education has failed, and many Americans seem to share that view.[2] They blame teachers' unwillingness or inability to offer suitable instruction, or school administrators' unwillingness or incapability to require better work from teachers, or organizational defects that inhibit solid professional accomplishment, or some combination of these conditions.

One response has been growing efforts to hold practitioners accountable for students' performance. These efforts have multiplied since the 1970s, and their popularity owes something to the simplicity of the central idea: if teachers were penalized for poor student performance or rewarded for good performance, or both, then they would have potent incentives to improve students' work and the work would improve. That was among the key ideas in state and local minimum competency testing programs that were popular in the 1970s and 1980s. It also became an important part of efforts, at about the same time, to improve education for disadvantaged children. Similar ideas turned up both in the recent congressional reauthorization of Title I of the ESEA and in the companion legislation titled Goals 2000. There also has been growing interest in broadly reorienting public schools to results produced rather than resources applied and in using performance rewards to do so. Though commentators and policy makers disagree about how it should be done, more and more agree that some system of performance rewards is needed in public education.[3]

One key similarity among recent performance reward schemes is their administrative character. Rather than substituting markets and consumer choice for state-administered schooling, these schemes would augment the state administration of schooling with scientific assessments of educational effectiveness and schedules of rewards and sanctions.[4] Performance rewards are an effort to improve the operation of schools within a state-maintained framework, not to change the framework.

As policy makers, practitioners, and researchers consider such schemes, they will want to know what sorts of performance reward systems might be considered and about the grounds on which they might choose among the alternatives. I consider both matters here. I begin by delineating the key issues in the design of any performance reward scheme and then discuss alternative ways that educators and policy makers could manage these issues. I also note several issues on which research could help.

Three broad themes run through my analysis. One is that despite many efforts to institute performance reward schemes, there is relatively little reliable professional or social science knowledge about their operation and effects. We know enough to rule out simplistic and punitive schemes—though that may not be sufficient to keep them from being adopted—but not enough to inform choices among more complex and sophisticated alternatives. A second theme is that performance rewards alone cannot solve the problems of weak school performance. Though we do not know nearly enough to design the best performance reward scheme, we know that even the best scheme would require critical additional elements to improve performance in the schools in which performance is worst. Yet much of the appeal of performance rewards lies in the idea that they would be a relatively simple and cheap solution to a complex and difficult problem.

A third theme is that though performance rewards would require unprecedented clarity about measures of performance, criteria of success, and fairness, these are matters about which Americans deeply disagree. The current schooling regime inhibits clarity because schools have been the vehicle for many different hopes and purposes, have been the site of many compromises over fundamental social issues, and in the process have accumulated many layers of purpose. Advocates of performance rewards propose to sweep such murk away and replace it with clear criteria of success and standards of fairness. It seems almost sure that such schemes could not work as intended if much greater clarity were not achieved, but it also seems very likely that the more clarity we achieved, the more disputes would ensue.

Design Issues: An Overview

When school officials consider performance reward schemes, they will have to decide several fundamental issues. To begin with, whose performances would the scheme focus on? Many accountability systems in elementary and secondary schools focus on students' performance on achievement tests. But many U.S. universities and a few school systems focus on instructors' performance in service, research, and teaching.

No less important, who would be rewarded for the performances thus produced? In the higher education schemes just mentioned, professors are rewarded for their service, teaching, and research; students' performance never enters the picture. In contrast, most performance reward schemes in K-12 education reward or penalize teachers for students' performance, an approach that assumes teachers have considerable leverage on students, or that teachers' and students' interests are quite close, or both. Different designs are possible. Students could be rewarded for their own performance, principals or central office staff could be rewarded for students' performance, or some combination of these.

Once those issues were settled, school officials would have to decide whether individuals or groups would be rewarded or penalized. If teachers were to be rewarded, would the consequences accrue to individuals or to entire faculties? Collective sanctions are thought to encourage cooperation, whereas individual sanctions are thought to encourage competition. Treating students as individuals does seem likely to encourage competition, whereas rewarding them as classes or entire schools could promote cooperation.

Finally, would measures of performance be internal or external to the performance situations? Many merit pay systems in K-12 education sought to hold teachers accountable for students' performance on tests that were created by some external agency—most often a testing or publishing firm. In such cases, teachers were held accountable for students' work on standards of performance that they had no hand in devising. But a few merit pay schemes in K-12 education, and many in higher education, are keyed to teachers' production of evidence about their performance on internally devised performance criteria. In some such cases, teachers had a relatively free hand to design their own portfolios, whereas in others, they report their performance on locally designed criteria.[5]

These issues suggest an enormous range of ways to interpret performance rewards, but there has been less variety in practice. Most schemes of recent vintage in K-12 schooling reward teachers for students' performance on some sort of external test. Very few schemes reward teachers for their own performance,[6] and very few reward teachers on internal rather than external criteria. Hence, I will focus on performance rewards for teachers that are keyed to students' performance on some sort of external test or examination.

Even with these restrictions, state or local school systems that were considering performance rewards would face several additional issues, including:

- Measures of performance: What sorts of student work would be rewarded?
- Criteria of success: What sorts of performance would be rewarded and punished on whatever measures were chosen?
- Professional capability: Would school professionals know enough to respond constructively to performance rewards? If not, how could such schemes be made to work?
- New and old incentives: Performance rewards would be introduced amid many extant incentives; how might the new incentives fit with existing incentives for school performance?
- Rewards and penalties: What would be appropriate ways to reward teachers for students' performance or to penalize them for poor performance?

Measures of Performance

In order to reward teachers for students' performance, that performance would have to be assessed somehow. Furthermore, a reward scheme could be valid only if such assessments accurately measured the performance that educators or policy makers wanted to reward, assuming that they could specify such a thing. Hence one must begin by asking: for what sorts of student performances teachers might be held accountable? Nearly all performance reward schemes contemplate using assessments of academic achievement as the central measure of performance. Hence state or local officials would have to decide what sorts of academic assessments made most sense, but they also would have to decide whether, in light of all the things that schools try to do, any such assessment offers an adequate account of desired school outcomes. Even if we begin by considering only academic performance, assessments of school achievement differ in at least three ways that would count for performance reward schemes: desired results, feasibility, and cost.

Desired Results

There are large differences in the ways that various assessments measure academic performance, and adopting one sort would emphasize academic outcomes to which others would give less attention. For instance, standardized norm-referenced tests tend to focus on facts and skills. Test questions offer a menu of possible answers, only one of which is right. Many researchers now argue that such tests reward students who can memorize disconnected bits and pieces of knowledge, and using such tests in a performance reward scheme would encourage didactic instruction that focused on mindless memorization.[7]

In contrast, authentic or performance assessments are intended to encourage students to make sense of serious practical and intellectual problems and to demonstrate how they reached an answer. Often the questions have no simple, single, right answer, and students' explanations and justifications of their work can count as much as the correctness of their answers.[8] Many researchers argue that such assessments would encourage more complex and thoughtful performances than standardized norm-referenced tests.[9] But the more complex and thoughtful the performances, the more likely it is that expert judges would have to be employed to read and rate the answers, an endeavor that would require educating such judges to use the same criteria to judge students' work. For without highly reliable judges' ratings of the same performances, such assessments would be deemed unfair in comparing students' performances.

Portfolio assessment—in which teachers or students compose collections of student work within particular domains—could draw on an even greater range of performance. Advocates argue that such assessments would encourage intellectually deeper and more adventurous classroom work because they would draw on a much greater variety of work within any domain. Assessment would not need to be limited by the time or format of common testing programs. But because portfolios and authentic assessments would be complex and more or less open-ended, students' performances would be rated by judges rather than scored by optical scanners. It is unlikely that such judgments could be comparable across diverse performances produced by students from different classrooms, schools, and districts.

Assessments thus take very different approaches to defining the academic terrain in which they purport to measure performance. Standardized norm-referenced tests are designed to sample performance within very broad domains—chiefly reading and mathematics—but to be independent of particular approaches to curriculum and instruction.[10] That is partly because they were not designed to be useful to instruction, but to monitor performance broadly in large populations. In contrast, criterion-referenced tests are designed to cover specific curricula, and items are selected with an eye more to topic coverage than to the distribution of responses. They are intended to be useful to instruction, for they report on how much of a given curriculum or set of objectives particular students have learned. Performance and portfolio assessments are a more recent development, and they are intended to be closely integrated with instruction. Both are seen as ways to probe students' knowledge that enable students to more fully display their capabilities and that enable teachers to learn more fully how students think and what they know. Although performance and portfolio assessments would cover specific fields of knowledge, no strong conventions exist concerning how they should do so. Several "authentic" assessments in mathematics have been drawn up with an eye on the NCTM curriculum standards, but at least some of these have paid as much attention to extant curriculum as to any more careful consideration of the field in question.[11]

Interest in performance rewards is growing at an odd and unsettled time in American education. Standardized norm-referenced tests are in bad odor because they have defined academic performance in fragmented and often quite limited terms. Authentic assessment rests on a more complex vision of academic performance, but it is a much less well-developed technology, and thus would be less useful for making the sorts of decisions that performance reward schemes would require.

Finally, we have little evidence about how well the newer assessments represent students' "understanding" of mathematics or reading, in part because this assessment technology is very young. It seems reasonable to think that performance assessments could do a better job than standardized norm-referenced tests, but researchers are only now turning their attention to what understanding might be, how it might be assessed, and what satisfactory assessment of understanding might be. But even if we had much more experience with such assessments, it is almost certain that testing experts still would disagree sharply about the nature of tests and their suitability for use in performance reward schemes. It is even more likely that disciplinary scholars would continue to disagree both about what is most important in their fields and about the nature of adequate performance in whatever they deemed most important, and that ordinary Americans would persist in differing about the sorts of academic performance that should be assessed.

Feasibility

Standardized tests would be the easiest assessment to use by far. They define knowledge in ways that are thought to be closer to established classroom practice than any of the newer and more ambitious assessments. The measurement technology is well developed and stable. These tests also are relatively easy for teachers and administrators to use, and they are familiar to students. They are not part of instruction and intrude on it only modestly. Educators also know how to administer them from much experience so that little new training would be required. And the tests are scored elsewhere; teachers' administrative responsibility ends once the answer sheets are collected.

Authentic assessments would be much more difficult. One reason is that they define knowledge in more open and complex ways than their better established cousins, which greatly complicates test construction and evaluation of students' performance. Another reason is that the technology for these novel assessments is young, and much remains to be done, including learning about the assessments' validity and reliability. Until the technology was more mature, assessment would be an uncertain enterprise, and that would be a major problem in schemes that attached rewards and penalties to the performances being assessed. A third source of difficulty is that such assessments have to be scored by knowledgeable judges—that is, teachers—and that would be costly in time and demanding in expertise. Fourth, these assessments are intended to be integrated into instruction by incorporation both as instructional goals and as evidence of students' performance. But to use them well for either purpose, most teachers would have to unlearn and learn a great deal about academic subjects and about new approaches to instruction and assessment; knowledge of all three is in short supply.

Portfolio assessments seem a promising way to relate assessment to instruction, but they would be very difficult to integrate into many performance reward schemes. One reason is that portfolios comprise materials that are produced jointly and over time—by students and their teachers, parents, and peers. Hence, they may not be a valid measure of individual performance, and they may not reliably relate to other performances of the same individual. Another reason for caution is that because portfolios are built in an open process rather than composed on demand, they would be especially open to the influence of parents, friends, and teachers that one would want to exclude from any performance reward scheme. It would not be easy to use such assessments in ways that were both fair and believed to be fair, especially when serious consequences for teachers and students hung in the balance. Still another reason for caution is that unless all schools in a performance reward scheme had the same curriculum and the same criteria for selecting materials, portfolios could in some sense be incomparable. And to the extent they were, ratings across schools—or even across classrooms within schools—could be an unsteady basis for making decisions about rewards and punishments. Efforts to create acceptable interrater reliabilities could be enormously time and energy consuming, and they still might not create adequate confidence in the results. Comparability among teachers and schools could be enhanced by carefully specifying the sorts of student work, the topics, and the like, but the more highly specified those terms of reference became, the more such assessments would resemble a districtwide take-home exam rather than a portfolio that allowed each student to present his or her unique strengths, perspectives, and modes of work.

Familiarity to parents, policy makers, politicians, reporters, and others concerned with schools is another dimension of feasibility. The more innovative an assessment was, the more difficulty such people would have in recognizing it as a valid and sensible instrument of education. The more intellectually ambitious assessments were, the more difficulty teachers and students would have, and the more students would do poorly—at least initially. As the recent debacle with the California Assessment Program revealed, innovative and ambitious assessments can be political dynamite, especially in a society in which cultural conflict over schooling is a favorite entertainment.

Cost

Standardized norm- or criterion-referenced tests are relatively cheap. Testing firms have been producing them for years, and can continue to do so for modest cost. Such tests also take little time to administer and are machine scored, thus holding labor costs down. But authentic and portfolio assessments are not being produced *en masse;* they are new and expensive to design—in part because in order to be usable, teachers need to be involved in design, field trials, and revisions. They also are much more expensive to use partly because they must be scored by well-educated observers and partly because they take a good deal more time than standardized tests.

At the moment, then, the assessments that many researchers and reformers consider least desirable are the easiest and cheapest to compose, administer, score, and use, whereas the assessments that many consider most desirable are the most difficult and costly to compose, administer, score, and use. School systems that contemplated performance rewards could be drawn to standardized tests for reasons of cost and feasibility while being drawn to newer assessment for reasons of desired instruction and results. Some standardized assessments, including the National Assessment of Educational Progress and some state assessments, have begun to add items that are intended to tap more higher-order knowledge and skill, but there has been little research on the extent or effects of these changes.[12] There also is only modest evidence on how standardized test performance correlates with performance on more innovative assessments, but the extant evidence suggests a weak relationship.

That may suggest that the new assessments measure very different things than the older tests, but it may be only that the new assessments are much less reliable than the older tests.[13]

We know only a little about how more innovative assessments would work in performance reward schemes, for there are only a few recent efforts to use them—those in Kentucky, California, and Vermont. California's experience has taught Americans how politically difficult innovative assessments can be, but we have nearly everything to learn about the other difficulties that will come up and how school officials and policy makers can manage them. More experience in Kentucky and Vermont may improve both assessments and the capability to use them.

Though this discussion tells us little about the actual effects of any particular performance reward scheme, it reveals that the effects on students and teachers are quite likely to vary with the measures of performance. My discussion also suggests that effects should be considered not only in student achievement, but also in professionals' time and energy in assessment administration and scoring, the complexity of assessment, difficulty of implementation, possible political conflict, and cost. There probably would be tradeoffs among these. For instance, some school systems that adopted performance reward schemes might wish to encourage complex student performance, but would not because of costs or the demands on professionals' time. One set of issues for research would concern how school systems dealt with these problems and what effects their solutions had on the design, implementation, and effects of performance reward schemes.

An additional effect of performance reward schemes concerns state and local testing programs. American schools administer more tests than any other country known to researchers. Some are part of inherited local assessment programs, others had their origin in state "back-to-basics" efforts, and still others are tied to specific programs, as with Title I testing requirements. These assessments are numerous, often burdensome, and sometimes offer contrary guidance for instruction. Would a state or local performance reward scheme give more coherence to the schools' assessment program by focusing attention on the scheme's measures of performance and drawing attention away from other assessments, or would the other assessments distract from the performance reward scheme? Such interactions between performance rewards and other state and local testing would be an important focus for research on performance rewards.

Finally, even though performance rewards focus on school achievement, that is not the only thing that Americans want from school or that responsible teachers and administrators care about. Educators also value the effort that students make, irrespective of their test scores. The qualities associated with effort—hard work, determination, dependability, and the like—also are attributes that many employers seem to value. Many parents and teachers also place a high value on discipline, by which they seem to mean some combination of respect for authority, obedience, and orderly behavior, and these too are qualities that many employers value. Finally, some teachers and employers recently report that they set a great store on such qualities as independence of mind and the capability to work with others. But if such social and affective features of schooling are essential to decent schools, they are more difficult to assess in a valid and reliable fashion than traditional versions of academic achievement. One reason is that many of these aspects of schooling are not obvious—discipline can be viewed and enacted in several different ways—and it would take careful instrumentation and analysis to fairly capture them. Another reason is that capturing them in any measurement effort would require much labor-intensive observation and many interviews.

Observing and assessing these social and affective features of schooling would greatly complicate the task of deciding on the quality of schooling because it would add more indices of quality and accomplishment and many puzzles about how to weight them. It also would add expense, time, and trouble to any scheme, so it is easy to understand why school systems and policy makers would prefer to ignore such matters. But one cannot teach or manage a school well without giving close attention to discipline, mutual respect, hard work, dependability, and the like. To the extent that a performance reward scheme reduced attention to these aspects and outcomes of schooling, then to that extent would such a scheme sooner or later contribute to a different sort of educational problem.[14]

Criteria of Success

However they defined and assessed the results of schooling, decision makers would have settled on only the type of school performance they wished to reward. They still would have to decide on criteria of success: given any set of measures of performance, what results would be good enough to warrant rewards, or bad enough to deserve punishment? That turns out to be a remarkably difficult matter because any criteria of success must satisfy various other criteria. For example, any defensible criterion of success or failure should be educationally sound, which requires taking account of various complex conditions that bear on instruction. But it is no less important that criteria of success be usable, for performance rewards could not provoke school improvement unless the scheme was easy for teachers, students, and parents to understand.[15] That requires clarity and economy, which could be at odds with the complexity associated with educational soundness. In addition, criteria of success must be demanding enough to raise performance, but not so demanding that they discourage students and teachers. Those criteria also must be unusual enough to be challenging but familiar enough to command broad assent from educators, students, and parents. Finally, criteria of success must be fair—an idea that is simple to write but knotty to decide.

Single or Multiple Criteria

The easiest way to decide what level of performance should be rewarded would be to settle on a single score on a single test. Schools with an average score of, say, sixty or above would be rewarded, whereas those with an average score of fifty-nine or below would not. Rewards would be decided on the basis of one school average at one point in time. The great advantage of such a criterion is its simplicity, but that also is its great weakness. For pass–fail is a rather crude distinction, and it would be difficult to decide on a single score that was educationally defensible. The original minimum-competency testing programs were simple: each state or local program set an absolute cut-off point on the test, and students with scores above it passed, whereas those below it failed.

Decision makers could instead fix several levels on a single test that distinguished higher and lower ranges of successful performance. Such an approach would enable school systems to make at least a few distinctions among acceptable work and perhaps schedule rewards accordingly while still marking off successful from failing performance. But one disadvantage is the possible dilution of incentives for improvement—that is, many teachers might settle for "passable" work rather than pressing for the best. School officials could try to solve that problem by offering more attractive incentives for higher performance, but there is a good deal of evidence that most educators, like other humans, prefer to satisfice than to optimize.

Decisions about criteria of success interact with the choice of assessments. Standardized norm-referenced tests offer little educationally defensible basis for setting fixed criteria of success because, as their name implies, they are referenced to national norms rather than to conceptions of adequacy. The norms are statistical statements about the distribution of performance and offer no principled answer to questions about what students should know. Setting multiple levels of success on norm-referenced tests would reduce the starkness of this problem but would not solve the underlying difficulty of finding an educational defense for criteria.

Criterion-referenced tests are somewhat less troublesome because they are referenced to specific domains. But having a more adequate test would not make it any easier to justify a single cut-off between adequate and inadequate performance. Setting several levels of success could be well defended if the tests had been built with such distinctions in view.

Authentic and portfolio assessments present even more acute problems in setting a single standard of success since these assessments are intended to complicate both instruction and the evaluation of students' performance. To use them as the basis for simple pass–fail scores would be at odds with the purpose of these assessments. Setting multiple levels of success would ease but not solve this problem; assessments that had been designed to embody different levels of performance would offer a more defensible basis for such criteria. As in so many matters, simplicity and ease of administration are at odds with justifiability and educational utility. Simple, single criteria of success would be easy to administer but difficult to either justify or use to educational advantage, especially with standardized norm-referenced tests. Multiple criteria would be somewhat more difficult to administer but easier to justify and use to educational advantage, especially with criterion-referenced or performance assessments.

Static and Dynamic Criteria

A deeper problem with any fixed criteria is that they treat school performance in static terms even though schooling is a dynamic process. Students achieve particular levels of performance at given points in time, but these are only snapshots at one moment in a much longer process of academic growth and social development. Though such snapshots are reasonable, students, parents, and concerned observers also focus on students' progress over time as on their rank order at a single moment. A scheme that pressed students and teachers to orient their work to set rank-order targets could have very different results than a scheme that was oriented to improved rates of learning. For instance, fixed targets could make it difficult to fairly accommodate the enormous variations in academic ability and achievement that are found in most schools or school systems. Officials might choose a target that was keyed to students' average ability or achievement in an effort to compromise out the differences, but average achievement could be too difficult for academically untalented students and too easy for very able students. If so, an average could be ignored by both sorts of students, or it could offer teachers incentives to ignore both sorts of students, or both. Decision makers might therefore try to set different targets for average, more able, and less able students, but that would be difficult to do in a way that was both fair and educationally appropriate. We have little basis in educational research or theory for deciding what such targets might be, and the explicit acceptance of different results for different groups of students could provoke a firestorm of protest.

Disadvantaged students present an especially significant special case of this problem. They do less well, on average, than students from more advantaged homes. Through what many observers would say was no fault of their own, these students have lower average test scores than their advantaged peers. If school systems used fixed and academically demanding criteria of success, it would be very difficult for schools that enrolled many disadvantaged students to ever do well enough to gain rewards, for the rank order of school average scores would closely parallel the rank order of school average parents' education. To base decisions about schools' success on such rank orders would penalize many poor students and their teachers for disadvantages that were not of their own making. These students and teachers could reasonably argue that they were playing on a field that was tilted against them, and grow discouraged about their prospects of ever doing well enough to be rewarded. That would defeat the purpose of performance rewards.

The only way that school systems could remedy this problem would be to adopt a dynamic approach to assessing school performance—that is, use a value-added approach to devising criteria for performance. To do so, school systems could adjust school or classroom average gain scores at each grade to remove the effects of nonschool factors on achievement. The point would be to restrict calculation of gains to those that schools may be presumed to cause in any given period, rather than those that could be traced to nonschool influences. Differences in how much schools added to student's achievement would be the key to rewards.[16] The most efficient way to make such adjustments is to statistically adjust students' fall-to-spring gain scores for differences in their prior performance, thus restricting the basis of rewards to effects that schools exert during the academic year.[17]

But such compensatory adjustments would not solve every problem of fairness. Many schools enrolling mostly disadvantaged students probably would make less progress, on average, than schools that enrolled mostly advantaged students, even after adjustments for initial scores.[18] That is especially likely if assessments focused on the sorts of ambitious knowledge and skills that many American teachers are only weakly qualified to teach. What might school officials or policy makers do in this event?

One likely response would be to set more modest gain score targets for schools that enrolled disadvantaged students, effectively basing target gains on student body composition or initial scores. Or officials could assign schools to performance gain streams, and compare adjusted gains only within them. If schools could not compete across these streams, the appearance of differential gains and levels would be hidden. But streamed competition could create potent disincentives for professionals to attempt dramatic increases in student performance. If so, such adjustments could further damage disadvantaged students. For if each school's performance was compared to only that of others in its own stream, schools could "win" more easily. There would be little incentive for teachers and students to try to outperform schools in higher streams, for the purpose of streamed competition would be to avoid such comparisons. Hence those in weaker schools might be kept in a sort of educational ghetto, in which lower performance was not only allowed but even encouraged. Differential performance targets might avoid some of the short-term political problems of comparing across the entire range of schools, but they could not only damage the schools and students in question, but also impair performance rewards by limiting the possible effects of incentives.

Though few would argue for educational performance ghettos, many could worry about comparing schools that enrolled mostly disadvantaged students with persistently smaller gain scores to schools that enrolled advantaged students and had larger gains. One possible solution would be to stream schools by average social status or initial scores, but also to compare each school both to schools in their own stream and to those in other streams. That at least would enable parents, students, and school professionals to consult a variety of evidence on effectiveness and to see differences among them. Alternatively, officials could stipulate that rewards would attach to gains among as well as within streams. Such a system would focus attention and effort on competition among all schools while still permitting schools to strive for rewards relative to others similarly situated. A scheme of this sort could even give larger rewards to schools whose gain scores moved them up a stream.

Another problem with adjustments could arise if teachers and administrators in some disadvantaged schools did substantially improve students' achievement, for their success could reduce the statistical associations between social and economic status and achievement. That change would be the ultimate mark of success for performance rewards, for the improved schools would have changed the social technology of education sufficiently to reduce the correlation between inherited social status and school achievement. Many would see that as a reason to change the adjustments for initial scores or inherited status, arguing that the associations that initially would have been used to statistically remove the effects of inherited status on achievement no longer were valid.[19] If the underlying relationships had changed for some schools, the original scheme for calculating success and assigning rewards might no longer be fair.

Some analysts and professionals as well as parents in advantaged schools could want the adjustments changed so as not to give an unfair advantage to schools that had learned how to educate poor children more effectively. But other analysts and professionals and parents in disadvantaged schools would be likely to argue instead that it was exactly the increased fairness, and possibly additional money, that enabled some schools to mobilize to weaken the association. To adjust the associations and perhaps reduce added monies could penalize schools for success and perhaps push them back into failure.

There is a troublesome paradox here. On the one hand, if the effective schools had changed the technology of instruction, why give them the handicap that they had when they were less effective? But on the other hand, changing the adjustments could make it more difficult for unsuccessful schools to change by reducing their incentive to do so—if they changed they would lose some advantages. A similar problem could arise if poverty got appreciably worse, for its effects might then also grow worse, leading some to argue for changes in the adjustments. The arguments about these issues could be methodologically complex and politically gruesome. But the issues that I have noted reveal that if educators did appreciably improve instruction and achievement, they would be rewarded with a really difficult problem: are performance rewards a transitional measure—a means to discover better approaches to education that then could be put into practice without additional incentives—or are they an essential continuing element of any improved instruction?

This discussion also reminds us of the tradeoffs between fairness and clarity. My account thus far suggests that the more fair a scheme was the more complex and costly it would become. But the more complex and costly a scheme became the less intelligible and useful it probably would become. The alternatives to streamed measures of performance that I sketched earlier have some appeal as a matter of fairness, but they could add complexities to an already complicated matter. A performance reward scheme of that sort could become the educational equivalent of Ptolemaic astronomy, with adjustments loaded onto adjustments until few could comprehend. Simple schemes are more likely to be unfair, but more complex schemes that are more likely to solve the problem of fairness also are more likely to be difficult to understand. Teachers, students, and parents could not respond constructively if they lacked a clear sense of how a scheme worked, what produced rewarded or punished scores, and what actions were likely to be productive.[20]

The problem extends further. The schemes that I have discussed here would not work unless school systems collected sound evidence with which to adjust student scores for the effects of prior performance. In high poverty schools, such adjustments almost surely would require evidence on student mobility, for without knowledge of who was in school for the entire performance period, adjustments could not accurately be made. Schools with high mobility rates work under a greater handicap than those that have quite stable enrollments, partly because students who were only there for half the year would not have had the same opportunity to learn as those enrolled for the entire year. If such distinctions could not accurately be made, it would be difficult to have confidence in the results, yet few school systems collect such evidence. Most rely on very crude aggregate data collected for other purposes. Without sound evidence, no one could convincingly defend the fairness of decisions about success, rewards, or adjustments to scores, but collecting the evidence could be complex and costly, and encourage political conflict and legal challenge. The political and fiscal costs of defensible data bases could keep many systems from doing a respectable job, but if state or local authorities attached serious consequences for students and teachers to analyses of school effectiveness, sooner or later officials would be pressed—politically, legally, and perhaps by a sense of professional responsibility—to collect the evidence and do the analyses in ways that met standards of decent social science. Though it seems clear that dynamic criteria of performance are more sensible than static ones, there may be deep problems in defining such criteria and calculating the added value of schooling.

It also is worth noticing that such determinations could be politically difficult. Criteria of success and fairness are quite murky under the current regime, for schools embody many purposes, conceptions of success, and fairness. Such murky complexity has been unavoidable in an institution that has been assigned many different hopes and purposes, that has been the site of many compromises, and in which many accumulated layers of purpose coexist. Yet performance reward schemes could not work as intended without much greater precision about criteria of success and standards of fairness, hence they would place much more educational and political pressure on any criteria and standards. One large question for research on performance rewards is whether either the criteria or the schools could bear those pressures.

What Gains Would Be Enough?

Even if a school system settled on a solid value-added criterion of success, officials still would have to decide how much added value would merit a reward. Many probably would incline to relative criteria of effectiveness—for instance, stipulating that schools with adjusted gains in the top quartile would be rewarded, or that all schools whose adjusted gain scores were above the district average of gains would be rewarded. There is no shortage of such relative criteria, and in all such cases, the cut-off for success would be set in relation to some statistical feature of the existing distribution of gain scores. Being above average or in the top quartile has considerable face validity and seems to avoid the need to justify performance levels in substantive educational terms.

From this perspective, decisions about how much of a gain warranted a reward would be a matter of selecting the proper reference group. Many advocates see performance rewards as a way to improve achievement for students at the lower end of the achievement distribution, especially students from disadvantaged circumstances. From that angle, the performance of advantaged or high-achieving students seems a reasonable reference for decisions about successful education. But there is no scientific or educational basis for determinations of this sort, and they could lock in mediocrity. If Podunk had low average achievement and little variance in annual school gains, then a school's rise to the average of the local distribution of local gain scores would not be a terrific achievement. One might ask what there is about Podunk that makes its top quartile of gain scores a defensible criterion of effectiveness.

That returns us to the problem that relative standards seemed to solve by avoidance: what is the educational justification for criteria of success? Many Americans recently have been convinced that something is deeply wrong with public education, that standards are not only too low but also aimed at the wrong target. Reformers argue that schools have been teaching outmoded facts and skills rather than advanced knowledge and critical thinking. If we want only a modest improvement in Podunk's low-achieving schools, perhaps the Podunk average out of quartile and gains is an acceptable standard. But if we believe that most schools in Podunk and America aim too low and at the wrong goals, then standards anchored merely to statistical features of extant score distributions leave much to be desired.

Relative criteria might be more appealing if they were tied to some better reference than the distribution of extant scores. If Americans could agree on substantive educational standards and if sound assessments that were tied to such standards could be devised, then students' progress toward those standards could be examined and compared. School average scores could be adjusted to eliminate the effects of initial achievement, and schools' contribution to students' progress toward the standards could be computed and compared. Such a scheme would combine value-added measures of improvement with educationally defensible standards of performance. This would leave the problem of deciding how much student progress toward standards would warrant the designation of successful, and that would re-present most of the problems that I have discussed earlier in this section, including differential progress. But sound external, generally agreed-on standards could offer substantive educational grounds for deciding how much progress was enough.[21]

Several difficulties stand in the way of this appealing formulation. One is that the very idea of such assessments is quite novel. American educators have just begun to devise the standards that would be required, and it would take much experience and investigation to refine them. It also would take extensive experience and investigation to devise assessments that embodied those standards and that could be defended as such—work that also has just begun. Much careful work also would be required to define criteria of success on such assessments that were both attainable and educationally defensible. Another difficulty is that efforts to devise more ambitious goals, standards, and assessments have stirred up terrific controversy. Some educators and many citizens reject Goals 2000, critical thinking, and related reforms. Much of Goals and its state counterparts may not survive the current educational warfare, and many states may not build a solid foundation for standards-based reform. At the moment, the criteria of success that combine the most appealing features in principle seem the most remote in practice.

Failing Schools

A last important issue concerning criteria of success is criteria of failure—that is, how should officials rate schools that did not win rewards? Should all of them be designated "unsuccessful" or "failed"?

That seems unwise, for it would label schools as either outstanding or awful rather than also being satisfactory or indifferent. Additionally, if the criteria for success were set relatively high, a pass–fail approach could produce a politically unacceptable avalanche of failures, with the likely result that criteria for success would be abandoned or set lower. Perhaps only especially low-performing schools should be rated as unsatisfactory, with those in the middle left unclassified. Such decisions would be consequential, for designating schools as "failed" or "unsatisfactory" might do more damage than the label of success could do good. Decisions about where to draw the line for failure thus would raise all the issues concerning criteria of success that I just discussed, perhaps with even greater stakes. There has been little discussion of this matter.

Some commentators might argue that there should be no designations of failure or unsatisfactory performance, that systems should focus only on success. But that seems a dubious strategy, for there is a good deal of evidence that a large fraction of schools, especially in disadvantaged neighborhoods, would not be able to mobilize themselves to substantially improve instruction even in the best-designed scheme with the most attractive incentives.[22] Devising and using a designation of unsatisfactory performance would be essential if state or local officials were to reliably identify the most difficult cases and try to improve them.

What might be sound evidence of failure? Performance rewards are designed to improve students' achievement, but the first thing to consider, especially in the early years of any scheme, would be whether schools' instructional capability was improving. One would expect changes in instruction and management to precede changes in achievement, even in improving schools.[23] And some instructional changes, such as more ambitious curriculum and teaching, would be likely to initially depress achievement, but it would be foolish to penalize schools for trying to accept more demanding goals. Additionally, some schools might make substantial progress in instruction and management but not achievement, whereas others might make no progress on either front. In any reasonable situation, the first sort of school would be candidates for assistance in making more change, and the second would be candidates for a different kind of treatment. It would be unwise to use a single blanket designation like "failed" for schools that were so different and required such different treatment.

But if these suggestions make sense educationally, they could have troublesome administrative consequences. My proposal would require schools to collect evidence on change in management and instruction, along with achievement, and to monitor both, at least in dealing with the schools most in need of improvement. To be done well would entail careful, costly, and time-consuming investigations by capable researchers. That, in turn, would add more evidence, reporting, and analysis, further complicating the tasks of parents, teachers, administrators, and policy makers. Moreover, it would only be the beginning, for if experience and research are any guide, it often would take extraordinary work to rebuild or replace troubled schools.

Professional Capability

That point leads us to a central paradox of performance rewards. The schemes are designed to solve problems that arise from failures of professionalism, but they could not succeed unless professionalism improved. Advocates of performance rewards often slide over this point because they want to focus on incentives to use resources more effectively. They argue that the quality of teachers' education, the quality of curricula and texts, the facilities in which teachers and students work, and the conditions of their work have improved greatly during the past century, all with no apparent corresponding increase in student performance. They point to many studies that report little or no relation between differences in schools' educational resources and test scores, once students' social status or beginning performance are taken into account. Advocates argue that unless there are incentives for professionals to use resources to improve students' achievement, more resources will have no useful effect. Since few school systems offer such incentives, the chief task for school improvement is said to be rewarding or penalizing teachers for students' performance. With such incentives in place, existing resources would be used more efficiently since teachers would either figure out how to produce the desired results or be replaced by others who could.[24] Only when such incentives were in place could rational decisions about additional resources be made.

Even if one grants everything in that formulation, incentives would not be automatic. They could work only through people and their organizations, and if those lacked either the capability to respond constructively or the means to readily acquire it, incentives could have no useful effect. Hence anyone interested in how performance rewards might work also should be interested in the professional capacities required for a constructive response. At one level this would concern individual educators, for performance reward schemes would not work unless they were able to somehow learn how to do a much better job than they had been doing—barring the invention of some way for students to succeed in school without teachers. At another level it would concern school systems, for many schools that failed to perform successfully would need assistance to improve.

Individual Capacity

Speaking very crudely, there are two sorts of individual professional capacity—will and skill. Professionalism includes pedagogical skill, knowledge of subjects, and the like, but it is not just technical. Professionals also must want to help students learn; they must take responsibility for students' work; they must care for students, respect their ideas, and believe in students' ability to learn. Without technical capacity all the values and commitments in the world would be useless, but without those values and commitments all the professional knowledge and skill in the world would be impotent.

Many advocates of performance rewards tend to assume that professional capability is not an issue. They appear to believe that most professionals have the skill but not the will because the extant incentive structure in schools frustrates their efforts. There is one respect in which that analysis may be close to the truth, for there is appreciable evidence that time is poorly used in most schools and classrooms. The National Education Commission on Time and Learning recently concluded that ". . . even within the confines of a 180-day school year, reclaiming the academic day should, alone, nearly double the amount of instructional time in core curriculum areas."[25]

Many teachers spend a great deal of time preparing for instruction rather than teaching core curriculum subjects; many spend a great deal of time on holiday and other special events rather than teaching these core subjects; many take weeks to settle into the new year; many use the instructional time that they do spend quite inefficiently; and a great deal of instruction consists of reviewing the previous year's work.[26] There also is evidence that students who spend more time on academic learning learn more than those who spend less. If incentives for performance simply persuaded teachers to allocate more time to academic instruction, performance might improve for many students and schools.

But even that conclusion must be carefully hedged. One qualification is that most or all of any such improvement would be in what Americans call basic skills because most teachers do not presently have the knowledge or skill to teach in much more advanced ways. Another is that better use of time would not begin to exhaust the possible improvements that could be made in basic skill instruction because it would only more efficiently use teachers' existing skills. Researchers have recently delineated several features of effective direct or active instruction that go far beyond the efficient use of time. For example, teachers who work effectively have clear goals for instruction, they recurrently assess students' progress in lessons, they make strong and plain links between the goals that they set and the assignments, lesson design, and questions they ask students. They also maintain a crisp pace and a clear focus in classwork.[27] These instructional actions rest on relatively complex knowledge and skills, and reflect significant professional norms. Research also suggests that only a modest fraction of teachers work in that way. For example, John Goodlad reported that most elementary teachers fail to make it clear to their students what is going on in the lessons so that many students are confused about what they are supposed to be doing, why they should do it, or both.[28]

A third qualification is that teachers would have much to learn simply in order to use time more efficiently at current skill levels. They would have to learn new methods of lesson preparation and format, pacing, classroom management, assessment of students' work, and much more. No small amount of teacher education would be required to help experienced teachers learn such things. Teachers also would have to learn to want to be more efficient—that is, to learn new professional values that would make their work lives much harder. Finally, they would have to learn that these changes would help students, which would require that they give much closer attention to students' work. Learning these things would be no mean feat, and there is no evidence that the capacity to offer the requisite professional education exists today. Though we know roughly what efficient teachers need to do, few professional developers offer such education.

Even in a basic skills approach to performance rewards, then, there seem to be two levels of response. In one, changes in existing skills and knowledge might be sufficient to improve achievement for many students if teachers were motivated to use instructional time more efficiently and learned the required skill and knowledge. These things would not be easy, but they would not require an instructional revolution. Much greater capacity development would be required if teachers were to make further significant improvement in basic skills instruction, for the needed changes in instruction would be fairly radical.[29]

The professional capacity to respond constructively to performance records thus is not generic; the capacities required would vary with the performances that were to be assessed and the criteria of effectiveness that were set. In that connection I should note that in addition to the two alternatives sketched, there is a third, in which schools promoted intellectually much more demanding work. That would require much greater professional capability, for teachers would have to cultivate sophisticated knowledge of subject matter and pedagogy, and most lack such knowledge and skills. They would need extensive opportunities to learn if they were to respond constructively.[30] There also is evidence that many teachers do not believe that most students can do intellectually challenging work. Hence they would have to acquire rather different professional beliefs about knowledge and students' capacities, and very different professional values to guide their teaching. These problems would be even greater for teachers who work with disadvantaged students.[31]

Advocates of performance rewards might object, saying that if strong incentives were attached to better student performance, teachers would somehow find ways to learn the necessary values, knowledge, and skills. On this view, greater demand would evoke an available but hitherto unused supply of professional knowledge and skill. But the evidence on professional development in education suggests that few suitable providers exist, even for improved basic skills instruction, and that the problem is most acute in schools that heavily enroll disadvantaged students. Hence, there is not only an appreciable lack of professional capacity to respond constructively to performance rewards, but the lack is greatest in those schools in which improvement is most needed and for those conceptions of instruction that are most ambitious.

Most public school systems that adopted performance reward schemes thus would not face the problem of mobilizing capacities already well developed but underused, but the much more difficult problem of developing and mobilizing barely existent capacities. That would be true even if one hoped only to squeeze more efficient time use out of the extant system, and it would be much more true for the more ambitious alternatives that I just discussed. State and local school systems have little experience with such work. Few seem to have any strategy for human resource development, except perhaps to identify areas like reading or mathematics for making professional development grants. Only a few have any capability for doing more. Most districts offer an array of brief and scattered professional development programs that reflect no particular strategy for human resource development and pursue no particular academic priorities.[32] These considerations suggest that improving individual professionals' capacity to respond to performance rewards would be a major task.

School Improvement

Improved professional capacity also includes changes in social organization, for the elements of capacity—values, commitment, and knowledge—are in some measure attributes of groups—that is, school and department staffs, and central office personnel.[33] Milbrey McLaughlin and Joan Talbert argue that schools and departments within schools are professional communities that differ dramatically in their academic effectiveness in part because of differences in their professional norms.[34] Anthony Bryk, Valerie Lee, and Peter Holland reach similar conclusions in their efforts to explain differences in secondary schools' effectiveness.[35] The capacity to respond to performance rewards should be understood as a problem of organization and culture as well as a matter of individual knowledge and values.

Organizational capacity is significant because spontaneously constructive responses to performance rewards could be expected only from a minority of schools that have extraordinary leadership or other unusual organizational resources. Studies of other school reforms suggest that many failing schools would be unable to correctly interpret the signals from a reform scheme, to fairly diagnose the problems and effectively devise means to improve instruction and raise students' performance.[36] Research on effective schools suggests that not many achieved and sustained high levels of student performance.[37] Though a minority of schools would be able to spontaneously and dramatically improve their own instruction and management and students' performance, it is very likely that a larger fraction either would make modest changes, inappropriate changes, or none at all. The existence of a group of schools that were mired in failure would tend to erode the credibility of any school system's improvement efforts and leadership, and that would be a reason for the leaders of such a system to take steps to improve failing schools. Yet those officials also would have reason to be cautious about promising help, for few systems have the capacity to provide much help. Most state and local systems do not even identify failing schools (New York has just begun), let alone assist them in improving instruction. Few seem to have staff that are knowledgeable about school improvement. And if local or state school officials tried but failed to help weak schools improve, their claim to be professionally capable educational leaders would erode further.

Launching a performance reward scheme without a capacity to improve schools could be politically perilous. But devising such a capacity would not be easy, and failing at the effort also could be perilous. The causes of school success and failure are not well understood, and there is scant experience with or research on systematic school improvement. There is, of course, no shortage of schemes to improve schools, but there is relatively little reliable knowledge about what works, and even less about how to make it work in one place after it worked in another. Worse yet, the most credible research in this novel area suggests that effective and lasting school improvement is not only rare but quite expensive.[38]

My account suggests that systematic learning from incentive schemes would be essential for even the hope of their success. School systems that instituted performance rewards should study the possible causes of school success and failure in order to learn from the results about how to improve individual schools.[39] If school systems collected evidence on academic achievement only in order to decide which schools deserved rewards, they would have no solid basis either for commenting on why some schools succeeded and others failed or for offering help to those that failed.[40] But it is much easier to argue for more evidence than to collect and use it. State or local systems would have to collect and analyze observational and interview, as well as survey, data on schooling processes, or to contract with some agency to do those things. Few systems have either the expertise for such work or the money to pay for it. To remedy that, school systems would have to develop staff capacity for school improvement, or find private firms that did such work effectively, and find a way to pay for it. They also would have to find ways to monitor the effects of assistance to learn how to do it better, to take corrective action when things went poorly, and perhaps to make defensible decisions about putting schools out of business when corrective action failed to help. Few school systems have anything like such capacities, and, in an age of increasing social problems and tight budgets, it is not clear how they might develop them.

Efforts to implement performance rewards thus would face a common dilemma of reform: the problems that reformers seek to remedy reflect the absent capacities that would be needed to solve those problems. The successful operation of a system of performance rewards would entail much more than creating rewards for performance. Professional education for many teachers and organizational and cultural change in many schools would be required in order to enable constructive responses to new incentives for performance. This conclusion would hold with greatest force in the schools that were most in need of improvement.

New and Old Incentives

Performance reward schemes generally assume that teachers are an effective lever on students' achievement, for they propose to reward teachers for improving that achievement. If there were grave doubts about teachers' leverage in such matters, the advocates of performance rewards would presumably instead propose incentives for students to improve their own performance. Teachers can, of course, influence students, but teachers and students work amid webs of incentives and disincentives that affect such influence. There are several reasons to be cautious about assuming that rewards for teachers would easily translate into better achievement for students.

One is that teachers depend on their students for professional success. Since the results for which teachers strive are produced in and by students, teachers can succeed as professionals only when their students succeed as learners. Teachers therefore need their students to succeed. Of course, carpenters need wood and nails, but students have minds and volitions, and can influence teachers' opportunities to succeed as professionals by the choices they make in working with teachers. Students can influence teachers in a way that wood cannot influence carpenters. Carpenters can produce results by themselves if they have the skills and knowledge of the trade, the will to work, and passable materials, for like workers in most occupations, carpenters address themselves either to inanimate materials or to ideas. But teachers, like therapists, organization developers, and other practitioners of human improvement, cannot produce results by themselves. Their art and craft are useless until students embrace the purposes of instruction as their own and seek them with their own art and craft. Of course, teachers need the will to work, and in this respect, they are just like carpenters and architects. But carpenters and architects do not require the will of their wood, paper, designs, and tools. Only teachers and their colleagues in other human improvement practices require clients who bend their own will and skill to the work.[41]

That fundamental difference among occupations bears on the mobilization of incentives for performance. It may make sense under certain conditions to focus external incentives exclusively on carpenters as a way to increase or improve the production of cabinets, for carpenters are the chief agent of cabinet production. But teachers are not the chief agent of student learning. Students are that agent, and teachers, however important, are ancillary. The instructional outcomes that advocates of performance rewards want to encourage are produced in and by students, with the help of teachers, parents, and others.

Teachers' dependence on students is no theoretical matter, for high school teachers who are eager to plunge into Shakespeare regularly encounter students who want only accounting. Teachers cannot succeed—or even proceed—unless they reach some agreement with students about the ends and means of their work together, and since those agreements are regularly unmade, they often must be remade. Teachers are continually enmeshed in negotiations about what students might do, and what teachers might do to secure students' commitment. Many of these negotiations occur in the privacy of teachers' minds as they try to anticipate students' response to their next move or to possible lessons, but many others occur directly with students in class.

To teach at all is to engage in some such negotiation and calculation, but teachers are pulled in contrary ways. On the one hand, if their professional success depends on students' accomplishments, there seem to be powerful reasons to press students for ambitious work since more success for students is more success for practitioners. From this angle, there are potent internal incentives for teachers to encourage high achievement. Yet from another angle those vanish, for learning can be both risky and difficult, and more substantial learning is substantially more difficult. Teachers who demand high performance run greater risks of student failure, or resistance, or both. Since teachers succeed only through their students, they also have incentives to ensure some success for themselves by avoiding failure for students.[42] One source of risk and failure is that many students seem uninterested in school learning. Another is that much learning entails unlearning. If one is to understand Newtonian physics, one must radically revise or abandon one's Aristotelian ideas about the motion of bodies even though the ideas are deeply rooted, serviceable, and difficult to cast aside. Another source of risk and failure is that learning often seems quite counterintuitive—for instance, that bodies once in motion tend to remain in motion, or that we don't "see" things but rather interpret sense data in one of several ways that it could be interpreted. These and other difficulties create incentives for teachers to set low goals since a little improvement would be better than none.

I imagine teachers caught in a dilemma: should they aim low, risking mediocrity in return for at least some success for students and themselves, or aim high, risking failure in return for great improvement for their students and equally impressive accomplishments for themselves? I further envision the advocates of performance rewards proposing to intervene in teachers' dilemma by creating incentives for high achievement. If teachers and students worked in circumstances in which all other incentives for and against high performance were roughly balanced, then introducing a performance reward scheme would be predictably positive: the new incentives would tip the balance for many teachers. They would have reasons to work harder for improved achievement, and everyone would be a winner.

But in fact teachers and students work in schools, communities, and societies that have all sorts of other incentives and disincentives for student performance, and it may not be reasonable to assume that those are balanced in a way that would endow performance rewards with a decisive influence. For example, one very important source of incentives for performance is selectivity of students. Selective schools and programs capitalize on and create strong incentives for students to work hard and do well, and that eases teachers' dependence on students. Students accept that they should work hard and do well, so teachers need not become agents for mobilizing learners' commitment, nor do they need to lower expectations to keep students engaged. In such cases, the social organization of practice does the work of motivating students that teachers in many less selective schools must struggle with if they want students to work hard and do their best.

Selectivity generally has been weaker and less consistent in the United States than in most Asian and European systems, where students have been increasingly selected by ability and effort as the grades rise. By the middle or secondary grades, many academic teachers in nations like France, Singapore, and Japan are presented with increasingly able and committed students. There are, of course, some selective U.S. public schools as well as top track classes in many public schools, but even top-flight U.S. schools regularly present teachers with classes full of indifferent or hostile students, or with a mix of committed and uncommitted students. If those teachers want students to tackle demanding work, they must persistently try to persuade students to do so, taking major responsibility both for motivation and learning. It is much easier for teachers in such circumstances to reduce their dependence by adjusting their expectations to suit students' wishes. There is considerable evidence that many teachers, especially in secondary schools, adjust their expectations to suit students' wishes rather than pressing for high performance.[43]

A performance reward scheme operating in such unselective schools and classes would offer teachers incentives to press students to do things that many students had other incentives not to do. Performance rewards would be working against the grain of the incentives arising from lack of selectivity. In itself that is not troublesome—teachers certainly should work hard to get students to do their best. But lacking any change in the larger structure of incentives for students, it is not clear that performance rewards would have the desired effect. They might only heighten conflict within teachers and classrooms.

The issue cannot be decided in terms of selectivity alone, for several other incentive structures are at work. Teachers and students are influenced by the higher education institutions that admit high school graduates and the business firms that hire them. Those institutions' consumption patterns send signals concerning the qualities and accomplishments that they desire. American colleges and universities send mixed but generally weak signals about the importance of hard work and strong academic performance. One group of higher education institutions has very modest requirements: students need only a thin record of academic accomplishment in high school, often only a C average, to be admitted. Only high school graduation is required for admission in still another group of institutions, and not even high school graduation is needed in still a third group. These arrangements offer many students a second chance, but they also signal that high school students need not work hard in order to get into college or university.[44] In those circumstances, it would be irrational for most students who aspire to higher education to work very hard in high school, just as it would be irrational for their teachers to press those students to try hard and do their best work.[45] There are exceptions, of course; a small number of highly selective colleges and universities do have demanding admissions standards, and they do send clear signals to interested applicants about the importance of high performance in high school. But these schools are unusual.

A similar situation holds for the employment practices of most U.S. businesses. Few firms seem to ask for students' high school transcripts or references from teachers when considering them for employment. And even when firms do request transcripts, only a tiny fraction of schools supply them.[46] The lack of employer interest deters students from thinking that grades, effort, or behavior count for jobs, and it deters teachers from thinking that their judgments about students could make a difference.[47] If students can get jobs without even presenting evidence about their grades, school behavior, and teachers' evaluation of their work, it would be irrational for them to work hard, or for their teachers to press them for their best work. There are cases in which employers create relationships with specialized vocational high schools and hire many of their graduates, but these are exceptions.

These arrangements are unusual in the world. Universities in Japan, France, and many other nations lay great weight on students' performance in high school, high school leaving and university entrance exams, or both. If students wish to enter university, they must work hard in school and get good grades, make special preparation for the exams, or both. In many cases, the external examinations become the target of cooperative efforts by teachers and students to ensure that students do as well as they can. There are many troublesome features of such systems, including that they screen out able students who do not do well on exams and offer students no second chance at high attainment. But these systems leave little doubt in students' and teachers' minds that hard work and good school performance are important.

Employers in Japan, the former West Germany, and many other nations also pay close attention to students' secondary school records in hiring decisions.[48] They routinely review transcripts and teacher references when high school graduates or early school leavers apply for jobs. In some cases, schools and employers work closely to place students in apprenticeship or regular work situations. Teachers know these things, as do students. It is understood that students who do not apply themselves and behave decently in school will have difficulty finding good apprenticeships or jobs. There are important rewards for academic effort and good behavior, even for students who have no ambitions for further education.

Given the broader incentive systems in which U.S. schools operate, schools could not adopt a performance reward scheme with much confidence about its effects. Teachers might be motivated to try to persuade students to work hard and do well in spite of the contrary signals from higher education and work. But lacking any change in the structure of incentives for students from firms and higher education, performance rewards might only heighten teachers' conflict, pushing them to push students in the opposite direction than students were being pushed by incentives from firms, higher education, and peers who knew the score on such matters.

Once again, the issue cannot be decided based only on the signals that firms and universities send students and teachers, for still other incentive structures bear on schools. Students and teachers also are influenced by broader attitudes about education, which are broadcast by the adults they know, as well as by newspapers, television, and other agencies. If these agencies sent generally strong signals that hard work and high achievement would benefit students of all sorts, perhaps the lack of clear signals from higher education and firms would be somewhat offset; if so, performance rewards might tip the balance toward effort and achievement inside schools. But many send quite contrary signals, for Americans are deeply ambivalent about intellectual work.[49] Attitudes and values vary, of course—The *New York Times* and Public Television are different from *USA Today* and the Fox Network—but we have long been inclined to value experience over formal education, and to value practical rather than intellectual content within formal education. Teachers are not held in high esteem, and a large fraction of those who enter the profession still do so with the idea that it will be a backup in case a better job or marriage does not materialize. There is little on commercial television or radio that supports academic learning, and much to suggest that it is irrelevant or useless. Adults further report that they value learning to get along, and job-related knowledge and skills more highly than academic learning.[50] For instance, 81 percent of the respondents in a recent Gallup poll said that the "chief reason" people want their children to get a formal education were job opportunities, preparation for a better life, better-paying jobs, and financial security. Only 15 percent said that the chief reason to get a formal education was to become more knowledgeable or to learn to think and understand.[51] Americans also seem to act on these beliefs: relatively few mothers report working closely with their children on academic tasks or offering support for hard work and success in school.[52]

Intellectual work and academic accomplishment are more highly regarded in many other societies. In Japan and China, for instance, parents take education very seriously and hold teachers in high esteem. Investigators report that Japanese and Chinese mothers also play a central role in their childrens' academic work, encouraging children, working closely with them on assignments, and creating an environment conducive to learning.[53] Japanese and Chinese mothers also seem to hold higher standards for their children and to have more realistic evaluations of their achievement than American mothers. Childrearing and adult values in these countries seem more conducive to successful schooling than in the United States.

In fact, America is distinctive for its deep divisions over schooling. We debate the value of intellectual independence versus obedience. Many Americans want schools to teach only basic skills. More and more campaign for home schooling to save children from schools' "propaganda," or they stage political shoot-outs over whether students should read *Catcher in the Rye* or *The Adventures of Huckleberry Finn*, or they argue about whether evolution, phonics, or critical thinking should be taught. Such matters barely surface in other nations. Our distinctive attachment to personal autonomy contrasts with more cooperative and deferential behavior in other societies, where people seem preoccupied with how they can fit in, work with others, and advance common values.

No one knows whether performance reward schemes would tip the balance of incentives toward high performance or would pit teachers against many students by pitting school incentives for stiff academic performance against a broad array of social, economic, and cultural incentives for weak performance. But the abundant indirect evidence suggests that performance rewards would not have a generally positive effect because so many other incentives encourage low performance. That is not a reason to avoid incentives for performance, but it is a reason to design such schemes in light of the situation. Alternative designs might include schemes that mobilize incentives for students and teachers at once, rather than teachers only. One example would be direct incentives to students and teachers for improved student performance. Another would be instructional designs that focused teachers' and students' attention on the quality of students' work in relation to demanding academic standards.[54] Still another would be competitions among groups of students for rewards that they would value. In any such scheme, it would be critical to design things so that the rewards were congruent, so that teachers would have reason to be resources for students' efforts to achieve. Another alternative design might include mobilizing broader social, educational, and economic incentives for student performance. One example would be persuading businesses to pay attention to students' grades and teacher references, and to let schools know that they were doing so. Another would be to persuade higher education agencies to adopt higher standards for admission. These alternatives recognize that the motivation for school performance has at least as many sources outside schools as inside them, and that one element of good policy design would be to get the several influences working in the same direction.

Rewards and Penalties

In a perfect world, one would not need to discuss rewards and penalties. Teachers would do the right thing because they could do nothing else. But rewards and penalties are essential in our imperfect world, for they help us decide what is most important out of all that we need and want, and they help us influence others' decisions. Rewards and penalties also can encourage us to cultivate or mobilize the capacities required to perform those tasks. The question is not whether various rewards and penalties are useful—they are essential—but what sort are best suited to improving student achievement.

Six assumptions, roughly derived from the discussion thus far, guide my response. The first is that we know only a little about the central issue: what suitable and serious rewards and penalties might be, and how to distinguish them from their too trivial or heavy-duty brethren? That distinction would be critical in designing any scheme, but experience with and research on incentives in education are both quite modest. Much would have to be learned before we would have anything like sound design principles in this matter. It seems more appropriate to offer ideas that might guide the design of a scheme than to specify a design.

A second assumption is that one cannot intelligently discuss rewards and penalties apart from the other chief design elements of a scheme, for rewards and penalties would not operate in isolation. The design elements would specify the situation in which rewards and penalties would operate, and thus would offer at least a rudimentary basis for considering how they might work. My remaining assumptions fill in the most important design elements. One is that although incentives for students are as important as those for teachers, they do not substitute for each other, for teachers' perceptions and interests are far from identical with those of students in most American public schools. Incentives for teachers to improve student performance should be complemented by incentives for students to improve their own performance. Though those incentives might be different, they should be aimed at the same results and designed to encourage the same sorts of academic behavior.

Another assumption is that any serious performance reward scheme would aim at higher level knowledge and intellectual skills, which could include demanding versions of traditional instruction.

Still another is that such a scheme would sharply increase uncertainty, and that would become more troublesome as learning goals became intellectually more ambitious. Such learning goals are more complex, open more room for disagreement than those associated with basic skills, and thus create more uncertainty in and around classrooms. Advocates argue that incentives for results would have a salutary effect on learning because they would focus attention on results and thus produce better performance. But that assumes a stable and well-known instructional technology, which does not exist for intellectually demanding work. Though many teachers care deeply about results, they often focus on instructional processes partly because they find learning to be so uncertain. It is, for example, often difficult to know when students know something: those who seemed to know two-digit multiplication on Monday often seem not to know it on Friday; those who seemed to know it when problems were written one way seem not to know it when they are presented in another.[55] It is much easier to tell students to work two-digit multiplication problems on a worksheet than to probe their knowledge deeply—that is, ask them to solve the "same" problems in several different forms at several different times. A scheme that offered potent incentives to focus on results would be likely to increase exactly those uncertainties that most trouble most teachers. Lacking stable, effective, and well-understood systems of instruction, many teachers would respond to performance rewards by fixing on process indicators that seemed to be proxies for the required results, or mechanically imitating instructional approaches that they thought would produce those results, or both.

A last assumption, closely related to these comments, is that any performance reward scheme that aimed higher than low-level skills would require fairly extensive teacher learning. Rewards and punishments should not only encourage teachers and students to boost student performance, but should also encourage teachers to learn what they would need to know in order to do so.

There are at least several ways to design schemes that would fit with these ideas, and we are far from knowing enough to specify the One Best Design. But one way to make close connections between the performances for which students and teachers would be rewarded would be to make students' academic work the focus of teachers' work—that is, to organize schooling so that teachers devoted considerable attention to understanding students' work and learning how to improve it. Linda Darling-Hammond terms this "learner-centered instruction."[56] Such an approach could create a basis for linking teachers' and students' learning by making students' work the agenda for teachers' learning. The teachers' curriculum would begin with students' work, with teachers' efforts to improve it, with the subject matter in which students' work was situated, and other related matters.

Teachers' work on students' work thus would focus partly on efforts to improve students' performance, dealing with such questions as "how good is this answer?" and "why is it as good as, or better than, that answer?" and "how could I have helped this student do better—and how do others do it?" One result of such work would be examples of desired performance that teachers could use in their work together, as well as in their work with students. In order for such a scheme to work, teachers would have to agree on results and judgments of quality, and come to some common understanding of acceptable variation. Teachers could not do much of that without opportunities to work together on students' work, on their understanding of it, their views of its quality, and their grasp of the underlying material.

Those ideas also imply the existence of common assessments that teachers and students also would use to guide their work. And that in turn suggests that there would have to be something like a common curriculum—at least agreement on the content to be covered, as in the Advanced Placement program. For if teachers did not have a common range of topics to work on, it would be extremely difficult to frame common assignments, to develop common ideas about quality, and to develop common understanding of how to improve teaching and learning. Without such things, no scheme could have any broad validity or application.

The point in such an approach would not be to "restructure" schools, but to revise instruction so as to create extensive opportunities for teachers to focus on students' work and its improvement, and, to that end, to improve teachers' knowledge of subject matter, teaching, and learning. Situating those collective efforts to improve students' performance in instruction would create a basis for rewarding teachers and students jointly for improved performance, but it would initially increase uncertainty and teachers' workload. If done well, it could help teachers learn what they would need to know in order to deal with the increased uncertainty of a performance reward scheme, by building a foundation for common judgments about the quality of students' work and what knowledge counts most. Such an endeavor also could reduce mechanistic instruction and create extensive support for teachers' learning.

A scheme of this sort could mobilize many internal incentives for teachers and students. For instruction that enabled students to learn more, and more effectively, would generate powerful satisfactions for teachers and students, and thereby incentives to sustain the effort. Such internal incentives would have to be central to any serious performance reward scheme, for teachers and other practitioners of human improvement depend on clients for their success. Lacking a way to mobilize those mutual satisfactions of teaching and learning, it is difficult to imagine external rewards and penalties that would be potent enough to produce high levels of performance.

But even if such internal rewards and penalties became central to teachers' and students' work together, they could not carry the entire weight of the reforms discussed here. For the transition to a more intellectually ambitious and performance-oriented sort of instruction would be difficult, unsettling, and in some important ways quite unsatisfying for teachers, not to mention students and parents. More palpable and less subtle rewards and penalties also would be important. Salaries, working conditions, and how superiors respond to their work all matter to teachers and would be suitable material for performance rewards. It probably would make sense to combine various sorts of rewards—financial and professional, individual and collective—rather than focusing entirely on one or the other. Suitable financial rewards could include free tuition, money for instructional improvement, and salary bonuses, whereas suitable external professional rewards could include career advancement, public recognition, improved working conditions, and the like. No medium is pure—money rewards for good work with students would be more than money, for they also would signal some professional recognition and might lead to opportunities for advancement or improved working conditions. But the emphasis among these can differ considerably. One reason for a mix of rewards is that it could reflect the rewards of teaching. Another is that professional taste varies—many would prefer one sort of reward to another, but few would flatly reject either. Still another reason to mix rewards is that the scheme I have sketched would require much collective work by teachers, and it could be damaging to assign individual rewards for collective effort. It probably makes sense for the balance among these rewards to be locally designed, or at least to be open to local redesign.

Finally, one must decide whether the absence of rewards is a penalty and, if so, whether it is a sufficient penalty, especially in the schools most in need of improvement. If not, what penalties would be suitable? The answer to the first query depends partly on the perceived fairness and legitimacy of the scheme. If both were high, and if knowledge of the scheme were broadly and thoroughly available, then the absence of success and rewards probably could seem to be a penalty. But such penalties seem likely to be sufficient only for schools that could relatively easily be improved, and those probably are a minority of the schools that most need improvement. Hence, additional penalties should be considered, including:

- Pressuring principals and teachers to improve
- Replacing the principal and other school leaders
- Teachers losing assignments or tenure and replacements being hired, handing over the school to an external improvement team, or closing the school and reopening it as a new unit with new leadership, staff, and mission

These alternatives remind us that the schools most in need of improvement would be least affected by the absence of rewards or the presence of penalties because they would have the least capability to read the situation, to consider approaches to improvement, and to take effective steps. That, after all, is one of the chief reasons that such schools are poor. Hence, we confront the likely inefficacy of incentives alone to provoke action that would broadly improve schools. My analysis suggests that externally provoked and operated school improvement also would be required.

Conclusion

I have repeatedly alluded to the limits of this little exercise in design. A scheme that moved schools toward a focus on results would increase teachers' uncertainties, especially if it also moved toward intellectually more ambitious conceptions of results. Many classroom problems for teachers and students would predictably follow from these changes, and they would be likely to generate pressures for simpler and more familiar assignments and assessments. That was the fate of the 1950's curriculum reforms, and as I write, reform in California, South Carolina, and other states is under attack on such grounds among others. A movement to press schooling back toward basics has been gathering force for a few years, but the further school systems moved in the direction of such simplification, the more performance reward schemes would be trivialized or regressive.

These matters could profoundly affect the design of any performance reward scheme, but they are not matters that designers could control. Designers might at best devise measures of performance and rewards and penalties that could ease the probable political pressures and perhaps restrain them from corrupting the design. One way to do that would be to devise assessments that covered several conceptions of knowledge and learning, and another would be to design rewards and penalties in consultation with parents and others interested. Performances and rewards should be understood as much in political as educational terms, for in America no scheme to improve performance will operate well educationally unless it works well politically.

Discussing the politics of performance rewards calls to mind their economics. Many advocates find these schemes appealing because they promise cleaner, more efficient, and perhaps leaner school systems. But I would mark that down as one of several central issues for research. My analysis suggests that serious performance reward schemes would be unlikely to work without a considerable additional investment in professionals' learning and school improvement, and those would entail more administrative responsibility and costs. Performance-oriented school systems might be differently organized and better, but they seem unlikely to be less expensive, or to have less potent central offices. The political and fiscal price of greater effectiveness may be steeper than many imagine.

Though this essay has covered a considerable waterfront, I have so far said nothing about how much improvement would be enough. I suggested criteria of success that were linked to substantial educational goals and standards, but no one knows how much scores should improve. Should state or local schools expect modest gains? Large gains? Should the entire distribution of achievement rise, should we aim for less inequality overall, or both? Research sheds little light, either on what reasonable expectations might be or on how much time improvement should take. These would be critical issues in the public as well as the professional evaluation of performance reward schemes, but researchers and professionals have barely made a start on them.

That point and many others like it show that performance rewards in schools are mostly unknown territory.[57] A polite way to put it is to note how much research could improve understanding of performance rewards. We don't know enough about incentives or school improvement to estimate, for example, the size or types of inventives that would be most compelling for teachers. In a rational world, such weak knowledge would incline public officials and others interested to create opportunities to systematically learn from experience. It would, for instance, be appealing to devise some sort of quasi-experimental or planned variation design in order to improve learning from innovation. But such things are costly, politically troublesome, and methodologically difficult in the best of times. And our own time is distressingly irrational, marked by expanding ideological conflict and contracting budgets; it makes experiments and other efforts to systematically learn from experience seem a bit remote.

Notes

1. This paper was written in connection with a forum on Incentives and Systemic Reform, sponsored by The Consortium For Policy Research in Education (CPRE) and The Pew Forum on Education Reform. I am grateful to Marshall Smith and Richard Murnane, whose dissatisfaction with an earlier version prodded me to rework it. Murnane also helped me think about how to revise, as did Tony Bryk, Susan Fuhrman, Helen Ladd, Jennifer O'Day, and Janet A. Weiss. My thinking about problems of professionalism was improved by comments from Brian Rowan and Joan Talbert, and Gail Baxter had helpful comments concerning assessment. My understanding of several issues was improved by discussions on performance-based approaches to school reform that Helen Ladd organized at the Brookings Institution. Of course none of these people are responsible for my views.

2. The literature on trends in student performance is very mixed, and researchers disagree. Eric Hanushek (Hanushek et al., 1994, chapter 3) argues that during the last three decades student performance on standardized tests has declined or, at best, remained unimproved. In their study of historical trends in literacy, Lawrence Stedman and Carl Kaestle qualify critics' and reformers' claims of declining test scores by

noting their failures to account for changes in test-taking populations and contradictory evidence (Stedman and Kaestle, 1987, pp. 18–23). They are inclined to think the scores have held roughly steady despite large increases in the enrollment of educationally disadvantaged students. Gerald Bracey takes much more sharp issue with claims of educational failure that cite declining test scores (Bracey, 1992). Like Stedman and Kaestle, he believes that demographic changes need to be factored into longitudinal comparisons of average student test scores. But Daniel Koretz argues that achievement has declined since the 1950s, even after compositional changes in the school population have been taken into account (Koretz, 1986; Koretz, 1987).

3. Linda Darling-Hammond argues against many sorts of accountability on the grounds that rewards and sanctions tied to student performance exacerbate existing educational inequalities and preclude meaningful inquiry into teaching and learning at school and classroom levels though she supports certain other sorts of accountability (Darling-Hammond, 1994a, pp. 14–16, 23–25). But Eric Hanushek asserts that incentives linked to student performance are "the best hope for getting on a path of long-run improvement" (Hanushek et al., 1994, p. 88). Chapter 6 of his book offers a taxonomy of performance incentive schemes, including schemes to reward or penalize teachers based on student performance.

4. This sort of scientifically augmented state administration could be compatible with market solutions. States could operate schools and permit new schools to enter the market and permit consumers to choose another school if theirs was low performing. But most accountability schemes do not go that far—they rely on state administration augmented with evidence on effectiveness and some sort of penalties and rewards.

5. For a report on several long-lived merit pay schemes, an explanation of why most have very short lives, and useful bibliography, see Murnane, R. J. and Cohen, D. K. (1986) and Cohen, D. K. and Murnane, R. J. (1985). For a general survey of research on performance rewards, see National Research Council (1991), and for a recent treatment of performance rewards in education, see Ladd, H. (1995).

6. Passing the National Board For Professional Teaching Standards exams is one exception to this generalization.

7. See Frederiksen (1994, pp. 532, 535), Kirst (1994, p. 385), Baker (1994, pp. 454–455), Resnick (1994, pp. 512–513, 522–523), and Darling-Hammond (1994a, pp. 6, 11, 13).

8. Gail Baxter, Anastasia Elder, and Robert Glaser provide evidence of a strong positive relationship between student scores and sophistication of thinking activity on a science performance assessment (Baxter et al.,

unpublished manuscript, pp. 14–26). Norman Frederiksen reviews a number of instructional and assessment technologies that support higher-order thinking by stimulating real problem situations (Frederiksen, 1994, pp. 550–558). Lauren Resnick acknowledges the praise that individual performance assessments receive for promoting higher-order knowledge and skills, such as those identified by the authors just cited, but she notes the absence of evidence for performance assessments' collective construct validity (Resnick, 1994). She attributes the absence of such evidence in part to a lack of consensus over the content to be measured by performance assessments (pp. 522–525).

9. Lauren Resnick provides a hypothetical sketch of a portfolio and performance assessment system that illustrates the greater capacity of portfolio assessment for representing variety of student work (Resnick, 1994, pp. 513–516).

10. Test items are selected by first sampling topics, problems, and other materials from a variety of texts and curricula, developing pools of test items, trying them out, and selecting only items that produce normal distributions of responses. That rules out items that many students get right or wrong.

11. Silver and Kenney, op. cit.

12. Ibid.

13. Gail Baxter, Richard Shavelson, Susan Goldman, and Jerry Pine find only "moderate" correlations between student performances on standardized multiple choice science tests and more innovative hands-on science investigations (Baxter et al., 1992, p. 12; Shavelson et al., 1992, p. 25). In addition, they find stronger correlations between standardized tests and measures of general cognitive ability than they do between innovative assessments and ability measures. Taking these two findings in combination, they conclude that standardized and innovative assessments measure different aspects of science achievement, with the former being more related to students' general knowledge and skills (Baxter et al., 1992, pp. 11–13; Shavelson et al., 1992, p. 25).

14. Bryk, A. (1995).

15. See Elmore, Fuhrman, and Abelman, "The New Accountability in State Education Reform: From Process to Performance," in *Holding Schools Accountable.* Washington, D.C.: The Brookings Institute, 1996.

16. Dallas has such a scheme, and it is terrifically controversial. For one account, see Helen Ladd and Charles Clotfelder's chapter in Ladd, op. cit. Linda Darling-Hammond and Ernesto Cortes, in personal communications, argue that the Dallas scheme is fatally flawed, among other reasons because the most disadvantaged schools are effectively excluded from the scheme.

17. One bit of additional support for value-added approaches to criteria of success is evidence that students in high-poverty schools seem to progress at roughly the same rate during the school year as students in more advantaged schools—the rates diverge during the summers (Heyns, B., 1975). This study suggests that using fixed criteria would bestow advantages on schools in privileged communities that would not accrue if districts used gain scores that were adjusted for inherited status, prior scores, or both, and did not include summer learning. But Heyns's data are nearly twenty years old, and more studies of relative gains would be needed to probe the issue further.

18. Whether that turned out to be the case would be an important issue for research on performance reward schemes. But many commentators expect that one effect of setting more demanding educational goals and standards—à la Goals 2000—is that more advantaged students would be able to do much better on them than disadvantaged students, both because of the educational consequences of social and economic disadvantage and because instruction in disadvantaged schools often is less effective than in more advantaged schools.

19. Whether schools were able to become much more effective in a stable fashion year after year would be one of the most critical issues for research on performance rewards.

20. Elmore, Fuhrman, and Abelman, op. cit, report that Mississippi recently adopted such a scheme and that it is quite difficult for teachers and parents to understand. Few seem to comprehend why schools that gained rewards did so, or why others did not. Mystification and mistrust seem to mark responses to that state's scheme, which do not bode well for its effect on practice.

21. That appears to be roughly the approach envisioned in Title III of the Clinton administration's central school reform legislation, Goals 2000. That statute invites states to adopt "internationally competitive" instructional goals and content and performance standards. Once those were developed and in place, assessments keyed to them would be devised or selected. Title III of the statute seems to urge educators to use assessment of (at least) students in disadvantaged schools to decide about movement toward new state standards. But, as I write, Title III is dead.

22. There is some evidence from both the South Carolina and Dallas plans, and from the Chicago reform, that quite a few schools would fall into and remain in such a category. See Ladd and Clotfelder, op. cit.

23. Bryk, A. Bryk, A. Easton, J., Kerbow, D., Rollow, S., and Sebring, P. (1993).

24. Hanushek et al., op. cit.

25. National Education Commission on Time and Learning (1994, p. 32).

26. National Education Commission on Time and Learning (1995).

27. Brophy, J. (1988); see also Brophy, J. and Good, T. (1987).

28. Goodlad, J. (1984, pp. 111–112).

29. Even such work would not be easy despite the focus on basic skills. Though most observers agree that classroom work is generally oriented to basic skills instruction, and that most teachers have not been educated to do much more, few have been educated to do such work very effectively. Doing so is considerably more demanding than ordinary classroom work. As a result, efforts to create more effective basic skills instruction run into appreciable obstacles. For example, Jane Stallings, reported in studies of the implementation of a direct instruction program in northern California, that students' achievement improved as long as teachers were being trained but that scores slipped once training was withdrawn.

30. Cohen, D., McLaughlin, M., and Talbert, J. (1993, chapters 2–5).

31. For example, teachers of disadvantaged students hold their students' academic abilities in lower esteem than teachers of advantaged students (see U.S. Department of Education, 1993, pp. 84, 87), and many teachers attribute their students' weakness to family circumstances. The frequently implied conclusion is that schools and teachers can do little to help. Increasing professionals' capability to respond constructively to performance reward schemes would require change in such beliefs, for teachers could hardly boost students' achievement if they thought them incapable of learning very much, or if they assumed that teachers were not responsible for producing better results, or both. Skill and will work together when they work. To be instructionally effective, teachers' sense of responsibility for students would have to be linked to an extensive repertoire of instructional actions and to criteria for judging the results. For instance, in order for educational professionals to take responsibility for students' work, they would require high internal standards for the sorts of things they should do to interest students in the work, to maintain students' commitment, and to encourage students to work hard. If such teachers had students who failed to measure up, they would revise their approach and try again. If they failed to notice a student's problem that later came to light, or if they noticed it and failed to take appropriate action, they would question their judgment or motivation, and try to figure out how to correct the problem.

32. See Judith Warren-Little (1989, pp. 173–177).

33. See, for example, Bryk, A. and Lee, V. (1993).

34. McLaughlin and Talbert (1993, pp. 5–11), Talbert and McLaughlin (1994, pp. 128–143), and Talbert and Perry (1994, pp. 5–19).

35. Bryk and Lee, op. cit, chapter 11.

36. Bryk et al., op. cit.

37. Purkey, S. and Smith, M. (1983).

38. Slavin, R. and Karweit, N. (1993, chapters 2–3).

39. Bryk, A. (1995).

40. The need for systematic learning also follows logically from the arguments made by advocates of performance rewards that we lack solid knowledge concerning the links between school resources and school achievement because under the present regime there are insufficient incentives for performance. Only when such incentives were in place would there be fertile ground in educational reality in which valid knowledge about instructional improvement could thrive—whether in the form of craft knowledge or a well-specified production function. These ideas suggest that the existence of performance rewards would be an occasion to create the knowledge and skills that would be needed to operate performance reward systems and help failing schools improve.

41. Some readers may say that nearly all occupations try to improve humanity and that nearly all have managers who work on other people and try to produce improvements. But consider the nature of the improvements and the means by which they are cultivated. Surgeons do not try to make their patients into apprentice surgeons, nor do salespeople try to improve their clients' capacity to sell vacuum cleaners or encyclopedias. Moreover, most managers assiduously avoid trying to help their subordinates become managers, let alone better managers. In occupations like sales, physical medicine, and many branches of management, practitioners typically strive for a distinctive sort of result: items sold or manufactured, profits earned, bones and organs repaired, and the like. Betterment of clients' minds and souls, or improvement of their knowledge and skill are subsidiary at best, and typically either irrelevant or merely decorative. In contrast, teachers succeed only by helping students acquire some elements of their own specialized expertise: knowledge of a subject, skill in communicating about it, a repertoire of strategies for solving problems, and the like. When psychotherapists succeed, it is typically by helping their patients acquire elements of their own distinctive therapeutic expertise: insight into emotional problems, understanding their sources, skill in noticing symptoms, and a grasp of the barriers to improvement. Only teachers and practitioners in sister trades must cultivate their clients' capacities to become adept practitioners of their own improvement, for only in these professions must clients become such practitioners in order for professionals to succeed. Hence, though there are elements

of human improvement in many modern occupations, there also are important differences between human improvement professions and other occupations in which people are processed.

42. For examples, see Powell, A., Farrar, E., and Cohen, D. (1985); Hollinghead, A. (1937); Lynd R. and Lynd H. (1928); and Coleman, J. (1961).
43. Powell, Farrar, and Cohen, op. cit. See also Cusick, P. (1983).
44. Bishop (1989, pp. 12–14).
45. Trow (1989); Powell, Farrar, and Cohen, op. cit.
46. Bishop, op. cit.
47. James Rosenbaum and Takehiko Kariya conclude that institutional linkages between Japanese employers and high schools increase the influence of academic achievement (grades) on work-bound graduates' chances of attaining desirable jobs; consequently, they create clear incentives for students to achieve academically (Rosenbaum and Kariya, 1989, pp. 342–358). Rosenbaum and Kariya also find that Japanese junior high students develop their educational and occupational plans in direct response to their academic achievements (Kariya and Rosenbaum, 1987). The centrality of academic achievement to their planning results from the education system's exclusive reliance on achievement for high school admission selections.
48. Bishop (1987, 1989); Kariya and Rosenbaum (1987); Rosenbaum and Kariya (1989).
49. Hofstadter, R. (1966).
50. Lynd, R., Lynd, H., op. cit; Cusick, op. cit; Powell, Farrar, and Cohen, op. cit.
51. Elam and Gallup (1989, p. 48).
52. Stevenson, H. and Stigler, J. (1985).
53. White (1987, pp. 144–145); Stevenson and Lee (1990, pp. 85–87, 97–100). See also Shimahara (1986, p. 20).
54. Linda Darling-Hammond's proposals for learner-centered instruction (see her essay in this volume) are a promising case in point, for they recognize that teachers' success is intimately linked to students' success—that is, she assumes that most teachers have professional incentives to help students learn if they have the wherewithal to do so. It is not clear whether her proposals take account of the risk and difficulty that more ambitious instruction holds, and of the ways those things can push teachers to accept modest success through modest standards for students.
55. Lortie, D. (1975); Lampert, M. (1984); Ball, D. L. (1993); Cohen, D. K. (1993).
56. Linda Darling-Hammond, op. cit.
57. See, most recently, Hanushek, E., op. cit.

References

Baker, E. L. "Researchers and Assessment Policy Development: A Cautionary Tale." *American Journal of Education,* 1994, *102*(4), 450–477.

Ball, D. L. "With an Eye on the Mathematical Horizon: Dilemmas of Teaching Elementary School Mathematics." *The Elementary School Journal,* 1993, *93*(4), 373–397.

Ball, D. L., Cohen, D. K., Peterson, P. L., Wilson, S. M., Grant, S. G., and Spillane, J. P. *Contrasting Resources for Reform in Mathematics and Reading.* Papers presented at the annual meeting of the American Educational Research Association, San Francisco, 1995.

Baxter, G. P., Elder, A. D., and Glaser, R. *Cognitive Analysis of a Science Performance Assessment.* Unpublished manuscript, 1995.

Baxter, G. P., Shavelson, R. J., Goldman, S. R., and Pine, J. "Evaluation of Procedure-Based Scoring for Hands-On Science Assessment." *Journal of Educational Measurement,* 1992, *29*(1), 1–17.

Bishop, J. *Information Externalities and the Social Payoff to Academic Achievement.* Ithaca, N.Y.: Cornell University, Center for Advanced Human Resource Studies, 1987.

Bishop, J. *Incentives for Learning: Why American High School Students Compare So Poorly to Their Counterparts Overseas.* Ithaca, N.Y.: Cornell University, Center for Advanced Human Resource Studies, 1989.

Bracey, G. W. "The 'Education Crisis': More Rhetoric than Reality." *Education Digest,* Feb. 1992, 39–42.

Brophy, J. "Research Linking Teacher Behavior to Student Achievement." *Educational Psychologist,* 1988, *23*(3), 235–286.

Bryk, A., Lee, V., and Holland, P. *Catholic Schools and the Common Good.* Cambridge, Mass: Harvard University Press, 1993.

Bryk, A. *Chicago Accountability White Paper, Center for School Improvement.* Chicago: University of Chicago, 1995.

Bryk, A., Easton, J., Kerbow, D., Rollow, S., and Sebring, P. *A View from the Elementary Schools: The State of School Reform in Chicago.* Chicago: Consortium on Chicago School Research, 1993.

Cohen, D. K. *Practice and Its Predicaments.* Unpublished manuscript.

Cohen, D. K., McLaughlin, M. W., and Talbert, J. E. (eds.). *Teaching for Understanding: Challenges for Policy and Practice.* San Francisco: Jossey-Bass Publishers, 1993.

Cohen, D. K., and Murnane, R. J., "The Merits of Merit Pay." *The Public Interest,* 1985, *80,* 3–30.

Cohen, D. K., and Neufeld, B. "The Failure of High Schools and the Progress of Education." *Daedalus,* 1981, *110*(3), 69–89.

Cohen, D. K., and Spillane, J. P. "Policy and Practice: The Relations

Between Governance and Instruction." In N. Cobb (ed.), *The Future of Education: Perspectives on National Standards in America*. New York: College Entrance Examination Board, 1994.

Cusick, P. *The Egalitarian Ideal and the American High School*. New York: Longman, 1983.

Darling-Hammond, L. "Performance-Based Assessment and Educational Equity." *Harvard Educational Review*, 1994a, *64*(1), 5–30.

Darling-Hammond, L. (Ed.). *Professional Development Schools: Schools for Developing a Profession*. New York: Teachers College Press, 1994b.

Durkin, D. "What Classroom Observations Reveal About Reading Comprehension Instruction." *Reading Research Quarterly*, 1978–1979, *14*(4), 482–533.

Elam, S. M., and Gallup, A. M. "The 21st Annual Gallup Poll of the Public Attitudes toward the Public Schools." *Phi Delta Kappan*, 1989, *71*, 41–54.

Elmore, R., Fuhrman, S., and Abelman, C. "The New Accountability in State Education Reform: Process to Performance," in *Holding Schools Accountable*. Washington, D.C.: The Brookings Institute, 1996.

Frederiksen, N. "The Integration of Testing with Teaching: Applications of Cognitive Psychology in Instruction." *American Journal of Education*, 1994, *102*(4), 527–564.

Good, T., and Brophy, J. *Looking in Classrooms*. 4th ed. New York: Harper & Row, 1987.

Goodlad, J. *A Place Called School: Prospects for the Future*. New York: McGraw-Hill, 1984.

Hanushek, E. *Making Schools Work: Improving Performance and Controlling Costs*. Washington, D.C.: Brookings Institution, 1994.

Heyns, B. *Summer Learning and the Effects of Schooling*. New York: Academic Press, 1978.

Hollingshead, A. *Elmtown's Youth, and Elmtown Revisited*. New York: Wiley, 1978.

Hofstadter, R. *Anti-Intellectualism in American Life*. New York: Knopf, 1966.

Kariya, T., and Rosenbaum, J. E. "Self-Selection in Japanese Junior High Schools: A Longitudinal Study of Students' Educational Plans." *Sociology of Education*, 1987, *60*(3), 168–180.

Kirst, M. W. "The Politics of Nationalizing Curricular Content." *American Journal of Education*, 1994, *102*(4), 383–393.

Koretz, D. *Trends in Educational Achievement*. Washington, D.C.: Congressional Budget Office, 1986.

Koretz, D. *Educational Achievement: Explanations and Implications of Recent Trends*. Washington, D.C., Congressional Budget Office, 1987.

Ladd, H. (ed). *Holding Schools Accountable: Performance-Based Reform in Education*. Washington: Brookings Institution, 1995.

Lampert, M. "How Do Teachers Manage to Teach? Dilemmas of Practice." *Harvard Educational Review,* 1985, *55*(2), 178–194.

Little, J. W. "District Policy Choices and Teachers' Professional Development Opportunities." *Educational Evaluation and Policy Analysis,* 1989, *11*(2), 165–179.

Lord, B. "Teachers' Professional Development: Critical Colleagueship and the Role of Professional Communities." In N. Cobb (ed.), *The Future of Education: Perspectives on National Standards in America.* New York: College Entrance Examination Board, 1994.

Lortie, D. *Schoolteacher: A Sociological Study.* Chicago: University of Chicago Press, 1975.

Lynd, R. S., and Lynd, H. M. *Middletown: A Study in Contemporary American Culture.* New York: Harcourt, Brace and Company, 1929.

McLaughlin, M. W., and Talbert, J. E. *Contexts That Matter for Teaching and Learning: Strategic Opportunities for Meeting the Nation's Education Goals.* Stanford, Calif.: Stanford University, Center for Research on the Context of Secondary School Teaching, 1993.

Murnane, R. J., and Cohen, D. K. "Merit Pay and The Evaluation Problem: Why Some Merit Pay Plans Fail and a Few Survive." *Harvard Educational Review,* 1986, *56*(1), 1–17.

National Research Council. *Pay For Performance: Evaluating Performance Appraisal and Merit Pay.* Washington, D.C.: National Research Council Press, 1991.

National Education Commission on Time and Learning. *Prisoners of Time.* Washington, D.C.: Author, 1994.

Powell, A., Farrar, E., and Cohen, D. K. *The Shopping Mall High School.* Boston: Houghton Mifflin, 1985.

Purkey, S. C., and Smith, M. S. "Effective Schools: A Review." *Elementary School Journal,* 1983, *83*(4), 427–452.

Resnick, L. B. "Performance Puzzles." *American Journal of Education,* 1984, *102*(4), 511–526.

Rosenbaum, J. E., and Kariya, T. "From High School to Work: Market and Institutional Mechanisms in Japan." *American Journal of Sociology,* 1989, *94*(6), 1334–1365.

Rowan, B., Guthrie, L., Lee, G., and Guthrie, G. P. *The Design and Implementation of Chapter I Instructional Services: A Study of Twenty-Four Schools.* San Francisco: Far West Laboratories, 1986.

Shavelson, R. J., Baxter, G. P., and Pine, J. "Performance Assessments: Political Rhetoric and Measurement Reality." *Educational Researcher,* 1992, *21*(4), 22–27.

Shimahara, N. K. "The Cultural Basis of Student Achievement in Japan." *Comparative Education,* 1986, *22*(1), 19–26.

Silver, E., and Kenney, P. A. "The Content and Curriculuar Validity of the 1992 NAEP TSA in Mathematics." In *National Academy of Education, the Trial. State Assessment: Prospects and Possibilities.* Author: Stanford, Calif., 1994.

Slavin, R., and Karweit, N. *Effective Programs for Students at Risk.* Boston: Allyn and Bacon, 1993.

Stedman, L. C., and Kaestle, C. F. "Literacy and Reading Performance in the United States, from 1880 to the Present." *Reading Research Quarterly,* 1987, *22*(1), 8–46.

Stevenson, H. W., and Lee, S. "Contexts of Achievement: A Study of American, Chinese, and Japanese Children." *Monographs of the Society for Research in Child Development,* 1990, *55*(1–2), 1–116.

Stevenson, H. W., Stigler, J. W., Lee, S., and Lucker, G. W. "Cognitive Performance and Academic Achievement of Japanese, Chinese, and American Children." *Child Development,* 1985, *56*(3), 718–734.

Talbert, J. E., and McLaughlin, M. W. "Teacher Professionalism in Local School Contexts." *American Journal of Education,* 1994, *102*(2), 123–153.

Talbert, J. E., and Perry, R. R. *How Department Communities Mediate Mathematics and Science Education Reforms.* Paper presented at the annual meeting of the American Educational Research Association, New Orleans, 1994.

Trow, M. "American Higher Education: Past, Present, and Future." *Educational Researcher,* 1988, *17*(3), 13–23.

U.S. Department of Education. "Prospects: The Congressionally Mandated Study of Educational Growth and Opportunity." *The Interim Report.* Washington, D.C.: Author, 1993.

White, M. *The Japanese Educational Challenge.* New York: Free Press, 1987.

Part Two

Motivation and School Context

Chapter Four

Motivation for School Reform

Susan Albers Mohrman and Edward E. Lawler III

Elementary and secondary schools are experiencing significant societal pressure to improve educational outcomes so that our youth are prepared for a more complex society and increasingly demanding employment. These increased pressures come at a time when the job of educating is made more difficult by the diverse and multilingual population of students, and by other sociological trends that result in many children arriving less prepared for school and without the support and active involvement of the nuclear family. In short, schools are being asked to do more under more difficult circumstances. This chapter addresses motivational issues and organizational approaches to promote meaningful employee involvement in addressing this situation.

The systemic reform movement (Fuhrman, Massell, et al., 1992; Fuhrman, 1993) has emerged in part to deal with the formidable educational challenges facing our society. Changes are advocated in all aspects of the institutional web that surrounds and constitutes public education. Some of the focus is on reforming the complex maze of policy makers that provide direction and constrain schools in sometimes contradictory ways. Much of the focus of systemic reform is on what happens in schools. It deals with higher standards for all children, more demanding curriculum content and instructional methodology, measurement systems for accountability, and organization for high performance. In short, it asks school personnel to attain higher standards, carry out their tasks differently, and organize differently to do so.

Systemic reform represents large-scale change—that is, change in the character of an organization that enables it to achieve and sustain new kinds and levels of performance (Mohrman and others, 1989). Such fundamental change has been occurring by necessity in many organizations in all sectors of the economy as we enter a period of global competition, deregulation, and increasingly scarce resources, and an era of new technological capabilities in which computer technology and advanced telecommunications play a central role in the production of products, the delivery of services, and the distribution and creation of information and knowledge. Buzzwords abound. Organizations are being "rearchitected" (Nadler, Gerstein, and Shaw, 1992), and "reengineered" (Davenport, 1993; Hammer and Champy, 1993)—that is, members are examining their organization and its use of resources and making fundamental changes to become more effective at achieving their mission. Knowledge and expertise are being challenged: the customer-oriented organization is being put in place to ensure that the needs of customers, not just the preferences and assumptions of "experts," determine organizational activities. On the other hand, knowledge has become the currency of successful functioning, and organizations are striving to become "learning organizations" (see, for example, Senge, 1990)—that is, to become able to generate and disseminate the information and knowledge to continuously improve products, services, processes, and organization. This simultaneous need for increased responsiveness to diverse clientele and for increased generation and application of expert knowledge is no less true in schools than in other kinds of organizations.

The changes go beyond mere buzzwords. Organizations are clarifying mission, setting stretch goals appropriate to increasingly difficult environments, determining priorities, focusing resources, eliminating low value-added activities, examining and changing their work processes, reducing bureaucratic activity control and emphasizing outcomes, getting customers actively involved in product generation and service delivery processes, and in so doing, they are changing their shape, governance, and the roles of almost all employees. The environment is dictating that business as usual is not adequate. The massive amount of change is yielding higher performance (Galbraith and Lawler, 1993; Lawler, Mohrman, and Ledford, 1995) and placing immense pressures on the people involved.

Systemic reform probably requires change of this magnitude. School personnel will have to work to achieve new and higher standards and employ significantly altered instructional practices in order to teach all students for a higher level of understanding (Cohen, McLaughlin, and Talbert, 1993). They will have to establish new relationships with their communities and students in order to tailor the school experience to the needs of the local population and better utilize local resources. One component of systemic reform school-based management requires fundamental change in the school organization (Mohrman and Wohlstetter, 1994) in order to get school-level participants meaningfully involved in improving school performance.

If school reform truly points to change of this magnitude, the motivational issue becomes paramount. Large-scale change is uncomfortable to people because of the massive amount of personal change, effort, and insecurity that is involved. People are asked to perform their jobs differently, use new approaches, interact differently with others, and focus on new goals. Professionals, who have traditionally cared primarily about professionally defined excellence and organizational autonomy in carrying out their tasks, are being asked to focus on and be accountable for organizational results. Organizational experts are being told that clients, patients, customers, and society determine whether the results are satisfactory. People who have focused inward are being asked to focus outward—to see where things are being done more effectively and import new and better practices.

The motivational challenge is particularly thorny in schools, where tenured teachers have watched wave after wave of educational "reform," and skepticism abounds. New practices are often championed by transitory political powers; new school boards and legislatures bring ever-shifting directions. And all the while, the reality that educators confront becomes more difficult and not amenable to quick fixes. Teachers essentially control their approaches in their classroom (Johnson and Bales, 1994; Meyer and Rowan, 1977; Rowan, 1990; Shedd and Bacharach, 1991); however, there are often adversary relations between teachers and the administration that determines policies and allocates resources, thereby creating the conditions within which teachers work. There is no tradition of monetary incentives in schools; in fact, there is considerable resistance to the use of performance incentives in an atmosphere of distrust, political control of resources, and strong belief in professional control (Shedd and Bacharach, 1991; Odden and Conley, 1992).

It is clear that unless organizational conditions are created so that the huge number of educators are motivated to change the way they deliver educational services, we will not successfully address the educational challenges in our society. In this paper, we will examine basic models of employee motivation and the high-involvement organizational approaches that have been found to create conditions where employees are motivated to participate in organizational improvement. Finally, we will talk about the motivation to change.

In this paper, we restrict ourselves to examining motivational issues of school-level personnel. We do not deal with the equally challenging issues of motivating district-level employees, policy makers, students, and the community to change. Systemic reform requires changes in the roles and behavior of all aspects of the institutional network in which our schools are embedded. Given the complexity of this network, however, it is not possible in one short chapter to examine the complex motivational factors at work in all its elements. However, it is our belief that the best place to start is with the educators who are in closest contact with the students and who collectively deliver the educational services of the school.

Conditions for Motivation

A dominant model underpinning the study of motivation in organizations is Expectancy Theory (Vroom, 1964; Lawler, 1973; 1994). This theory has withstood the test of time through hundreds of empirical studies in diverse organizations despite fundamental changes in how they operate (Lawler, 1994). It rests on the fundamental premise that behavior is need driven and that people are motivated to perform in a manner that leads to need fulfillment. It posits that a person's motivation to exert effort in a particular direction is a function of two personally held expectations, or expectancies, and of the value one attaches to the anticipated outcomes of achieving the targeted performance. One expectancy is the extent to which one believes that one's effort will lead to success in the achievement of the intended performance. The second expectancy is the extent to which one believes that achieving the intended performance will lead to important personal outcomes. Research has found that individual expectancies are not always objectively accurate, but that it is the expectancy that drives the behavior.

Personal value of outcomes is a rough, subjective calculation of the desirability of the various outcomes that a person experiences as a result of achieving a performance. Individuals differ in the value they attach to outcomes because needs vary across people. For any work performance, individuals are likely to experience both positive and negative outcomes. For example, teachers may believe that they will get a sense of satisfaction if they can successfully employ new approaches to achieve increased student achievement, but they also may feel that they will suffer personal costs such as long hours of work and time away from family as they learn and use these new approaches. Expectancy theory posits that positive and negative personal values (valences) are attached to the extrinsic and intrinsic outcomes that are believed to be likely and that are salient to the individual. Positively valued extrinsic outcomes might include recognition and increased pay or promotion as a consequence of achieving high levels of performance. Feelings of satisfaction and accomplishment are positive intrinsic outcomes that might be expected. Stress, social discomfort, and fatigue are possible negatively valued outcomes. Although there are large individual differences in the extent to which various intrinsic and extrinsic outcomes are valued, the behavior of most people in employment situations is motivated by a combination of intrinsic and extrinsic factors (Locke and Latham, 1990; Lawler, 1994). Motivation results from a subjective balancing of the various outcomes.

In short, people are motivated to try to achieve a certain performance if they believe it is attainable and that achieving it will lead to outcomes they value. Using the terms of this volume, the "incentive" to perform well derives from the combination of outcomes expected; the motivation to perform well is a function of the expectancies and the value of the expected outcomes. Educators, for example, are more likely to exert personal effort to try to implement the new approaches to teaching and to participate in the new organizational approaches that are part of systemic reform if they believe that doing so will make new levels of student attainment possible, if they have faith in their abilities to be successful in the execution of these new approaches, and if they believe they will experience valued personal outcomes, such as satisfaction, recognition, or increased pay, as a result.

What Shapes Expectancies?

Expectancy theory is a cognitive theory of motivation. Expectancies and the values attached to expected outcomes are believed to be in part a function of individual personalities, but also a function of cognitions gained through experience, including occupational and organizational experiences. For example, people form an expectancy of their ability to achieve certain performances based on their experiences of success or failure. This aspect of the organizational motivational cycle relates very closely to theories of self-efficacy (Bandura, 1986) that focus in particular on people's needs to experience a sense of competence, effectiveness, and achievement. If teachers have had experience working to implement new approaches that failed to achieve their objectives, they may not have an expectation that working hard to implement the approaches being advocated in systemic reform will lead to improved student performance.

Individuals form an expectancy of what outcomes they will experience based on the outcomes they have experienced in the past as a result of succeeding or not succeeding in accomplishing a targeted performance. If teachers have had experience working hard to implement new approaches at personal cost and with no recognition or reward, they may expect that successful implementation of new approaches as part of the systemic reform movement will likewise lead to no positive personal outcomes.

Expectancies are shaped by the organization and its processes and structures. For example, does the school have processes and structures that enable teachers to identify and obtain the resources required for successful implementation? Do the reward systems acknowledge excellent performance and the implementation of new approaches? The nature of the work that is done also relates to expectancies. A particular aspect of teaching stands out in this regard: the outcomes of the teaching process depend only in part on teacher performance. Student behavior and performance are also key ingredients of success. If teachers do not believe that students are willing or able to carry out their part of the equation, teachers may have low expectations that their hard work will lead to better educational attainment by the students.

In approaching systemic reform, it is not possible to reverse expectancies that have been formed through years of experience. It is, however, possible and desirable to establish new organizational conditions that will enable new expectations to be formed because teachers begin to encounter new organizational experiences. Some of the factors that influence the effort-to-performance expectancy are whether the individual believes that he or she has the skills and knowledge required, whether there is a clear understanding about the nature of the performance that is to be attained and it is viewed as attainable, and whether the individual believes that there is situational support for the performance (resources such as time, information, and supporting performances by other people). Three aspects of the organization are especially related to the motivational cycle and can be consciously designed to support the motivation for high performance: the goal-setting processes in the organization, the design of work, and the reward system.

Goal-Setting Processes

Goal-setting is a linchpin of organizational motivation. Goal-setting theory (see, for example, Locke and Latham, 1990) is highly compatible with the expectancy theory of motivation (Lawler, 1994). The effort–performance expectancy depends on the existence of a clearly defined performance. Goals define the targeted performances and provide the gauge against which individuals measure their own success and the organizational members measure the success of the organization. In a sweeping review of the goal-setting literature, Locke and Latham (1990) have concluded that in employment situations, goals and incentives are highly effective in motivating behavior, even when employees are strongly intrinsically motivated. They dispute conclusions drawn by Deci and others (Deci and Ryan, 1985) that the use of extrinsic outcomes such as rewards will undermine intrinsic satisfaction. In the arena of organizational change, numerous empirically based models emphasize the importance of shared vision and goals in energizing and directing change activities (see, for example, Tichy and Devana, 1986; Beer, Eisenstat, and Spector, 1990; and Bennis and Nanus, 1985).

Goals are an important, even if underutilized, aspect of motivation in schools. A number of models of effective schools have found that they are characterized by a shared vision and shared goals (Wohlstetter and Smyer, 1994). Schools where teachers' attention is focused on clear, coherent goals do a more effective job of educating students (Rosenholtz, 1985). Multiple and sometimes conflicting goals and the lack of goal consensus have limited the ability of schools to establish clear, shared goals (Rowan, this volume). Beyond that, norms of professional noninterference have limited the ability of school districts and schools to establish standards and objectives that are experienced by teachers as anything other than efforts to control them (Shedd and Bacharach, 1991). In the absence of clear and shared school- or district-level goals, teachers have exercised freedom to establish their own outcome standards (Rowan, 1990), with little realistic feedback about whether these are aligned with the needs of the clientele.

Design of Work

The *design of work* heavily influences performance expectancies and, consequently, motivation. Motivating characteristics of work include variety, the performance of a whole task (task identity), and task significance, all of which contribute to personal meaningfulness. In addition, feedback provides knowledge of results, and autonomy provides a sense of responsibility for work outcomes. Well-designed work promotes psychological states that are associated with intrinsic satisfaction and promote high performance (Hackman and Oldham, 1980). The jobs of teachers would appear to be potentially quite motivating given the importance of the task to society, the variety and relative autonomy inherent in being fully in charge of a classroom, and the immediate feedback available from students.

Given the importance of teacher skills in affecting student achievement (Darling-Hammond, Wise, and Klein, 1995), motivation to increase competencies is a particularly important issue to consider in the design of work. Here, the way the school is organized can detract from the motivational quality of the work. Specifically, how teaching jobs are structured and the organizational processes at work can work against the collective, collegial attention to continual improvement by closing off meaningful feedback from peers about performance and meaningful discussion among peers about school improvement (Shedd and Bacharach, 1991).

Work design theory points out that some work requires a team because performance necessarily results from the interdependent work of multiple people. In these situations, team work design should optimize the motivating characteristics of work at the group level—that is, the team's task should have variety, identity, and significance; the team should get feedback; and the team should be as autonomous as is feasible (Hackman and Oldham, 1980; Hackman, 1987). In such settings, designing work to optimize individual performance may actually detract from overall performance. In schools, for instance, it has been suggested that significant improvement of performance cannot be achieved by concentrating on the behavior of individual teachers in their individual classrooms. Although the work of teachers would appear to be highly motivating at the individual level, true task identity is not possible given that the education of students is a complex composite of a myriad of educational experiences occurring concurrently in different classes and longitudinally across a series of experiences. Reform intended to focus on overall educational outcomes will depend on achieving better coordination and collaboration between the multiple teachers who collectively educate populations of students (Shedd and Bacharach, 1991). A team work design may enable such coordination and provide a more motivating work environment.

Reward System

Motivation also depends on the expectations for achieving valued extrinsic outcomes and thus is related to the organization's *reward system*. The work of Lawler (1990) and others has shown that money can be an important motivator when significant amounts of it are delivered in a manner that is tied to performance, and when a line of sight exists for individuals so that they can see how their personal activities contribute to the performance for which they are rewarded. There are many possible purposes for a compensation system, including establishing a culture and attracting and retaining a qualified workforce, and some organizations choose not to use it as a performance motivator by not making pay contingent on performance. Using compensation as a motivational tool to foster behavior that enables the organization to achieve its mission depends on linking pay to the outcomes or performances that the organization requires in order to achieve its strategy. For example, if the strategy of an organization calls for increasing particular outcomes such as customer responsiveness or quality of service, rewards should be linked to performances that achieve targets and result in improvement in these areas.

Although there is increasing experimentation in school districts with linking rewards to well-specified standards (see Rowan, this volume), schools have in the past not been very successful at linking rewards to performance. The political systems in which schools exist create a context in which the public may clamor for more linkage of rewards to performance, but teachers do not believe that the money for such rewards will actually be available. In addition, teacher norms of equal treatment run deep, their distrust of administrator's ability to evaluate performance objectively is strong, and there is not general agreement on standards or on tests that accurately measure the important aspects of a teacher's performance. All this results in strong resistance to attempts at differentiating pay (Odden and Conley, 1992).

Most attempts at pay for performance in schools have been merit pay systems, often based on measures of performance that focus on behaviors that are easy to measure rather than important for student achievement (Shedd and Bacharach, 1991). Such approaches fit with a traditional organizational mode of hierarchical control, discourage learning, and can promote competitiveness rather than the cooperative, collegial behavior required for a school to be excellent. Odden (this volume) argues that pay for performance was not appropriate in bureaucratic school organizations but may be more suitable in emerging collegial, school-based management settings.

The appropriate level for rewards—individual, team, or a larger organizational unit such as a school—depends on the level at which performance is attained. If the education of students is indeed a collective endeavor, it may make more sense for rewards to be delivered at a team or school level. Individual contribution may be acknowledged by tying compensation to a teacher's mastery of an enhanced repertoire of skills and knowledge required to effectively carry out new technical approaches or expanded roles (Firestone, 1994; Mohrman, Mohrman, and Odden, in press). Skill-based pay has been particularly popular in team-based organizations where the flexible deployment of its members to perform multiple tasks is one of the performance improvement tools available to the team (Ledford, 1990). The organization and work design in many schools currently isolate teachers and limit the feedback and interaction that allow ongoing teacher development, which may limit individual and collective skill development. The development of teachers' skills and knowledge is more likely to occur in schools where there are strong norms of collegiality (Little, 1982) and norms that support skill development and high performance. A combination of team or school-based rewards and a base pay system that rewards development of competencies would seem to be compatible with motivation of teachers for individual development and school performance improvement (Odden, this volume).

Involving Teachers in Performance Improvement

Organizational theorists writing about high-performance organizations increasingly advocate systemwide change to enable the new levels and types of performance that are required to be successful in changing environments (see, for example, Galbraith, Lawler, et al., 1993; Nadler, Gerstein, and Shaw, 1992; Mohrman and Cummings, 1989). High-involvement management is a systemic change model that describes approaches to organizing that create an environment where employees are motivated and empowered to become active in improving organizational performance (Lawler, 1986). These approaches strive to create organizational designs where motivating conditions are in place, where employees develop strong expectancies of being able to perform successfully, and where valued outcomes will result. The basic aim is to move away from the traditional control-oriented hierarchy where managers at the top are responsible for strategy, direction, and organizational performance, and where employees feel victimized and constrained by a context they cannot influence. High-involvement management establishes a situation where control is spread throughout the organization, all organizational members focus on organizational performance and contribute to strategy and direction, and employees are able to influence decisions that shape their expectancies. For example, teachers arc able to flexibly apply resources and methodologies to attain educational goals and to participate in the determination of school goals in the first place.

High-involvement management represents a systemic change involving most aspects of the organization rather than a program or an attempt to employ one key lever such as training or rewards. Systemic change is increasingly advocated in the educational literature where it is recognized that schools are not currently designed to promote the collegial interaction and control required for the level of development and coordination that will be required to support new educational standards of higher-order thinking for all children (Shedd and Bacharach, 1991; Elmore et al., 1990). Many school restructuring proposals are quite compatible with the high-involvement framework; they often focus on how to empower teachers, students, and parents to exercise increased influence in school decisions (Elmore, 1990). School-based management, an important element of systemic reform models, is an approach to restructuring that in its full embodiment requires the creation of a high-involvement school (Mohrman and Wohlstetter, 1994). Elsewhere in this volume, Darling-Hammond describes high-performing schools that have most of the characteristics of high-involvement organizations.

The high-involvement framework entails increasing the presence of four key organizational resources at the technical core of the organization. These resources, which we list here, are believed to be closely linked to employees' capability and motivation to contribute to enhanced performance.

- *Information* about the performance, strategy, mission, and goals of the organization as well as ongoing task feedback to underpin operational decisions in the organization. This information enables individuals and teams to form goals that are in alignment with organizational direction, and provides feedback that enables better targeting of activities, identification of areas that require development, and informed systematic problem-solving and work-process improvement. Receiving ongoing feedback can also promote a sense of accomplishment when goals are accomplished and performance is improved.

- *Knowledge and skills* that enable employees to more fully understand and contribute to the improvement of organizational performance. Expansion in this arena contributes to the individual and team expectations of successful performance as well as to the number of ways they can contribute to performance and consequently to job variety.

- *Power* to make decisions that influence organizational practices, policies, and directions. This enables employees to have more influence not only about what work they do and how they do it, but also about the organizational goals and the context or situation in which work is performed. Ideally, employees can create organizational conditions that enhance their expectations of successful performance. They can collectively set goals that they believe in and experience satisfaction when they are accomplished.

- *Rewards* based on the performance of the organization and the capabilities of individuals. These increase the expectations that individuals will experience valued outcomes as a result of their effort to achieve new skills required to support new organizational directions and to contribute to organizational performance objectives. This aspect of the high-involvement model aligns self-interest with organizational performance.

High-involvement frameworks have been found to be particularly appropriate in settings where the work is nonroutine and employees have to deal with high levels of variety of input and uncertainty about what means will lead to what ends. Under these conditions, work cannot be fully programmed in advance, and employees are called on to use judgment and tailor approaches to the case at hand. These conditions characterize education (Rowan, 1990; Rowan, Raudenbush, and Cheong, 1993). High involvement is also appropriate where there is high interdependence between various contributors—that is, where the work of various contributors has reciprocal impact and needs to be coordinated in a manner that cannot be fully preprogrammed (Mohrman, Lawler, and Mohrman, 1992). In private sector service and manufacturing organizations, the implementation of high-involvement practices has been found to positively influence a number of organizational conditions, including levels of work quality, innovation, introduction of new technology, customer satisfaction, and quality of decision making; employee outcomes such as quality of work life and satisfaction; and financial outcomes such as efficiency and competitiveness (Lawler, Mohrman, and Ledford, 1995).

Different organizational design features can be employed to ensure that information, knowledge and skills, power, and rewards are available to employees. Lawler (1992) has identified three levels of employee involvement, each of which offers different improvement potential and affects the expectancy motivational framework in different ways: parallel suggestion involvement, job involvement, and organizational involvement. These three approaches, which we discuss separately, represent an escalating commitment to changing the organization to promote high involvement.

Parallel Suggestion Involvement

Parallel suggestion involvement includes mechanisms for involving employees in solving problems, generating ideas, and making recommendations that influence how the organization operates. This approach provides avenues for employees to address aspects of the situation in which they work and the way in which work is done that can be changed to enable more effective task performance. Quality improvement teams and task forces are examples of parallel suggestion involvement. These approaches are parallel to the ongoing activities of the organization in the sense that they coexist with a more traditional work organization—people participate through special participatory forums and carry out their regular jobs in their normal work setting. Parallel structures have been advocated in the organizational literature as a way to enable two kinds of activities to go on simultaneously in an organization: efficiency in carrying out work processes and critical examination and improvement of the organization (Stein and Kanter, 1980).

Parallel suggestion approaches increase the power of partici-pants because they provide mechanisms for raising issues to the offi-cial agenda of the organization. In that sense, they enable employees to begin to deal with some of the obstacles to perfor-mance, and they may be expected to yield changes that will improve expectations of being able to perform successfully. Participants in parallel structures generally receive increased information and may develop new skills. The increases in these two resources are partic-ularly noticeable in organizations where there is widespread rather than limited participation. Sometimes parallel involvement is accompanied by rewards, often in the form of a gain-sharing or bonus program funded from the savings generated by the involve-ment process.

Parallel suggestion involvement has been quite successful in generating improvements to the way work is done, and organiza-tional participants often report high levels of satisfaction with the opportunity to influence organizational decisions. However, this approach does not represent a major shift in the way control-oriented organizations deal with most issues. Generally, the allo-cation of resources or changes of policy that are recommended by the involvement groups remain the purview of management; implementation depends on approval and support from a man-agement structure that may remain relatively unchanged. The basic design of the organization remains intact except for the superimposition of the "parallel" structures on the organization. Thus, parallel suggestion involvement may not strongly influence motivation in the day-to-day work of the members. Furthermore, since most U.S. organizational improvement programs do not give all employees the opportunity for ongoing participation, the sense of accomplishment that comes from such involvement is often lim-ited to a small number of employees. In fact, a split may be created between those who participate and those who do not, making it hard to generate employee support for some recommendations (Ledford, Lawler, and Mohrman, (1988). Finally, changes gener-ated through this approach may lack adequate management sup-port for full and lasting implementation.

More recent approaches to parallel involvement, including advanced total quality management programs (Deming, 1986; Juran, 1989) and some reengineering approaches (Davenport,

1993), have in some companies created the conditions for successful stable use of parallel approaches to generating continuous organizational improvement. These companies have changed the role of management to support change generated from those doing the work, and in some cases flattened the management structure and downsized the staff groups that once were relied on to generate and enforce changes from the top. They have provided participants with more powerful organizational process improvement tools that lead to a very systematic critical examination of the organizational processes that are most strongly related to organizational outcomes and that deliver value to the customer. They have incorporated computer and telecommunication technology in new ways that extend capability of their human resources rather than just supplement it. Even in knowledge-oriented and service organizations, great strides in productivity have been made by following systematic processes, focusing on organizational outcomes and customer-defined values, opening up the assumptions of organizational participants to critical scrutiny, and being willing to use information technology that changes what people do. The resulting productivity strides have freed up organizational resources to escalate the rate of learning and the generation of innovation.

In some cases, the changes in the work processes of the organization that are generated by task teams and other parallel structures stimulate the kinds of organizational design changes involved in the more fundamental approaches to employee involvement that we will describe in the next two sections. New approaches to the design of organizations enable these task teams not only to generate new ways of doing work, but also to create an organizational design that is compatible. The sociotechnical approach to work design starts by critically examining the work processes and then strives to create an optimal social system in which employee motivation and performance outcomes are jointly optimized (Pasmore, 1988). In many cases, new work processes require an organization to be designed so that discretion is moved downward and decisions are made laterally between co-workers. The next level of high involvement, job involvement, is made possible by such redesigns.

Job Involvement

Job involvement focuses on designing work in ways that motivate high levels of job performance. Enriched jobs consist of a variety of tasks that compose a whole piece of work, ongoing feedback about performance, and influence over how the work is done. Direct responsibility for a defined customer base enhances the perceived significance and often the personal meaningfulness of work. Individual job enrichment provides a direct line of sight between an individual's effort and job performance, and with good measures, it is possible to attach a performance-dependent reward. This job involvement approach is appropriate when the technology of work allows an individual to complete a whole task independently.

Increasingly, the principles of job design are being applied in team settings, with the establishment of teams that have responsibility for a larger piece of work. This design allows interdependent contributors to work together and to have complete responsibility for a set of customers. In school settings, this might be a teaching team or a "house" in a larger school. These empowered teams may have responsibility for the application of resources (including their own internal expertise), for setting performance targets and determining how best to accomplish them, and for working collaboratively and influencing each other in order to continually improve performance. When teams comprise multidiscipline contributors, they collectively have the responsibility for coordinating across disciplines. The team approach frequently results in teams doing many of the tasks previously done by managers and by specialized support groups. Teams designed according to these principles have been referred to variously as self-managing teams, semiautonomous work groups, or work teams. The team approach may be accompanied by a team incentive system and is often reinforced by a skills- or competency-based system, whereby different team members may be skilled in different aspects of the "whole task," and each member is paid based on skills demonstrated and used. This approach is often used in combination with parallel suggestion involvement so that teams have a way of influencing the larger organizational situation in which they perform.

Job involvement has significant implications for how an organization is structured and managed. Significant authority is vested in the enriched job or team. Individuals and team members have to develop new and expanded skills and knowledge, receive ongoing performance feedback and other information such as customer requirements and trend data relevant to how they go about their work, and take responsibility for an expanded range of decisions. Team members perform their own coordination and scheduling, and often their own personnel functions such as hiring and firing and attending to the development needs of team members. They may also perform tasks previously carried out by support departments, such as guidance counseling. Team rewards may be a part of a team model although organizations often have teams without putting in place true team rewards. A frequent approach is to alter the individual reward system to be based on competencies that the team needs or to retain an individual merit component that is weighted by contribution to team performance. Increasingly, peer evaluation is part of the team process.

Job involvement approaches particularly emphasize intrinsic satisfaction since they strive to create conditions where the individual or the team controls most factors that influence performance. Extrinsic satisfaction may be addressed by a competency-based pay system or team rewards. It should be noted that for some individuals, team rewards actually are perceived as lengthening the line of sight—by rewarding them for performances where they have to depend on other team members. On the other hand, team structures increase the opportunity for positive social outcomes, such as the satisfaction of working collaboratively with a group of peers and the opportunities for feedback, recognition, sharing, and mutual learning.

Unlike parallel suggestion approaches, job involvement affects the day-to-day work activities of all individuals. It is not a special or parallel activity; it is a new way of managing and carrying out the work of the organization. This approach to organization often moves support activities into the teams, and members are often cross-trained to play these roles. Formal management positions are often substantially reduced since team members take on a variety of management responsibilities. A variety of leadership roles emerge, often occupied by team members. Job involvement approaches require substantial change in the roles of people in remaining management and support positions.

Organizations have reported large performance gains through the use of this approach. The limitation of job involvement lies in its almost exclusive focus on operations at the individual or team level. This focus can lead to suboptimization if individuals or teams focus entirely on their own bailiwick and fail to consider how they need to contribute to the larger organizational unit (Mohrman, Cohen, and Mohrman, 1995). When the activities of all teams and individuals are shaped by a common context, such as overall policies and resource allocation of a school, job involvement may provide insufficient employee influence on these organizationwide issues. These limitations have led many organizations to pursue a higher level of organizational involvement.

Organizational Involvement

The organizational involvement approach focuses all employees on the success of the organization, not simply on their own job success or team success. This approach often incorporates parallel and job involvement. It may include enriched jobs, work teams, and task teams that focus on schoolwide process and organizational improvement. It goes beyond these approaches in that it designs the organization to make it more likely that employees will be concerned about and knowledgeable about what is required for the school as a whole to be successful. Employees will continue to receive information about their own or their team's job performance, but they also receive information about how the overall organization is performing. They develop knowledge about the organization as a whole, how strategy is formed, environmental pressures, policy formulation and organizational tradeoffs, and financial and resource optimization. They can put on an organizational hat when making decisions rather than being advocates only for their piece.

Mechanisms for influencing decisions may include multistakeholder governance groups. Another structural approach is to break up the larger organization into minibusinesses or customer-focused units rather than functional units, and to vest in each unit a larger set of decisions, such as strategy, resources, structural decisions, and whatever policy decisions do not absolutely have to be uniform across the larger organization. This has the impact of breaking up larger organizations into smaller units with entrepreneurial motivation to optimize their performance.

School-based management, when taken to its logical endpoint, is an embodiment of organizational involvement (Mohrman, Wohlstetter, et al., 1994). Within a larger school, houses or schools within schools is a way to break down a large impersonal system and create a smaller social system where people truly feel they can influence and be held accountable for the unit's performance and, by implication, for the full education of a defined group of students. Accountability is a key aspect of this approach. These performing units should be independent enough to control most aspects of their functioning. Services can be shared between them where definite economies of scale are offered and where it can be demonstrated that these shared services can meet the needs of each unit. Responsiveness to the performing units should be the performance accountability of all shared services. Their evaluation should be performed by these internal customers.

Tying extrinsic rewards to organizational or minibusiness performance is an important part of organizational involvement. These rewards should be significant enough to convey a clear message that it is not sufficient to focus on only the job you do individually or even your team alone. Individuals may also be rewarded for their contribution, but because they are asked to contribute in many ways and at different levels, a competency-based pay system is better suited than a job-based pay system for acknowledging individual contribution. A combination of these two approaches to rewards creates a situation where individuals are motivated both to improve their individual competencies and to contribute to the larger organization. It also makes it more likely that norms will develop where peers will take an interest in each other's development and recognize each other for outstanding performance because everyone will do better if each person does better (Lawler, 1994).

Organizational management positions are kept at a minimum because most control is now vested in performing subunits. However, the leadership role of organizational management is more important than ever, going far beyond an administrative or control function. The organizational involvement model requires leaders who can work with members of the organization to create a shared direction; to ensure that multidirectional influence is effective; to ensure that effective organizational structures and meaningful goals are in place and that resources are being allocated throughout the organization in a way that results in overall organizational performance; to monitor overall performance as well as the performance of each performing unit; and to initiate activities to further develop organizational capabilities of individuals and teams, and improvement of the work processes that are employed.

The organizational involvement approach can potentially create a superior motivational environment by combining intrinsic and extrinsic sources of motivation, and by creating joint focus on individual, team, and organizationwide performance. It calls for the most extensive change in organizational design and roles, as well as for a simultaneous organizational focus on performance and capability development at all levels. For schools, this organizational design approach complements the recognition within the educational literature that school reform will require systemic change—in instructional approaches, teacher capability, and the situation in which teaching occurs (Rowan, this volume). It takes an organizational view of capability development and puts the responsibility for developing a situation where effective learning can occur squarely on the shoulders of organizational participants. In her chapter describing schools that are characterized by high levels of organizational involvement, Darling-Hammond finds a strong positive effect on student outcomes, which is, of course, the ultimate performance toward which high involvement is directed.

Motivating for Large-Scale Change

We have argued that the systemic reform movement calls for a large-scale change in the educational establishment, and that the generation of school-level improvements may require that schools become high-involvement organizations. The conversion to high-involvement management is in itself a large-scale organizational change—one that may be required to unleash the vast potential of teachers to find better ways to educate all children. Teachers and principals are not being asked simply to do their jobs better; they are being asked to do different jobs. Principals are being asked to lead an organization as it transforms itself organizationally and as the participants collectively seek new and more effective approaches to teaching and learning. Teachers are being asked to participate in improving the capabilities and performance of the school; to collectively generate new approaches; to generate new ways of relating to each other, to students, and to the community.

Establishing a high-involvement organization—where the conditions are in place for participants to be motivated to continually improve organizational performance—entails a great deal of effort. The transformation process requires developing systems to measure results and share information; developing broader and deeper skills and knowledge; putting in place rewards for performance; and establishing effective new structures and processes for school participants to exercise influence in governance, organizational improvement, and enhanced service delivery.

A major challenge in producing large-scale organizational change is motivating individuals to change in such fundamental ways to assume new and expanded responsibility. As indicated by the expectancy model, motivation is shaped by the expectations of positive and negative outcomes. Motivation for significant change entails making clear the negative consequences of not changing as well as the positive consequences of changing. What are the individual, institutional, and societal costs of maintaining the status quo? What are the benefits of changing? Motivation requires a clear picture of the intended performances. A shared understanding of the new approaches will have to be developed so that there is a picture of the performances for which the organization is striving. Standards is one piece of this picture, but it includes far more. Large-scale change generally entails a change in the definition of successful performance. For example, schools may need to see their responsibility as organizing and teaching in a manner that meets the needs of their clientele, not in a way that is a generalized picture of professional practice. This requires changes in the roles of individuals and in what it means to be competent and perform well. Educators will need to develop new understanding of the skills they must develop to be effective in a high-involvement organization, the information that will be relevant to them, and the way that they will be able to influence how things are done. These changes may violate people's assumptions and perhaps even values about how the organization should run and what their role should be, and some educators may not be able to develop comfort with their new roles in a high-involvement organization.

Many factors work against being able to create positive motivation to change. People fear losing their positions, comfort, and status. They don't want to work as hard or make the personal sacrifices that are required by large-scale change—for fundamental organizational change occurs simultaneously with ongoing work. They resist being put into a situation where they may not be fully competent. They have low expectations that this change will be lasting or successful—they have seen many fads come and go. Managing through this uncertainty and negativity requires using the collective capabilities of the organizational employees to focus on purposes; open up one another's thinking; consider and try out new approaches; learn from one another; achieve, celebrate, and build on successes; and gradually build up a set of positive expectancies concerning the new directions. It requires tearing down the walls that have separated people from one another (Senge, 1990).

Large-scale change is facilitated by strong leaders who can define a compelling case for change, define the new performance requirements, and create the conditions for the immense amount of learning and personal transition that has to occur. Although leadership can and should be shared throughout the organization, most successful large-scale change occurs when the formal leader is a strong visionary and enlists organizational members in the collaborative work of effecting fundamental change (Bennis and Nanus, 1985). Where the workforce is represented by unions, their involvement as partners in the process of change has been found to contribute to the success of the implementation of high-involvement practices and to their impact on organizational performance (Lawler, Mohrman, and Ledford, 1995).

Change is facilitated by very clear performance definitions and by creating conditions of accountability where the transition cannot be construed as voluntary—that is, a social system such as a school cannot achieve fundamental change and substantial performance improvement if change is viewed as optional by employees. Schools where large numbers of teachers refuse to participate in improvement activities have great difficulty effecting change (Robertson, Wohlstetter, and Mohrman, 1995). The performance management system in the organization, particularly the goal-setting and feedback systems, are critical during transitions. These systems target performance, provide an opportunity to learn, enable the organization to measure success, and demonstrate that the organization is serious about the change.

A number of factors in schools make change of this magnitude especially difficult and present special challenges. The loose coupling of various aspects of schools (Weick, 1976) and the isolated functioning of teachers work against taking a systemic approach to change. A school community will have to be established in order to successfully implement high-involvement approaches. Schools do not have a tradition of strategy formulation and goal-setting, nor are accountability and performance management systems well developed or accepted. School participants will have to get used to examining results, talking about goals and how to achieve them, watching trends collectively, problem solving, and being held accountable. Finally, administrators are frequently not encouraged to be leaders, either by their bosses or by the people they would lead. In fact, the wedge between teachers and administrators in many school buildings turns school-based management into tug-of-wars for power and control between the two parties (Wohlstetter, Smyer, and Mohrman, 1994). Principals will have to be selected, developed, and supported in their new leadership role so that they can provide support to their staff as the school community goes about the process of generating change and improving performance.

Preceding sections of this chapter provided a theory-guided picture of an organization that builds in the conditions for motivation for school improvement. This section has argued that creating these conditions for high involvement is itself a fundamental organizational transition for schools. Surely if large numbers of educators are to seriously embark on change of this magnitude, they will need evidence that it will lead to more effective schools. There is a pressing need for experimentation and evaluation of new forms of school organization.

There is already some supporting evidence. A number of models of effective schools are currently yielding demonstration schools that have a number of high-involvement characteristics (Wohlstetter and Smyer, 1994); these include the School Development Program schools (Comer, 1980), Accelerated Schools (Levin, 1987), and Essential Schools (Sizer, 1984). Darling-Hammond (this volume) has described high-performance schools with many high-involvement characteristics. Robertson, Wohlstetter, and Mohrman (1995) have found that school-based management schools having success in reforming their approaches to teaching and learning were also characterized by high levels of knowledge and skill development, information sharing, and many ways of exercising influence.

More research is required to fully test the efficacy of the high-involvement approach. Much of this will have to be action research: the creation and evaluation of field demonstration pilots and naturally occurring experiments. Models will have to be generated and tested for new information systems, skills and knowledge development approaches, structures and processes for sharing power, and rewards that fit the technology and professional nature of teaching. The application of new ways of rewarding performance, in particular, is highly relevant to the question addressed in this volume: how to provide incentives for school reform. In addition, new approaches to the development and role definitions of school leaders are required.

Conclusion

In this chapter, we have argued that systemic school reform requires large-scale change in schools. It entails fundamental changes in how educational services are delivered and how expert resources are deployed to meet the needs of the population being educated. It changes the goals, content, and pedagogy of schools. It requires new skills and knowledge and new organizational capabilities. Effecting such change requires the creation of motivational conditions where educators believe that such change is possible and that it will lead to valued outcomes.

We briefly reviewed the basic expectancy model of motivation and the closely related arenas of goal-setting, job design, and reward theory. We then provided an overview of three different approaches to the creation of increased employee involvement. The high-involvement framework is an approach to designing organizations that build in the conditions for motivating the involvement of teachers in creating successful reform.

Many of the organizational approaches described in the high-involvement framework are in place to some extent in high-performance schools. Some schools have broken up into smaller units and provided a group of educators with increased autonomy in determining how best to educate their group of students. Advanced school-based management districts often remove many contextual constraints and enable school-level participants to try out approaches that they believe will lead to better performance. However, many schools remain populated by teachers who stay in separate classrooms with little or no collective learning or engagement in improvement activities. For many districts, the road to being able to prepare a population for the twenty-first century is a long one. Judging from the experiences of many organizations in other sectors of the economy, educators may be at the front end of envisioning what schools will look like in the future, and the change process may be just beginning.

References

Bandura, A. *Social Foundations of Thought and Action: A Social-Cognitive View.* Englewood Cliffs, N.J.: Prentice-Hall, 1986.

Beer, M., Eisenstat, R. A., and Spector, B. *The Critical Path to Corporate Renewal.* Cambridge, Mass.: Harvard Business School Press, 1990.

Bennis, W. and Nanus, B. *Leaders.* New York: Harper Collins, 1985.

Cohen, D. K., McLaughlin, M. W., and Talbert, J. E. (Eds.). *Teaching for Understanding: Challenges for Policy and Practice.* San Francisco: Jossey-Bass, 1993.

Comer, J. *School Power.* New York: Free Press, 1980.

Darling-Hammond, L., Wise, A. E., and Klein, S. P. *A License to Teach: Building a Profession for the 21st Century,* Boulder, Colo.: Westview, 1995.

Davenport, T. H. *Process Innovation: Re-engineering Work Through Information Technology.* Cambridge, Mass.: Harvard Business School Press, 1993.

Deci, E. L. and Ryan, R. M. *Intrinsic Motivation and Self-determination in Human Behavior.* New York: Plenum Press, 1985.

Deming, W. E. *Out of the Crisis.* Cambridge, Mass.: Center for Advanced Engineering Study, Massachusetts Institute of Technology, 1986.

Elmore, R. F. "Introduction: On Changing the Structure of Public Schools." In R. F. Elmore (ed.): *Restructuring Schools: The Next Generation of Educational Reform.* San Francisco: Jossey-Bass, 1990.

Elmore, R. F. et al. *Restructuring Schools: The Next Generation of Educational Reform.* San Francisco: Jossey-Bass, 1990.

* Firestone, W. "Redesigning Teacher Salary Systems for Education Reform." *American Educational Research Journal,* 1994, *31* (3), 549–574.

Fuhrman, S. H. (ed.). *Designing Coherent Education Policy: Improving the System.* San Francisco: Jossey-Bass, 1993.

Fuhrman S. H., Massell, D., et al. *Issues and Strategies in Systemic Reform.* New Brunswick, N.J.: Rutgers University, Consortium for Policy Research in Education, 1992.

Galbraith, J. R., Lawler, E. E., et al. *Organizing for the Future: The New Logic for Managing Complexity.* San Francisco: Jossey-Bass, 1993.

Hackman, J. R. "The Design of Work Teams." In J. Jorsch (ed.): *Handbook of Organizational Behavior.* Englewood Cliffs, N.J.: Prentice-Hall, 1987, pp. 315–342.

Hackman, J. R. and Oldham, G. R. *Work Redesign.* Reading, Mass.: Addison-Wesley, 1980.

Hammer, M. and Champy, J. *Reengineering the Corporation.* New York: Harper Business Press, 1993.

Johnson, S. M. and Bales, K. C. "The Role of Teachers in School Reform." In S. A. Mohrman, P. Wohlstetter, et al.: *School-Based Management: Organizing for High Performance.* San Francisco: Jossey-Bass, 1994, pp. 109–138.

Juran, J. M. *Juran on Leadership for Quality.* New York: Free Press, 1989.

Lawler, E. E. III. *High-involvement Management.* San Francisco: Jossey-Bass, 1986.

Lawler, E. E. III. *Strategic Pay.* San Francisco: Jossey-Bass, 1990.

Lawler, E. E. III. *The Ultimate Advantage.* San Francisco: Jossey-Bass, 1992.

Lawler, E. E. III. *Motivation in Work Organizations.* San Francisco: Jossey-Bass, [1973] 1994.

Lawler, E. E. III, Mohrman, S. A., and Ledford, G. E. *High Performing Organizations: Employee Involvement and Total Quality Management Practices and Results in the Fortune 1000.* San Francisco: Jossey-Bass, 1995.

Ledford, G. E., Jr. "Effectiveness of Skill-Based Pay Systems." *Perspectives in Total Compensation,* 1990, *1* (1), 1–4.

Ledford, G. E. Jr., Lawler, E. E. III, and Mohrman, S. A. "The Quality Circle and Its Variations." In J. P. Campbell and R. J. Campbell (eds): *Frontiers in Industrial/Organizational Psychology, II: Individual and Group Productivity in Organizations.* San Francisco: Jossey-Bass. 1988.

Levin, H. "Accelerated Schools for Disadvantaged Students." *Educational Leadership,* 1987, *44* (6), 19–29.

Little, J. W. "Norms of Collegiality and Experimentation: Workplace Conditions of School Success." *American Educational Research Journal,* Fall 1982, *19,* 215–340.

Locke, E. A. and Latham, G. P. *A Theory of Goal Setting and Task Performance.* Englewood Cliffs, N.J.: Prentice Hall, 1990.

McLaughlin, M. W. and Talbert, J. E. "Introduction: New Visions of Teaching." In Cohen, D. K., McLaughlin, M. W., and Talbert, J. E. (eds): *Teaching for Understanding: Challenges for Policy and Practice.* San Francisco: Jossey-Bass, 1993.

Marsh, D. D. "Change in Schools: Lessons from the Literature." In S. A. Mohrman, P. Wohlstetter, et al.: *School-Based Management: Organizing for High Performance.* San Francisco: Jossey-Bass, 1994, pp. 214–252.

Meyer, J. W. and Rowan, B. "Institutionalized Organizations: Formal Structure as Myth and Ceremony." *American Journal of Sociology,* 1977, *83,* 340–363.

Mohrman, A. M. Jr., and others. *Large-Scale Organizational Change.* San Francisco: Jossey-Bass, 1989.

Mohrman, A. M. Jr., Mohrman, S. A., and Odden, A. R. "Aligning Teacher Compensation with Systemic School Reform: Skill-Based Pay and Group-Based Performance Rewards." *Educational Evaluation and Policy Analysis,* in press.

Mohrman, S. A. "Making the Transition to High-Performance Management." In S. A. Mohrman, P. Wohlstetter, et al.: *School-Based Management: Organizing for High Performance.* San Francisco: Jossey-Bass, 1994, pp. 187–214.

Mohrman, S. A., Cohen, S. G., and Mohrman, A. M. Jr. *Designing Team-Based Organizations: New Forms for Knowledge Work.* San Francisco: Jossey-Bass, 1995.

Mohrman, S. A. and Cummings, T. G. *Self-Designing Organizations: Learning How to Create High Performance.* Reading, Mass.: Addison Wesley, 1989.

Mohrman, S. A., Lawler, E. E. III, and Mohrman, A. M. Jr. "Applying Employee Involvement in Schools." *Educational Evaluation and Policy Analysis,* Winter 1992, *14* (4), 31–57.

Mohrman, S. A., Wohlstetter, P., et al. *School-Based Management: Organizing for High Performance.* San Francisco: Jossey-Bass, 1994.

Nadler, D., Gerstein, M. S. and Shaw, R. B. *Organizational Architecture: Designs for Changing Organizations.* San Francisco: Jossey-Bass, 1992.

Odden, A. R. and Conley, S. "Restructuring Teacher Compensation Systems." In A. Odden (ed.): *Rethinking School Finance. An Agenda for the 1990's.* San Francisco: Jossey-Bass, 1992, pp. 41–96.

Pasmore, W. A. *Designing Effective Organizations: The Sociotechnical Systems Perspective.* New York: Wiley, 1988.

Robertson, P. J., Wohlstetter, P., and Mohrman, S. A. "Generating Curriculum and Instructional Innovations Through School-Based Management." *Educational Administration Quarterly,* August 1995, *31* (3), 257–276.

Rosenholtz, S. J. "Effective Schools: Interpreting the Evidence." *American Journal of Education,* May 1985, 352–388.

Rowan, B. "Commitment and Control: Alternative Strategies for the Organizational Design of Schools." In Cazden, C. B., (ed.): *Review of Research in Education.* Washington, D.C.: American Educational Research Association, 1990.

Rowan, B., Raudenbush, S. W., and Cheong, Y. F. "Teaching as a Non-Routine Task: Implications for the Management of Schools." *Educational Administration Quarterly,* 1993, *29,* 479–500.

Senge, P. M. *The Fifth Discipline: The Art and Practice of the Learning Organization.* New York: Doubleday Currency, 1990.

Shedd, J. S. and Bacharach, S. B. *Tangled Hierarchies: Teachers as Professionals and the Management of Schools.* San Francisco: Jossey-Bass, 1991.

Sizer, T. *Horace's School: Redesigning the American High School.* Boston: Houghton-Mifflin, 1984.

Stein, B. A. and Kanter, R. M. "Building the Parallel Organization: Creating Mechanisms for Permanent Quality of Work Life." *Journal of Applied Behavioral Science,* 1980, *16,* 371–386.

Tichy, N. M. and Devanna, M. A. *The Transformational Leader.* New York: Wiley, 1986.

Vroom, V. *Motivation and Work.* New York: Wiley, 1964.

Weick, K. E. Educational Organizations as Loosely Coupled Systems. *Administrative Science Quarterly,* 1976, *21* (19), 1–19.

Wohlstetter, P. and Odden, A. "Rethinking School-Based Management Policy and Research." *Educational Administration Quarterly,* 1992, *28* (4), 529–549.

Wohlstetter, P. and Smyer, R. "Models of High-Performance Schools." In S. A. Mohrman, P. Wohlstetter, et al.: *School-Based Management: Organizing for High Performance.* San Francisco: Jossey-Bass, 1994, pp. 81–108.

Wohlstetter, P., Smyer, R., and Mohrman, S. A. "New Boundaries for School-Based Management: The High Involvement Model." *Educational Evaluation and Policy Analysis,* Fall 1994, *16* (3), 268–286.

Chapter Five

Restructuring Schools for High Performance

Linda Darling-Hammond
with the assistance of Lori Chajet and Peter Robertson

Over the last decade, school reform proposals have shifted from efforts intended to make the current educational system perform more efficiently to efforts intended to fundamentally rethink how schools are designed, how school systems operate, how teaching and learning are pursued, and what goals for schooling are sought. The enormous complexity of today's world, and the even greater complications of tomorrow's, signal a new mission for education: one that requires schools not merely to "deliver instruction" but to ensure that all students learn—and to do so in more powerful and effective ways. Students are entering a society and an economy that will require them to manage complexity; create ideas, services, and products; use ever-evolving technologies; and plan and evaluate their own work.

If schools are to meet this new challenge, they must find ways to dramatically enrich the intellectual opportunities they offer while meeting the diverse needs of students who bring with them varying talents, interests, learning styles, cultures, predispositions, language backgrounds, family situations, and beliefs about themselves and about what school means for them.

Unfortunately, the bureaucratic school created at the turn of the twentieth century was not organized to meet these needs for intellectual development or for individual responsiveness. Today's schools were designed when the goal of education was not to educate all students well but to process a great many efficiently, selecting and supporting only a few for "thinking work." Strategies for sorting and tracking students were developed to ration the scarce resources of expert teachers and rich curriculum, and to justify the standardization of teaching tasks and procedures within groups. This, in turn, enabled greater routinization of teaching work and less reliance on professional skill and judgment, a corollary of the nineteenth-century decision to structure teaching as semiskilled labor.

For the masses of students, the goal then and now is to instill rudimentary skills and the basic workplace socialization needed to follow orders and conduct predetermined tasks neatly and punctually. The rote learning needed for these early twentieth-century objectives still predominates in today's schools, reinforced by top-down prescriptions for teaching practice, mandated curriculum packages, standardized tests that focus on low cognitive level skills, and continuing underinvestment in teacher knowledge.

The school structure created to implement this conception of teaching and learning is also explicitly impersonal. Students move along a conveyer belt from one teacher to the next, grade to grade, and class period to class period, with little opportunity to become well known over a sustained period to any adults who can consider them as whole people or as developing intellects. Secondary school teachers may see 150 or more students a day, precluded by this structure from coming to know any individual student or family well. Teachers work in isolation from one another, stamping students with lessons with little time to work with others or share their knowledge. Students, too, tend to work alone and passively, listening to lectures, memorizing facts and algorithms, and engaging in independent seatwork at their separate desks.

In urban areas, these school structures are likely to be huge warehouses, housing 3000 or more students in an organization focused more on the control of behavior than the development of community. With a locker as their only stable point of contact, a schedule that cycles them through a series of seven to ten overloaded teachers, and a counselor struggling to serve the "personal" needs of several hundred students, teenagers struggling to find connections have little to connect to. Heavily stratified within, and substantially dehumanized throughout, most students are likely to experience such high schools as noncaring or even adversarial environments where "getting over" becomes important when "getting known" is impossible. For adults, the capacity to be accountable for the learning of students is substantially constrained by the factory model structure that gives them little control over or connection to most of what happens to the students they see only briefly.

It is becoming increasingly clear that the task of educating very diverse learners to much higher standards of learning in a world with fast-changing educational demands will require more skillful teaching and more responsive school organizations than current educational bureaucracies allow. Many argue that new school organizations—like those being created to replace ossified bureaucracies in business and industry—will need to rely on much greater knowledge, skill, and judgment from all "front-line workers" (in this case, teachers), along with collaborative and flexible forms of planning and problem solving more responsive to the needs of clients and the realities of change (Darling-Hammond, 1993; Lee, Bryk, and Smith, 1993; Mohrman, Lawler, and Mohrman, 1992; Senge, 1990).

This chapter uses the lens of "high-involvement" management to examine how several extraordinarily successful schools in New York City operate. The analysis is organized around four aspects of organizational functioning that are commonly identified as central to high-involvement workplaces: the decentralization and reconfiguration of *power, knowledge, information,* and *rewards* (Lawler, 1986; Wohlstetter, Smyer, and Mohrman, 1994). The analysis illustrates how decentralization of these organizational resources and enhanced teacher participation allow schools to redesign education in ways that are significantly more successful for students.

Organizational restructuring in both the corporate and education sectors is seeking to replace the bureaucratic forms of organization dominant throughout the twentieth century with new organizational designs that are less rigid and more adaptive, more able to accommodate diversity, and more capable of continuous invention. Efforts to invent nonbureaucratic twenty-first-century organizations tend to use incentives and structures that motivate through collaboration rather than coercion; build strong relationships rather than rely solely on rules for governing behavior; encourage quality by structuring work around whole products or services rather than disconnected piecework; and create information-rich environments that support widespread learning and self-assessment among workers rather than rely primarily on hierarchical design and supervision of work routines. Such organizations aim to stimulate greater thoughtfulness and creativity rather than focusing largely on enforcing compliance with predetermined procedures. Their success, then, depends on the creation of new opportunities for teacher and school learning, new modes of accountability, and new kinds of incentives for continual improvement and problem solving.

Characteristics of High-Performing Schools

As reforms in both the business and education sectors mature, striking parallels are emerging between the organizational strategies of "high-performance, high-involvement" corporations and those of extraordinarily successful schools. Research has begun to identify common characteristics of more successful school organizations that intersect with research on the features of high-performance businesses. Studies of effective schools frequently find smaller, more personalized structures with less departmentalization, greater use of teaching teams, and substantial teacher participation in school redesign and improvement (Braddock and McPartland, 1993; Wehlage et al., 1989). Such "communitarian" school structures that reduce fragmentation and create stronger relational bonds between and among students and teachers are more effective than traditional bureaucratic high schools (Lee, Bryk, and Smith, 1993). Structures for collaboration among teachers in these settings increase knowledge sharing and promote horizontal communication that focuses "a faculty's collective technical expertise on specific problems within the school" (Lee, Bryk, and Smith, 1993, p. 221).

Small size is one important factor. A substantial body of research shows that, all else equal, smaller schools or school units (in the range of 300 to 500 students) are associated with higher achievement (Howley, 1989; Howley and Huang, 1992; Haller, 1992b), as well as better attendance rates (Lindsay, 1982), fewer dropouts (Pittman and Haughwout, 1987), and lower levels of student misbehavior (Garbarino, 1978; Gottfredson and Daiger, 1979;

Haller, 1992a). They are more effective in allowing students to become bonded to important adults in a learning community that can play the role that families and communities find it harder and harder to play. They are also more effective in creating good inter-personal relationships and in providing opportunities for students to participate in extracurricular activities and to take leader-ship roles (Fowler, 1992; Green and Stevens, 1988; Haller, 1992a; Howley, 1989; Lindsay, 1982, 1984).

Size is not the only factor at work here, however. Most effective are those schools or school units that create structures for caring—forms of organization that enable close, sustained relationships among students and teachers—rather than structures determined by bureaucratic divisions of labor. Typically, this is achieved by redesigning teaching assignments and grouping practices so that teachers work for longer periods with smaller total numbers of students, for example, by teaching a core interdisciplinary curriculum to one or two groups of students rather than a single subject to five groups, or by teaching the same students for more than one year. In smaller schools or houses within a school, students may work with the same stable group of teachers over several years and become well known to them as a team.

Such structures, which enable teachers to know students and their families well, are associated with heightened student achievement, more positive feelings toward self and school, and more positive behavior (NIE, 1977; Gottfredson and Daiger, 1979; Wehlage et al., 1989). These outcomes hold for all students, but are especially pronounced for low-income students. Such outcomes are not surprising because teaching involves much more than conveying subject matter to passive recipients. Effective teaching requires knowledge of students and their experiences, their prior knowledge, and the ways in which they learn. It also requires opportunities for staff to interact about both students and the school's academic work.

Many of the highly successful schools exhibiting these features are alternative schools in central cities such as those affiliated with the Center for Collaborative Education (part of the Coalition of Essential Schools) in New York City (Darling-Hammond et al., 1993; Darling-Hammond, Ancess, and Falk, 1995); Philadelphia's charter schools (Fine, 1994); and a number of schools associated with early shared decision making and restructuring initiatives in Louisville, Kentucky; Hammond, Indiana; Dade County, Florida; and southern Maine (Darling-Hammond, 1994; Elmore, 1990; Lieberman, 1995). These features are also prominent in restructuring schools in Victoria, Australia (Odden and Odden, 1994), and elsewhere.

The efforts of several such "high-performance" schools, described in this chapter, draw on the same principles of learning, motivation, and organization that underlie the restructuring efforts of businesses that are seeking to rebuild their competitiveness and effectiveness by adopting more lean and flexible management techniques, flattening hierarchies, and decentralizing decisions. In both kinds of settings, more responsibility and resources are invested in the knowledge and capacities of front-line workers, who are organized to design their own work and solve problems in cooperative teams.

These schools also approach teaching and learning in distinctive ways. They are *learner centered,* in that they are deliberately organized to attend to the individual needs of learners, and *learning centered,* in that their work is clearly focused on developing powerful learning and proficient performances (Cohen, McLaughlin, and Talbert, 1993; Gardner, 1991). They organize their work around learners' needs for active, inquiry-based learning opportunities that build on prior experience and support individual talents and learning styles. Learning is organized around complex and integrative tasks that lead to major products and performances; students and teachers are grouped in ways that are sufficiently personalized for teachers to come to know their students well (Sizer, 1992). The schools also acknowledge students' needs for affiliation and belonging, for close oversight and affirmation through the ways in which they structure adult–student and student–student work and relationships.

The use of teaching teams enables a more integrated and holistic view of students and a more interdisciplinary and in-depth approach to teaching and learning while supporting teacher learning. Performance assessments and documentations of learning in process are used to better capture the outcomes of more challenging work and to examine how children think and learn as well as what they can do (Resnick, 1987; Kornhaber and Gardner,

.993). Teacher and parent involvement in shared decision making forms a basis for creating shared goals, strategies, and commitments. In short, these "high-performance, high-involvement" schools are structured as "knowledge work organizations" for adults and students alike (Schlechty, 1990).

Case studies of these schools suggest that decentralization of decisions is not alone sufficient to explain their success. Organizational redesign in all these settings is consciously aimed at *personalizing education for students and creating close relationships with families, addressing higher-order learning goals* (sometimes in defiance of external accountability and reward structures), and *engaging students as workers and decision makers in the learning process.* These three features are linked to explicit goals and values the schools have adopted, which provide the framework within which work redesign operates. The combined result of these goals—a set of well-developed structures and participatory processes for achieving them, and deeply-embedded incentives for maintaining them—is a highly effective system for learner-centered accountability, one that ensures that students make progress toward valued learning goals and do not "fall through the cracks." I discuss the incentives that support these practices and outcomes in the final section.

Organizational Considerations

In what follows, I examine how work is organized and how teaching and learning are structured in high-performance schools, in addition to examining the decentralized management of organizational resources like power, knowledge, information, and rewards that are noted in the literature on participatory work organizations (Lawler, 1986, 1992; Wohlstetter, Smyer, and Mohrman, 1994). As Mohrman and Wohlstetter (1994) note, work that is complex, uncertain, and group oriented is often best accomplished when the delivery of service is directly connected to the processes of planning, allocating resources, and controlling performance through employee involvement strategies.

The conception that workers should be involved in planning and evaluating their own work as well as performing it confronts the Tayloristic job structures and the "trickle-down" theory of knowledge prominent in bureaucracies. These structures and assumptions are well dug into school systems that have sought to standardize and simplify jobs through age grading, tracking, and departmentalization, and that have created elaborate administrative and supervisory structures for designing and overseeing the work in each cell of the elaborate organizational matrix thus created. Expertise is presumed to reside at the top of the system and is used to design work specifications (curriculum; textbooks; tests; decision rules for grading, promotion, and grouping of students; and so on) for routine implementation by workers.

The increasingly apparent shortcomings of Tayloristic work management has provided a rationale for high-involvement management that is closely related to the argument for enhanced professionalism in teaching and other complex occupations. As Benveniste (1987) notes in *Professionalizing the Organization*:

> Since rules and routines work well when tasks are predictable, unvaried, and well understood, they are used extensively. However, when tasks are varied and unpredictable, when learning is important in the task situation, and when adaptability is required, discretion is necessary. Discretion and trust have to replace routines. This where the professional in the organization takes on new importance. . . . In an uncertain environment and task situation, the professional has the necessary knowledge and experience to act independently. The professional can search for solutions, determine which alternative to adopt, and implement new approaches (p. 256).

Greater knowledge and information are needed by professionals acting with greater discretion. So, I will argue, are work structures that enable them to reduce some of the uncertainties in the environment and task situation. As David Cohen (this volume) notes, teaching work has distinctive features that must be taken into account in any discussion about work organization and incentives. These include the intrinsic uncertainty of the teaching–learning process and the teacher's dependence on students— their motivation, will, and capacities—for the production of learning. This uncertainty is a function of the complexity of the task, the uniqueness of each student and each teacher, and the stunning number of interactions between them and the many aspects of the environment that influence learning. Lee Cronbach

(1975) observed many years ago that the number of interactions between student characteristics and teaching treatments that can influence outcomes comprise "a hall of mirrors that extends to infinity" (p. 119), severely limiting any sweeping generalizations that can be made about the effects of specific teaching behaviors.

Cohen notes that these uncertainties and complexities are heightened when teachers are asked to teach in riskier ways toward more difficult and uncertain ends, as teaching for understanding requires. This kind of teaching, because it relies on active learning in which students construct knowledge rather than having it fed to them for passive consumption, is more challenging and indeterminate than rote teaching, which is more teacher centered, less intellectually demanding, and more easily controlled. My analysis suggests that to manage these risks, teachers need both high levels of skill and school structures that are conducive to more complex teaching and more extended, intensive kinds of learning.

Teachers who are given the opportunity to develop greater pedagogical knowledge and skill can reduce some of the risk of what Cohen calls "ambitious teaching." Knowledge that enables teachers to more effectively understand and appraise student learning, to create the necessary scaffolding to enable complex learning, and to adapt their strategies to the diverse learning approaches and needs of students can be enhanced through more effective professional preparation and ongoing, job-embedded professional development. This includes supportive structures that allow teachers to collaborate and seek help from one another, and shared work that allows them to focus on academic issues across the entire school. In addition, teachers need to be able to reduce some of the uncertainties related to student motivation, understanding, and performance by having the kind of extended time and close connections with students that enable deep knowledge of students' lives and learning, as well as strong relationships that can leverage motivation and commitment.

Structures that provide teachers with extended access to students' time and that enable close, sustained relationships around common goals are as important to the success of high-performing schools as are participatory management structures. If teachers ultimately have greater knowledge, information, power, and rewards without more learner-centered structures in which to work, they will be far less able to undertake the risks of ambitious teaching and to succeed.

The discussion of how successful schools treat these structural and management dimensions of their work addresses the following questions:

Work Structures That Enable High Performance

How is work organized to create greater focus on learning and effectiveness in teaching?

How are work units (teams, departments, houses, committees) structured to be relevant to and functional for the work to be done? How are these units connected in a single, functional organization?

What processes does the school use for creating and changing work structures and technologies and for evaluating and improving its own work?

Decentralized and Shared Power and Authority

How are decision-making processes decentralized? What decision-making units exist, what are their powers, and how do they function?

In what ways are work teams permitted to manage their own performance and within what constraints? How are schoolwide issues dealt with?

Who is involved in hiring, firing, and evaluating organizational members and how? How are individuals and teams appraised? Is appraisal multidirectional?

Decentralized and Shared Knowledge and Information

How are individual and group learning supported? How do work structures encourage knowledge building and knowledge sharing?

Are staff encouraged to extend their expertise and develop skills in new areas?

How is information about performance shared within and across teams and other units?

Are information-sharing and accountability systems set up to ensure wide dissemination of information relevant to the performance of individuals, teams, and the whole school?

Decentralized and Learning-Focused Rewards and Incentives

What rewards and incentives appear to operate to motivate effort and continued improvement for both staff and students?

Are rewards and appraisal systems set up to support increased knowledge, ability to contribute to the organization, and collective achievement of goals?

Examples of High-Performing Schools

A growing number of schools associated with New York City's Center for Collaborative Education, a network of more than 30 schools, could be selected as examples of high-performing, high-involvement organizations that achieve outstanding success with diverse student populations. Case studies conducted by the National Center for Restructuring Education, Schools, and Teaching (NCREST) detail the outcomes of many of them, documenting the high success rates of students who would have been expected to achieve much less well in traditional schools and analyzing the structures and practices that support this success (Ancess, 1995; Darling-Hammond, Ancess, and Falk, 1995; Darling-Hammond et al., 1993; Snyder et al., 1992). These outcomes are striking: graduation and college-going rates of more than 90 percent in high schools serving primarily low-income students of color and recent immigrants, and high levels of academic attainment as measured by early grades progress and later grades placements for elementary school students. A recent follow-up of the graduates of Central Park East Elementary School, a school founded in 1974 that was the inspiration and initial birthing place of many of the others, found remarkable sustained effects on continued academic and later life achievement of former students after more than a decade since they had left the school (Bensman, 1994).

It is noteworthy that so many of the CCE schools have similar successes along with similar organizational features and educational commitments. Each has arrived at different manifestations of twelve common principles that build on the core principles of the Coalition of Essential Schools, of which CCE is an affiliate. The twelve principles treat:

1. *School purposes* (*helping young people learn to use their minds well*)
2. High and universal *academic standards*
3. *Curriculum* that is interdisciplinary, multicultural, and focused on powerful ideas
4. *Small size and personalization*
5. Commitment to a goal of *student as worker and student as citizen*
6. *Assessment* that is performance based and aimed at clearly stated competencies
7. *Tone and values* that emphasize unanxious expectation and decency
8. *Involvement of families*
9. *Shared decision making*
10. *Commitment to diversity* among students and staff
11. Selection of the school by student *choice*
12. *Administrative and budget targets*: a student load of no more than eighty, substantial shared planning time for teachers, and a budget no more than 10 percent above that of other schools

In a discussion of success and incentives, it is important to understand how the commitment to student choice influences both the clientele and the incentive structure for these schools. None of the schools uses choice as a means for "creaming" students: they explicitly seek an economically, ethnically, and educationally diverse student population; give first preference to neighborhood children in their high-poverty communities; and will often accept a low-achieving student who needs their support over a high-achieving student who does not. However, choice is important to the schools' success because it allows them to be more educationally adventurous, since parents and students have selected the kind of nontraditional teaching and organization they offer rather than having it foisted on them, and it creates stronger bonds among student, parent, and school. As Central Park East founder Deborah Meier explains, "We work harder where our loyalties are tapped and where we believe we have some power, if only the power to make a move. (Choice) creates conditions that reinforce a sense of membership in a community, a quality that parents, teachers, and youngsters are missing in most areas of their lives today" (1995, p. 101).

Although the schools share common values, their diverse strategies for achieving these are informative as well. Because these strategies are important to understand as they fit together in a coherent whole, I use one school as the center of my analysis, adding examples of specific practices from other schools to elaborate on selected points in the later discussion.

The school that serves as the center of this analysis, Central Park East Secondary School (CPESS), is one of several alternative high schools in New York that have been in existence long enough to establish themselves as securing extraordinary success for their students serving quite distinct student bodies and using different organizational features. In addition to CPESS, I discuss International High School (IHS), which accepts only recent immigrants who score below the 20th percentile on New York City's language achievement battery; Manhattan International High School, a new school launched on the IHS model and serving a similar population of students; and the Urban Academy, which serves students who have generally dropped out of other high schools. Case studies of these schools and their outcomes can be found in Bensman (1994, 1995); Darling-Hammond, Ancess, and Falk (1995); Jacobson (1994); and Ancess (1995).

In contrast to the norms for such students in traditional New York City comprehensive high schools—who graduate at rates below 50 percent and attend college at rates less than half that—these schools typically graduate more than 90 percent of their students. Every one of the first class of graduates of both International High School in 1988 and Central Park East Secondary School in 1991 was accepted to postsecondary education, and more than 90 percent of them were accepted to four-year colleges, a rate several times higher than surrounding area high schools. College-going rates for graduates at these schools and the longer-standing Urban Academy have remained above 90 percent over the years.

These schools have been among the partner schools helping to launch other small high schools in New York City, more than fifty of which have opened their doors in the last three years. The Coalition Campus Schools Project, which is opening twelve new Coalition schools on the campuses of failing comprehensive high schools that are being closed down, is one of several school-launching initiatives. In early assessments of the first six of these new schools, improvements in student attendance and achievement are indications that the similar organizational features these schools have adopted make a difference in school and student outcomes (Darling-Hammond, Ancess, MacGregor, and Zuckerman, forthcoming). It is important to look across these many school examples because of the tendency to dismiss high-performing schools like CPESS as the anomalous results of charismatic leaders or a unique band of unusual teachers.

There are also a number of affiliated elementary schools that could be analyzed as high-performance, high-involvement settings that share many organizational and educational features. These include the Brooklyn New School, the Bronx New School, River East, and Central Park East Elementary Schools I and II. Because the generally smaller size and less bureaucratized structures of elementary schools create a different set of management issues, these schools are not analyzed here. However, it is useful to note that many of the student-centered features of Central Park East Secondary School grew explicitly from its connection to Central Park East Elementary. (CPESS was created in 1985 to provide a continuing experience for many of CPE's students.) The founder of both schools, Deborah Meier, concurs with faculty in many other CCE schools that bureaucratized secondary schools could take many fruitful pedagogical and organizational lessons from less departmentalized and fragmented elementary schools.

Central Park East Secondary School

Central Park East Secondary School has been carefully designed from its inception to support students and teachers in their work together. The school is small and intimate by city standards: its 450 students in grades 7 through 12 are largely drawn from the local community, and many attended one of the three alternative elementary schools out of which CPESS grew. The students and their parents choose CPESS from among other junior high schools in District 4's choice system, but the school does not screen students to create an elite student body. In 1991, when the research for this case study began, 85 percent of the students were from Latino and

What happens to students who do not fit the program?

African-American families, mostly in the neighboring East Harlem community; 60 percent qualified for free or reduced price lunch; and 25 percent were eligible for special education services. CPESS shares a building with two other schools but maintains its own character and values in the midst of the overwhelming size, density, and impersonality that tend to characterize New York City Public Schools.

Curriculum and Teaching

Students' intellectual development at CPESS is guided by five Habits of Mind, which embody the goals of the school and permeate the entire curriculum:

1. Weighing evidence: How do we know what we know? What is the evidence, and is it credible?
2. Awareness of varying viewpoints: What viewpoint are we hearing, seeing, reading? Who is the author and what are his or her intentions?
3. Seeing connections and relationships: How are things connected to each other? Where have we heard or seen this before?
4. Speculating on possibilities: What if . . .? Can we imagine alternatives?
5. Assessing value both socially and personally: What difference does it make? Who cares? (CPESS, 1990).

The Habits of Mind are prominently displayed in classrooms throughout the school. They guide the assessment of student work throughout CPESS and appear as criteria incorporated into assessment instruments for the required Graduation Portfolio. In developing its graduation requirements, CPESS staff engaged in a process of "planning backwards" (McDonald, 1993), asking first, what kind of graduate do we want? Then, how do we get there? And, finally, how will we know when we have arrived? This third question has led CPESS to develop graduation requirements—and structures within which students prepare for these requirements and for later life—that reflect the values and goals of the school for what students ought to know and be able to do.

School Structures

A number of structural features of the school support students and teachers in their work (see Figure 5.1). In divisions I and II (two-year blocks that are the equivalent of grades 7 through 8 and 9 through 10), students pursue a common core curriculum, which includes two interdisciplinary courses: humanities and social studies, and mathematics and science, along with an hour-long Spanish course and a one-hour advisory. These courses take place within houses of four to five teachers and seventy-five to eighty students each. Along with the advisories, these help personalize students' experience of the school. They remain with the teachers and students within their house for two years until they "move up" to the next division.

By reorganizing teacher work, CPESS has reduced the student–teacher ratio in individual classrooms to 18:1 and the total student load per teacher to 36 students in contrast to the 150 or more common in most high schools. In divisions I and II, each teacher is responsible for two subject areas—math and science or social studies and English—which are taught together in two-hour blocks of time to two groups of students each day. In addition to classroom teaching, however, teachers are responsible for advisories, college and career counseling, and certain administrative and governance responsibilities. The reductions in class size and load and the creation of shared planning time for teachers are a result of resource allocation decisions that debureaucratize the functions of the school: there is much less specialization of functions and very little administrative overlay. CPESS has spent most of its funds on classroom teachers rather than on nonteaching or auxiliary personnel. Thus, there is only one art teacher for the school, a part-time social worker, and a librarian shared with another school in the same building. There are no guidance counselors, attendance officers, assistant principals, supervisors, or department heads. The co-directors teach classes themselves and have responsibility for advisories. This staffing pattern is dramatically different from that in a typical large comprehensive high school, in which 40 to 50 percent of staff are nonteaching personnel, and staff–pupil ratios of 1:14 translate into class sizes of more than thirty students.[1]

Figure 5.1. Central Park East Secondary School Structure.

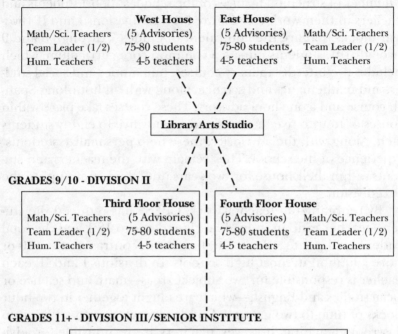

GRADES 7/8 - DIVISION I

West House		East House	
	West House	**East House**	
Math/Sci. Teachers	(5 Advisories)	(5 Advisories)	Math/Sci. Teachers
Team Leader (1/2)	75-80 students	75-80 students	Team Leader (1/2)
Hum. Teachers	4-5 teachers	4-5 teachers	Hum. Teachers

Library Arts Studio

GRADES 9/10 - DIVISION II

Third Floor House		Fourth Floor House	
	Third Floor House	**Fourth Floor House**	
Math/Sci. Teachers	(5 Advisories)	(5 Advisories)	Math/Sci. Teachers
Team Leader (1/2)	75-80 students	75-80 students	Team Leader (1/2)
Hum. Teachers	4-5 teachers	4-5 teachers	Hum. Teachers

GRADES 11+ - DIVISION III/SENIOR INSTITUTE

Senior Institute 150 Students

Core Seminars
Academic Courses
Mentorships/Internships   In-House Faculty of 10
Preparation for Graduation
Post-Graduation Planning

DIVISION I AND II DAILY SCHEDULE

8-9	Spanish
9-1	2 hours each of Humanities and Math/Science
1-2	1/2 hour educational options and 1/2 hour lunch
2-3	1 hour Advisory
3-5	Extended day options

Note: 1 day per week for school/community service occupies the first 2 1/2 hours of the day for students while faculty meets for curriculum planning

The advisory is one of the school's key strategies for ensuring that students cannot "fall through the cracks." Each professional staff member works over a period of two years with a group of twelve to fifteen students and their families, providing academic and personal supports of many kinds. The advisory period is used as a study time; an opportunity for quiet reading and writing; for discussion of health, social, and ethical issues; and for one-on-one and group advising and counseling. The advisor is the "expert" on the student, meeting frequently with the family and with other teachers to ensure communication about the student's needs and progress, to "tap the family's expertise" (CPESS, n.d.), and to guide the student through courses, exhibitions, and graduation requirements. Parents attend conferences four times a year, with the advisor, teachers, and student present to look at the student's work together. Advisors also maintain contact with families through frequent phone calls to follow up on student problems and progress. This ensures that parents, teachers, and the student are all working with the same understanding of goals, standards, and processes, and that there is a high degree of mutual effort toward these goals.

Students in divisions I and II spend two and a half hours weekly in a community service program, tutoring younger students, working with senior citizens, and working in community settings like museums and other nonprofit organizations. While these experiences help them understand the adult world, explore occupations, and develop a sense of social responsibility and initiative, the community service time also allows their teachers to spend at least one full morning a week engaged in team planning. This allows teachers to share expertise to discuss how specific students are doing and to plan a coherent curriculum.

In the Senior Institute, a roughly two-year capstone experience that is the approximate equivalent of grades 11 and 12, students design their course of study within the broad guidelines of core requirements in literature, social studies, mathematics, science, and Spanish. In addition, each student participates in a work-related internship and attends at least two courses on college campuses. These two curricular components place students outside the school in the "adult" arenas of work and college where they are evaluated by "real-world" standards. Rather than trying to create courses or tests that would seek to predict, probably poorly, whether students are likely to succeed in college or in employment settings, the Senior Institute puts them in these situations, where they are evaluated and can test themselves directly against the actual criteria for performance such experiences call for.

Graduation Requirements

In order to graduate, students complete a portfolio of their work that reveals their competence and performance in fourteen curricular areas, ranging from science and technology to ethics and social issues, from school and community service to mathematics, literature, and history. This portfolio is evaluated by a graduation committee comprising teachers from different subjects and grade levels, an outside examiner, and a student peer. The committee members examine all the entries and hear the students' oral "defense" of their work as they determine when each student is ready to graduate.

For students and faculty to be able to undertake such ambitious goals, teaching and learning time is structured much differently than it is in traditional schools. Senior Institute teachers have time for their roles as advisor, mentor, tutor, coach, and assessor both because CPESS allocates almost all its staff to the classroom and because it uses external learning experiences such as coursework at local colleges and required internships in lieu of some classes.

These strategies allow Senior Institute teachers to spend about half of their time "advising students" rather than "teaching classes." They teach traditional courses about twelve hours a week, spending another five hours weekly leading their twelve-member advisories and many more hours working on portfolio development and graduation committee meetings with their individual advisees.[2] Senior Institute teachers also have two forty-five-minute blocks during the week for meeting as a staff to deal with curriculum, assessment, or student issues. Given that Senior Institute advisors accompany their advisees on college visits as well as support them through courses and internships, help them conceptualize their portfolios and locate resources, and serve as facilitators, backstops, and cheerleaders, their student-focused time is a critical investment in students' later success.

All these strategies help develop knowledge about students as well as about subjects. This is a critical form of knowledge in learner-centered schools that is substantially absent in highly departmentalized settings. The CPESS structures and curriculum provide many means for teachers to come to know individual students and their learning needs exceptionally well. The advisory structure, close family relationships, and the multiyear house structure help teachers build this kind of knowledge. In addition, curriculum and teaching are structured to access information about students' experiences, concerns, interests and views. During the early grades, students conduct oral histories, develop family trees, write poems and narratives about themselves, and talk and write about the areas they feel are their talents and needs. In their graduation portfolios, students write an autobiography and develop a postgraduation plan. This enables their teachers to know something about where their students are coming from and where they are going. In contrast to traditional schools, which are structured on the presumption that knowing students is irrelevant to teaching them, CPESS explicitly creates knowledge-building structures and strategies that take into account the central need to understand students in order to develop teaching that will help them learn.

Shared Standards and Collective Accountability

One of the guiding forces for curriculum planning is the internally developed assessment system that promotes a high level of coherence around goals and standards, as well as providing exemplars of high-quality work. CPESS teachers say the assessments are a primary means of reflection on what is being taught and how it is being taught (Darling-Hammond and Ancess, 1994a). Senior Institute math and science teacher Edwina Branch notes that "developing standards for mathematics or science portfolios makes teachers think about what they're doing in their classrooms." She feels she and her colleagues have revamped the kinds of projects they expect of students so that they are closer to "what we all said we wanted as a standard for the kids," and she constantly uses the portfolio scoring grid, based on the five Habits of Mind, as a way to talk to students about the criteria they should be applying. Explicit criteria help the whole school focus on its mission. Branch recalls that when she first came to CPESS,

Teachers pushed each other to answer "why are we doing this? And what do we want kids to get out of it?" (The grid) is understood to be something we need as an entire school. . . . I can't imagine right now trying to teach without thinking about assessment all the time. It's easier to be in your own little world and not be accountable to anybody. It's much easier for me to be in this room doing what I want. But it's not the best thing for the kids, and it's not really the best thing for my teaching.

One of the most powerful vehicles for sharing knowledge and information is the graduation committee. All faculty in all divisions serve on graduation committees, as do upper-level students and some parents. This creates a conversation about standards throughout the school and a set of shared norms for the quality of student work. Because of this participation, lower grades teachers are much more aware of what they need to do to prepare students to succeed on their portfolios. The public defense of student work brings focus to the educational experience. As parent Darwin Davis explains:

(The graduation committee presentation) was certainly in my mind the clearest and most focused time that I had as a parent, knowing what the expectations were of my daughter in terms of her academic work and performance. It lays it out fairly clearly for the student as well. This is the goal I must reach. And not only must I reach it but I must be able to convince five other people, some of whom are selected (by the student), that this in fact reflects the capability that I have and I bring to this particular subject area.

The committee meetings are a moment of truth in which all the members of the CPESS community can see the fruits of their labors. There is no escaping what has worked, what has not worked, and what needs more work. As a consequence of the highly visible exhibitions students undertake at graduation and in the years before, conversation about teaching and learning is enriched. The assessment system has served as a vehicle for staff development and for school development. It has provided a concrete, student-centered focus for staff collaboration and shared learning, with student work at the center. The negotiation and use of the standards has served to strengthen shared goals and values, the sense of the school as a whole entity with common direction.

Each year, in a set of retreats and other meetings, CPESS staff review the portfolio process and products, look at student work and standards of performance, and make changes in the assessment process and the school's operations to improve their practice. In addition, external reviewers—professors from local colleges, researchers, local employers, teachers and administrators from other schools—convene annually to provide another set of perspectives on the student performances demonstrated in the exhibitions. These reviewers meet with staff and look at student work, commenting on the extent to which the work measures up to the standards they would employ in college courses, employment circumstances, and other schools. These processes build knowledge about internal and external standards as well as occasions to share knowledge about teaching and learning.

Faculty find that the assessment process raises schoolwide questions for them to work on: What must the school do to help students produce work of depth and quality? What must happen within classes and in advisories, resource rooms, and elsewhere? Do new courses, such as research writing labs, need to be invented? Meier notes that the process of working through portfolio requirements, standards, and evaluations motivates improvement of teaching across the entire school. By tackling the question of graduation standards with authentic examples of student work as the focus of the conversations, "We've created a school that's more collective in its practice."

Discussion

Central Park East Secondary School illustrates a number of strategies for organizing work structures and teaching processes so that they focus on students and their learning, creating both high standards and high supports. Similar strategies enacted by equally successful schools, including International High School, Manhattan International High School, and the Urban Academy, help illuminate the core features of "high-involvement, high-performance" schools. In this section, I discuss how these schools have decentralized and restructured authority and work, knowledge and information sharing, and rewards and incentives in much the same way that high-involvement firms have done (Lawler, 1986; Mohrman, Lawler, and Mohrman, 1992).

Decentralized Authority:
Faculty Collaboration and Decision Making

These highly successful schools share several features that allow for decentralization of authority in a manner that supports greater accountability and effectiveness with students. Decentralized power, knowledge, and information (Lawler, 1986) are a byproduct of faculty decision making through committees that deal with educational issues and work units that are responsible for groups of students. Teaching teams maintain a focus on whole students and their learning and provide a venue for surfacing issues and problems. Committees and teams engage in democratic decision making rather than representative governance or merely advisory input.

Governance

Both the elementary and secondary schools associated with CCE have deeply rooted faculty governance systems that include shared decision making about curriculum, assessment, instructional, and personnel issues at the team and school levels. This work operates in the context of strong shared norms and values (each school's version of the twelve CCE principles) that are made real throughout the organization as teachers use them in hiring their colleagues, developing evaluation systems, engaging in peer review, making curriculum decisions, setting standards for assessing student and teacher work, and deciding on professional development. Each school has articulated its own set of educational ideals that is a touchstone for every organizational decision. This provides the coherence that enables decentralization to operate responsibly. For most public schools that have not had the opportunity to work through what they stand for and what all staff will commit to, this will be a necessary first step toward responsible decentralization. Otherwise, there is no basis on which to make shared decisions or to evaluate their appropriateness.

Faculty governance occurs at both the school and team levels. All the schools have schoolwide councils, and teachers serve on multiple teams and committees that function horizontally and vertically to communicate ideas and enhance participation throughout the organization. The schools use a variety of strategies to maximize participation while maintaining a whole-school perspective. Many decisions reside in teaching teams or other workgroups; these are either conducted within a framework established at the school level (for example, a consensus about curriculum goals) or are returned to the school council for final approval (for example, a staff hiring decision). At the Urban Academy, which is small enough to function as a committee of the whole, ad hoc committees and workgroups are kept fluid to reduce the territoriality that can emerge when subgroups remain static and to increase the opportunities for people to develop shared perspectives and to learn from one another.

Student or parent involvement in governance is also common. Parents and students are involved in school-level decision making at CPESS. At the Urban Academy, International High School, and Manhattan International High School, student representatives from each advisory meet to discuss schoolwide issues of concern and make recommendations. At Urban, students provide input to the hiring of new teachers on the basis of demonstration lessons taught by the candidates.

Because the schools are deliberately small, governance engages every teacher; this enables the collective decision-making practices that create a high-involvement work setting. In larger settings, it is difficult to enact democratic decision making in ways that allow every member to participate. Typically, large schools use representative forms of governance, such as school-based decision-making councils, that involve a small number of faculty in decisions, leaving out and sometimes alienating the others (Lieberman, Darling-Hammond, and Zuckerman, 1991).

At International and Manhattan International High Schools, each teacher serves on one of several decision-making committees dealing with staff development, personnel functions such as staff hiring and peer evaluation, curriculum, or parent involvement. A coordinating council includes the school's administrators, union representative, PTA president, student association president, and a representative of each of the six teaching clusters. This supports vertical and horizontal communication throughout the school. In addition, teachers at International see this democratization as a key to transforming classroom teaching:

> There is a relationship between the management style of a
> school and the learning style in the classroom. When the man-
> agement style is authoritarian, the learning style in the classroom

is authoritarian and teacher driven. When we change the management style to a more democratic, collaborative style, it becomes a model for learning in our classrooms (Defazio and Hirschy, 1993).

The Manhattan International teacher contract makes explicit the responsibilities created by shared decision making:

> We firmly believe in the school based management and shared decision making model of school governance and that all members are co-participants in such a governance body with the understanding that they intend to abide by staff decisions, and take responsibility for the school's work, its outcomes and daily practices.

At CPESS, decision making occurs in both divisionwide and schoolwide meetings. School committees are involved in interviewing and hiring staff, in planning and implementing professional development, and in other functions that cut across the concerns of house and division teams. Smaller groups of staff often work on certain issues together, bringing them back to the whole staff to decide policy. This gives staff the chance to be involved in the final decisions and maintains coherence and unity of purpose in the work of the school.

Teams

It is significant that teacher work units organize teachers' collaborative work primarily around shared groups of students rather than around subject matter, as traditional high school departments do. In houses, teams, or divisions, groups of teachers assume common responsibility for a relatively small number of students, working with them across multiple subjects and counseling them over multiple years. Thus, together, teachers can assume full responsibility for the welfare and success of students rather than for the delivery of content lessons to conveyer-belt pass-bys for whom no one takes responsibility. These structures, and others that I describe later, increase teachers' influence over what they do, provide information and feedback, and "give them a whole piece of work" (Hackman and Oldham, 1973, quoted in Mohrman, Lawler, and Mohrman, 1992, p. 350). They allow for decentralization of decision making in a manner that is likely to lead to greater accountability for student learning rather than greater fragmentation. They also motivate teachers by increasing their expectancies of success: as team structures increase teachers' reach over students' lives and their control over the total learning process, they reduce uncertainty, increase student success, and thus increase teacher success and willingness to invest even more effort (Rosenholtz, 1989; Mohrman, Lawler, and Mohrman, 1992; Rowan, this volume).

A very strong feature of the organizational designs at CPESS and Manhattan International is that faculty work in two kinds of teams: one that focuses on a shared group of students and their needs, and one that focuses on curriculum planning and teaching strategies. Thus, within houses, a math and science teacher works with a humanities teacher and a resource room teacher or counselor with whom he or she shares a common group of students for two years. At CPESS, these teachers have seven hours weekly during planning and extended lunch times to meet together. In addition, each teacher meets with a discipline-based (math/science or humanities) curriculum team one morning a week to plan curriculum across divisions and houses while students are participating in community service activities. These cross-functional teams help teachers focus both on learning standards and on students while ensuring that information is widely shared throughout the organization.

Another strategy for collaborative curriculum work is seen at the Urban Academy, which enables staff to work through issues of curriculum and pedagogy in twice yearly schoolwide projects that all students and teachers work on together and in twice monthly curriculum meetings where issues are raised about how students are engaging content, how they are developing skills in the school's proficiency areas, and how teaching can better support their progress. These occasions, along with staff reviews of the needs of individual students and collective work on graduation portfolios, keep the faculty continually talking and thinking about how to improve teaching and learning.

In all these schools, staff members, including administrators, take responsibility for "family groups" or "advisories," in which a small number of students meet regularly with a staff member (or at Manhattan, a pair of staff members), who also take responsibility for continuous communication with the students' families by phone and through parent conferences, typically four annually. The focus of this work is academic as well as personal. Students feel well attended to in this arrangement. As they describe their experience:

> Teachers know about the students. When you don't understand something, they know when you need help.

> The teachers know us. They talk with our parents about our problems, our personality. They give us counsel.

> They know you because in the school and in the home, it's the same. They see if you're working, if you're good friends with other students, they see if you're behaving well. They ask if you have problems.

All these arrangements create functional workgroups for teachers while personalizing education for students, providing continuity of relationships over time as well as a team of teachers focused on their progress. A variety of strategies for creating work teams focused on students have been tried. At International High School, staff are now divided into six cross-functional clusters that take complete responsibility for groups of approximately sixty-five students each thirteen weeks. These groups of students are in turn divided into "strands" of twenty to twenty-five students who spend all day with each other during that thirteen-week cycle, taking classes with four teachers who compose an interdisciplinary team that has full responsibility for managing the entire instructional day for their students. Guidance counselors are attached to teams, giving them a lower per pupil load and stronger connections to both teachers and students. The team decides about scheduling, curriculum, teaching strategies, discipline, grading, and other issues related to individual students. Over the course of students' four years at International, they will take several cycles with the same teachers.

Teachers developed this new cluster arrangement, which also features longer (seventy-minute) periods that are more conducive to collaborative group work for students, after experimenting with other schedules over the years. When one group of teachers experimented with the first interdisciplinary cluster course, they found that the performance of students in the course was significantly better than that of students in their regular singleton courses because of the more intensive, focused attention they received. Several years later, after intensive deliberation, the entire faculty decided to convert to the cluster approach, concluding that this arrangement increases teacher responsibility for students as well as their control over the conditions of teaching and learning. As teacher David Hirshy explains:

> Our new schedule has given us confidence that we, as teachers, can affect the learning environment of the students we serve in real and concrete ways. The shift toward students sharing and learning from each other, rather than teachers teaching, has been facilitated. Our role has been expanded to include planning and designing the learning community in which we work each day. It has demonstrated that, given time and real decision making power, teachers can exercise careful and visionary judgment.

Faculty at International insist that in all aspects of the school it is important that students and teachers engage in the same kinds of experiences: collaborative work, shared decision making, portfolio assessment. Thus, moving teachers into tighter more interdependent teams enables them to more effectively work with students who are themselves working in groups. Teacher Steve Lindberg explains:

> The teachers are now working in the same ways that the students are. The students in most classes work in groups (and) rely on each other to do things. There's responsibility. When people aren't working up to par, the group suffers. When people do very well and support each other, then the group goes well. . . . The idea that in groups, people are responsible to each other as they learn, that people can rely on others, this is one of the core values of the school.

At the much smaller Urban Academy, which serves only 100 students who come in with varying academic backgrounds and course-taking needs from the schools they have left, formal teaching teams that create smaller units are less necessary, and a common core curriculum for standard cohorts of students is less appropriate. Urban's more fluid structures feature interage grouping in courses, highly individualized programs for students, and frequent team teaching and regular visits to one another's classrooms by teachers. Each is responsible for an advisory of ten to twenty students. (The most senior teachers work with more students.) The instructional program is designed through a collaborative process in which teachers collectively discuss how they can create courses that will meet students' needs and the school's graduation proficiencies using what they know in conjunction with what local colleges offer.

At all the schools, teams have substantial freedom in enacting curriculum within the framework of school decisions about overarching curriculum goals and student proficiencies that must be demonstrated in portfolios or exhibitions for graduation. Although their students do take and pass the state Regents Competency Tests, the schools are not subject to the standardized Regents examinations, which are course-based examinations that substantially constrain curriculum, often focusing on superficial content coverage rather than in-depth mastery of concepts. Although the Regents are overhauling the current state tests, the CCE schools have developed their own graduation requirements and assessment systems that provide a framework for their curriculum development.

Collective Decision Making and Peer Review

The decentralization of authority does not mean unfettered individual autonomy but a greater collective authority for teachers coupled with greater professional accountability. Major curriculum decisions are collectively made by teams or by the entire faculty, as are many decisions regarding how students will be supported and evaluated in their work. Teachers must hash out the issues until they agree. As noted earlier, the graduation portfolios at CPESS serve as a major forum for creating a collective perspective. At the Urban Academy, consensual decision making about curriculum occurs in twice monthly schoolwide curriculum meetings. Additional three-hour weekly staff meetings are used to look at individual students and their needs, to examine how well the school is achieving its intentions, and to share specific classroom practices and problems.

Teachers in all these schools see themselves as giving up individual autonomy and subjecting themselves to greater peer review in order to gain collegial feedback, opportunities for sharing, and more success for their students. As a teacher at Manhattan International High School puts it:

> With my colleagues, we've had to work together on curriculum, look at each other's work. We're forced to be more collaborative. So there's kind of a loss of freedom to some extent. But I think it's compensated for by the lack of isolation and the feedback you get. With feedback, there's growth. Here you can't hide. It's kind of hard at first, but it's good for you.

At both International and Manhattan International, all faculty members serve on peer evaluation committees for their colleagues. This involves them in observing and being observed in their teaching, developing a portfolio of their work and responding to those of others, engaging in self-evaluation, and preparing and receiving written evaluations of teaching. Teachers are provided with supports for courses or other professional development they may need to improve performance in particular areas. The peer evaluation committees are empowered to grant tenure and to recommend continuation or dismissal. These decisions are taken seriously and are far from pro forma. Not all teachers are invited to stay. At International, administrators evaluate each team as a whole, and staff respond to an annual questionnaire in order to evaluate the principal. All these functions serve to expand knowledge and information across individuals and teams, as well as to create a press for accountability.

Shared and Decentralized Knowledge and Information

In order for decentralized authority to be handled responsibly, workers must have a steady flow of information needed for decision making and continuous opportunities to build their knowledge. At least five features of these schools support decentralized, shared knowledge and information. First, team planning and teaching allow teachers to share knowledge with one another and to create work structures that take advantage of distributed expertise that is continually growing as teachers fill in gaps in one another's base of knowledge and experience.

Team members help one another plan what they will do in

their classrooms, serve as a sounding board and a critical friend for one another, and provide additional disciplinary and pedagogical expertise. One of the felt needs in a more generalist model of teaching is to help teachers expand their expertise in the areas in which they have less training and experience. In this structure, teachers who are more experienced in the social studies will help those more experienced in English/language arts with their planning, and vice versa. The same interchange occurs for mathematics and science teachers. The opportunity for creating teams with distributed expertise is taken into account in hiring decisions as well as team formation.

Such opportunities for developing greater shared knowledge are needed in traditional secondary school settings as well, where over one-third of all teachers teach at least some courses outside their area of preparation because of shortages or logistical needs. These "out of field" assignments are typically not supported by team planning with other teachers in those fields to help share expertise and consciously build teachers' curriculum and teaching knowledge. Interestingly, schools in many European countries routinely prepare teachers to teach in more than one subject area and organize their work in teaching teams that support continuous learning about teaching within and across content areas.

Whereas curriculum teams allow teachers to share disciplinary knowledge, house teams help teachers share knowledge about students and integrate instruction. For example, humanities and math/science teachers may work together to integrate geometric studies of pyramids into a unit on ancient Mayan civilization. In addition, particular concerns about students and teaching can be raised in the context of house meetings so that collective problem solving can occur. Students' advisors can easily share information about students' concerns or situations within the context of team meetings, without having to chase down seven or eight different teachers with different schedules as they would in a traditional high school setting. The result is that students are seen more holistically, their families are consulted frequently, and their needs are more continuously addressed.

Second, cross-group structures for planning, communication, and decision making extend the benefits of group expertise to other groups and provide a web of horizontal communication throughout the school. Cross-team planning and learning occur in schoolwide staff development and staff meetings (conducted at least weekly in all the schools), shared governance contexts, and on assessment occasions, such as exhibitions and portfolio reviews that involve schoolwide planning and multiple faculty reviewers. At International, peer evaluation teams provide another place for people to exchange ideas and to share knowledge across boundaries.

Third, both team planning and professional development are built into the schedule and tied to ongoing, homegrown innovations that enable constructivist learning for teachers as well as students. For example, CPESS teachers have learned a great deal about students, teaching, and learning by their deep engagement in creating and continually revising the portfolio system, by linking this work to staff development, and by subjecting students' work and their own judgments to further scrutiny by outside reviewers. When teachers at International developed a portfolio-based peer evaluation strategy for themselves, they created new forums for knowledge sharing. Ultimately, this also led to more use of portfolio and peer review strategies within classrooms.

Fourth, rich communication vehicles such as narrative report cards, student and teacher portfolios, class and school newsletters, and widely distributed meeting notes augment the continual sharing of information about students, families, and classroom work in team and committee settings. These communication vehicles include the manner in which teacher development and evaluation are conducted. In the context of peer observations, teacher portfolios, and continuous collegial sharing of practice, communication about what teachers are doing and how it is working is constant and focused on daily problems of practice rather than behavioral checklists filled out in twenty-minute observations by the principal.

That these communication vehicles talk about and exhibit teaching and learning in first-hand detailed fashion is unusual in schools, where most communication deals with logistics and procedures (bus schedules, meeting dates, new guidelines) or uses proxy data about learning (grades, test scores) rather than concrete examples of student and teacher work. In these schools, extensive public examples and discussions of what students and teachers are doing proliferate.

Finally, highly visible shared exhibitions of student work and performance make it clear what the school values and how students are doing. Symbolically, perhaps, the walls of these schools are literally plastered with student work. Student writing, designs, models, and artwork cover hallways, classrooms, and offices. Teachers work collectively to create assessments and to document and evaluate student learning within and across classrooms. This serves to decentralize information about student learning and about teaching in other classrooms. As teachers look at the work of their own students, they learn what is working as they had hoped and what is not. They gain richer information than externally scored standardized tests can provide about what students are doing. As they look at the work of other teachers' students, they have a window into the curriculum and teaching strategies used in other classrooms.

Aggregated data about student performance are also regularly available and discussed. At International, for example, every individual has access to all measurable information about the performance of all students in the school. Thus, every team knows student pass rates for in-school and college courses, RCT scores, attendance rates, suspensions, college acceptance rates, drop-out rates, and faculty attendance rates as well as other in-school academic progress indicators. These are broken down by individual course or team where appropriate and included in an end-of-year evaluation report.

Shared information about how students are achieving can motivate greater accountability. One cluster team at International High School, for example, was disturbed that its students showed higher levels of incompletes than those of other clusters at the end of a cycle. In response to this information, they assigned themselves as mentors to each student who had an incomplete, working on their own time with former students in order to help them complete the work so that they could pass (Ancess, 1995).

In addition, the process of developing and evaluating performance assessments with other teachers enhances teacher learning about both their students and their teaching and learning more generally (Darling-Hammond and Ancess, 1994b). It sharpens their ability to think in a curricular way, to understand the scaffolding that is needed to produce high-quality performances, and to develop strategies that will help their students achieve the standards embedded in these complex tasks.

Rewards and Incentives for Teachers and Students

The concept of rewards and incentives in schools needs to be understood in organizational context. Public elementary and secondary schools are typically devoid of rewards that have to do with the core mission of the organization. Schools that serve low-income and minority students are especially heavily sanctioned environments. Because of bureaucratic rigidities and the low status of teaching, there are many ways in which highly committed staff are punished for taking on students who need more help in order to learn or for undertaking tasks that would improve the organization but that rock the bureaucratic boat. As Phil Schlechty notes, most schools are organizations in which the only reward is the lack of punishment.

A particularly dysfunctional aspect of rewards for staff in schools is that, to the extent that they exist, they usually are tied to student status and achievement rather than to the extent of growth and learning students experience, and to tasks that are relatively risk-free rather than those that are riskier and require more effort. Thus, high-status teachers are those who teach "honors" or "gifted" students who need little help in order to learn, or who teach in schools with more economically and educationally advantaged student bodies. Working with students who have more difficulty learning is a punishment handed out to new teachers or those with less clout. These students and their teachers also receive fewer resources at both the classroom and school levels (Darling-Hammond, 1995). This stands in contrast to the reward structure in some professions where the most capable practitioners gain status from working on the most difficult problems rather than handling easy cases.

Traditional schools provide few incentives to support the efforts of teachers who want to come to know the needs of their students well, who are willing to look for answers to the knottiest problems of teaching and learning, and who are willing to work with students for whom educational attainment is a riskier and more labor-intensive course. The incentives provided by traditional school structures are to depersonalize and standardize instruction so as to comfortably handle large numbers of students in short blocks of time; to use pedagogical strategies that are as simple, self-contained, and routine as possible and that undermine teaching for understanding (these are also often required by teacher evaluation procedures); and to try to avoid teaching high-need students by "moving up" to higher tracks or transferring out to more attractive schools with increased seniority.

Monetary incentives favor those who are furthest away from teaching. Higher pay and higher status are acquired by leaving the classroom for administration. Within teaching, monetary incentives for learning take the form of salary hikes that accrue for graduate course-taking. Earning a master's degree appears to have some positive effect on teacher effectiveness (Ferguson, 1991; Armour-Thomas, 1989), but course-taking incentives are crudely fashioned and only haphazardly emphasize learning aimed at more insightful teaching. In most districts, these salary incentives cease after a teacher reaches a certain education and experience level. Incentives for learning are also largely absent from the school environment, where there is usually no time provided for professional development and no intrinsic motivation for changing practice.

In the successful schools described here, a very different set of intrinsic and extrinsic incentives and supports operates for teachers and students. In case studies of these schools, teachers continually describe the intrinsic rewards that derive from their increased success with students as the most powerful factor that keeps them engaged in the intensive work of transforming their pedagogy and reforming their school organizations. Their reports are consistent with several decades of research indicating that the opportunity to be effective is a powerful motivator for entering and staying in teaching and for triggering commitment and effort (Rosenholtz, 1989; Firestone, 1994).

Students describe the incentives that come from being cared for and having clear, attainable goals to shoot for, with plenty of supports to ensure their success. This success is supported by the ways in which redesigned work structures create more extended time with students (and hence the opportunity for individual teachers to have greater effects on student learning), smaller pupil loads, and collegial help in solving problems of practice with respect to individual students and to overall questions of curriculum and pedagogy. Extrinsic incentives, including time and financial support for teacher learning, and teacher time available to students, support the attainment of intrinsic rewards.

Incentives for Teachers

Restructured Time

First, the ways in which schools have redesigned the use of time and have created smaller student loads, especially at the secondary level, enables more collegial learning and more personalization of instruction. This provides incentives for deep engagement in teaching and learning issues as well as peer pressure for using the time productively toward those ends. Structuring for success reduces the excuses that are virtually necessary for teachers who work with little or no planning time and more than 150 students a day. The use of that collegial time for curriculum planning, teaching discussions, and student reviews creates a continual conversation about standards and progress that motivates effort toward agreed-on goals.

Time for new faculty roles is built into the regular schedule. Each school does this differently but manages, through block scheduling and creative student programming, to create several hour blocks for joint teacher planning, staff development, and faculty governance. At CPESS and Urban, for example, teachers meet for a half day each week while students are engaged in community service activities. CPESS teams get another two and a half hours of shared planning time built into the schedule each week; on Fridays, students begin their days earlier than usual and are dismissed early in order to free up time for another two-hour meeting. At International High School, a clubs period for students on Wednesday afternoons provides three and a half hours for faculty staff development. At Urban, as in schools in Germany and Japan, teachers' desks are arranged in one large room so that teachers see each other all day long and have opportunities for constant interaction.

All the schools plan retreats and summer institutes each year for professional development purposes, and they allocate additional days for professional development. All this time is used for collective learning and shared decision making rather than for transmitting administrative directives, which is the usual use of faculty meetings in traditional schools.

Reduced Pupil Loads

Smaller pupil loads that allow for more personalization are achieved by creating more generalist roles for teachers that focus more on teaching students than transmitting subjects. That the CCE schools are deliberately creating new incentives is explicitly seen in the teacher contract developed by Manhattan International High School in its first year of operation (1993–1994). The contract states, in part, that:

> In return for smaller class size and smaller total student rolls, teachers will work with students in classes, family groups, clubs, teams, tutorials, seminars, projects and coaching individual students. . . . All faculty, in their roles as family group advisors, are expected to keep families informed of student work, progress and other concerns. We are committed to meeting with parents at least four times a year when they will receive a narrative assessment of their child's work, and when workshops of interest to parents will be held. As family group advisors, we are responsible for 18 to 25 students, meeting briefly with them each day and once a week for an hour. As advisors we are responsible for knowing our family well and serving their needs concerning school issues, health, career education and family life.

Ownership and Opportunity to Create

Teachers in these schools value the opportunity to create and to innovate. They are committed both to their schools and to the change process because of their role in developing the innovations they are undertaking. Teachers in these schools have gained greater individual autonomy by having agreed to operate in a collective manner when it comes to goal-setting, standard-setting, curriculum development, and schoolwide decision making. Within the parameters they jointly set and agree to—which are closely tied to the stated norms and values of the school—they have tremendous opportunity to invent their own practice.

All teachers have substantial responsibility for shaping and operating the school's work. This, too, provides incentives for effort. Co-director Paul Schwartz notes that "the teachers at CPESS feel as though they own the school because of the governance structure. They don't mind the extra time they have to put in because they are invested. It's like how the bodega owner feels about stocking the shelves and sweeping the floor, versus the McDonald's worker." Faculty members' discussions of their work confirm this view. They talk enthusiastically about the work they are in engaged in and the substantive changes they continually initiate rather than about extra chores they feel they are forced to take on. Teachers who previously worked in traditional high schools frequently talk about being "reborn," reenergized, and renewed by a chance to work in an environment that enables them to be so much more effective and creative.

The greater control over their own work that staff gain from their participation in decision making is itself a powerful intrinsic incentive to remain in the school and in the profession as well as to continue to be involved in transformational efforts. The psychology of positive action—of doing rather than being done unto—is important for developing self-efficacy and motivating purposeful effort.

Work Variety and Leadership Opportunities

Rather than a hierarchical career structure, all these schools offer teachers work variety that enables them to use and develop their talents in ways that are individually satisfying. For example, if there is a research project underway, any teacher can participate. If a teacher is particularly interested in an area of study, he or she can develop it within and across course structures. Interests ranging from the use of video to the study of ancient civilizations or applications of mathematical modeling can find their way into courses given the breadth of the essential questions that guide course development.

Teachers are known for their areas of expertise and are encouraged to lead and contribute to curriculum initiatives and related school projects based on those interests. There are leadership opportunities within the many committees and teams that operate in the schools. Some of these are compensated with modest stipends. Teachers are actively encouraged to take leadership in the profession as well. Teachers present at conferences, create study groups, and share their expertise with other schools and faculty in the CCE network. Grants are sometimes available to support the professional development work that teachers engage in within their schools or with other faculties interested in learning about the curriculum strategies or assessments they have developed.

At least three teachers from CPESS and two at International have left in the two years to start new schools as part of the movement in New York City to create new high schools, many of them partnered with existing schools as a means for supporting their growth. Teachers undertake these challenges knowing they are supported by a collegial network that will help them learn and problem solve in these new roles.

Internally Developed Standards

Standards and assessments provide incentives for both teachers and students. The description of student standards at CPESS illustrates how an iterative approach to standard-setting and continuing opportunities for students to meet high standards motivate effort and maintain focus. The power of schoolwide standard-setting and shared highly public assessment strategies is that they convey valued ideals in a concrete way; they provide occasions to recognize and celebrate student and teacher work; and they make clear the areas where more work is needed. All three of the other schools have developed or are developing schoolwide standards and exhibitions of performance as the basis for graduation. For faculty, the publicness of the process is an incentive to prepare students well for the exhibition; the gratification of student success is also an important incentive.

The highly developed peer review process for faculty at International and Manhattan International High Schools provides another powerful approach to standard-setting. Faculty gain insights into their teaching and that of others while shared standards of practice are developed through the conversations and observations that take place. Like students, teachers have continual incentives and opportunity to improve their practice with supports provided.

Incentives for Students

Standards and Supports

Managing high academic standards so that they serve as incentives for students, rather than as disincentives, is a delicate business. The standards carry stakes: students cannot graduate until they receive passing scores on all of their portfolios, and graduation committees enforce the standards by requiring revisions when work is not up to par. Especially in the first years of this graduation system, a number of CPESS students did not graduate in June, working through the summer and sometimes into the following year to reach the standards. At the same time, the supports to meet the standards are also present: teachers continue to work intensively with students until they succeed. If this were not the case, the standards would become demotivating, persuading students that they should give up rather than continuing to exert effort. Because students choose many of the topics they want to pursue, much of the work is intrinsically interesting to them. The combination of student choice, high supports, and high standards creates the motivation and opportunity to continue to work until success is achieved.

As Urban Academy teacher Nancy Jachim notes, the challenge a school faces is negotiating the tensions of the competing agendas of caring and academic rigor so that they serve each other:

> The teacher's agenda is curriculum. Students have a different agenda. If the teacher connects with the students, the students will accept the school values. They will achieve. The student's agenda is to relive the parenting experience—caring, personal contact. (Our) students need the caring and attention. . . . They are slouching toward success, not pursuing it ardently.

In all these schools, students voice over and over again how important it is to them that they are cared for. The personalized attention they receive and the doggedness with which teachers pursue their futures with them—taking them on trips to college campuses, coaching them through exhibitions, meeting with their parents—are the incentives that secure their commitment to work hard and to achieve. Because the schools are structured to allow teachers to care for students effectively, students develop trust and students begin to believe that accomplishing the school's goals will be important to their later success. This engenders the effort that teachers need from students to produce learning.

Home–School Connections

Another set of incentives for students evolves because of the tight connections forged between teachers and parents, which allow both parties to better understand and support the student's experience in school and to create mutually reinforcing incentives in the two environments. Because advisors tend to meet with parents at least four times a year and to talk with them much more frequently, needed supports can more readily be identified and established in the home and school, and problems can be worked through before they become crises. Sometimes other solutions can be worked out for students whose schoolwork may be suffering because of an after-school job or who have been taking on baby-sitting responsibilities at home. Sometimes the exchange of information simply makes it easier for parents and teachers to be delivering the same messages and working with students toward the same ends. When teachers can secure the interest and involvement of parents in supporting their efforts, the incentive system around the student begins to work in a synergistic way.

These strong connections are also important to create bridges and common cultural ground across the wide gulf that sometimes separates schools as middle-class Eurocentric institutions and minority communities that have experienced a history of exclusion (Ogbu, 1992; Comer, 1988). Connecting with parents to create common ground can help reduce cultural conflicts that create competing psychological incentive structures for students. The two International High Schools work especially hard at this, calling parents frequently; holding workshops for parents to help them learn English, deal with immigration issues, and complete college applications; publishing newsletters in multiple languages and arranging for translators at PTA meetings. In all the case studies, students talk appreciatively about how their teachers "keep after" them, meeting with and calling their parents so that they are not allowed to fail.

Choice, Participation, and Autonomy

Because they are alternative schools, all these schools operate as schools of choice. Although the schools are not selective, the act of choosing creates a different dynamic for the relationship between students and the school—one in which free will rather than coercion is the operant variable. Choice also operates in the curriculum since students have frequent opportunities to choose the topics for projects they will undertake, to pursue internships in fields of interest, and to select college courses. Students are always participants in shaping their own learning. They are part of parent–teacher conferences, part of the curriculum development process, and part of the ongoing decision making in classrooms.

In addition, students are very much involved in governance within the schools. They discuss and advise on a wide range of issues, and they are represented on school site councils. Visitors to the school are likely to be greeted and briefed by students, who also frequently participate in teams that represent the schools at conferences and meetings. Internship placements and an array of independent projects that allow students to take charge of their own inquiry are other ways in which students are enabled to take on the roles of increasingly responsible young adults. Students participate in portfolio reviews and on graduation committees for their peers as part of the assessment team, and they engage in ongoing self-evaluation. For developing adolescents who need both autonomy and affiliation, the opportunity to be heard and to be taken seriously is a major incentive to commit to the school environment.

Finally, much of the work students undertake is intrinsically interesting, and the opportunity to display their competence in public exhibitions that include parents as well as teachers and outsiders is highly motivating. Work that is engaging and that builds a sense of accomplishment operates as an incentive. As a member of the first graduating class at Central Park East Secondary School put it, "This environment gives us more standards. It makes us stand up straight . . . It makes us look at ourselves in the mirror and feel proud of our accomplishments."

Schools that take seriously the idea of "student as worker"—which involves students as well as teachers in shaping and leading the work—are able to construct incentives that engage the efforts of both teachers and students. Incentives and structures that take account of students' needs to be cared for and to participate in shaping their own work are as important as those that take account of teachers' needs for knowledge, information, and authority in structuring theirs. In applying the ideas of high-involvement, high-performance organizations to schools, it may be most productive to understand students and teachers as co-workers in the task of creating ambitious teaching and powerful learning together.

Implications for Policy

Many of the practices that create personalization and commitment in these schools are achieved on waivers or through exceptions from state and local policies governing curriculum, testing, the use of time, the hiring of staff, and staff allocation patterns. These include highly prescriptive state curriculum and testing policies that emphasize rote-oriented teaching and learning within narrow disciplinary boundaries. Because these are externally developed and prescribed, they also dissuade teachers from thinking deeply about curriculum goals, standards, and evaluation of student work. To create a healthy dialectic between externally developed and internally developed standards, proposed reforms in New York would create a more parsimonious system of high-quality, performance-based state assessments derived from the new state curriculum frameworks complemented by a rich set of locally developed assessments to be assembled in a Regents portfolio for graduation (New York State Council on Curriculum and Assessment, 1994). This new results-oriented system would also free schools from input regulations that currently prescribe the number of minutes to be devoted to each subject and the precise course configurations that must be used.

Staffing constraints that inhibit new ways of organizing teaching work derive largely from local collective bargaining agreements and New York City board of education policies that have, historically, assigned teachers to schools as though they were interchangeable cogs in a wheel and assigned staffing resources according to Byzantine formulas that presume highly bureaucratic staffing patterns and designations of duties and responsibilities. Collective bargaining agreements often reify these presumptions about the allocation of staff and duties because they grew up in tandem with bureaucratic management systems.

These systems too, are being challenged. In response to the demands of new high schools being created in New York, the board and union agreed to try a hiring process that allows faculties to interview and hire their colleagues. The practice was so successful that it has been written into the collective bargaining agreement as an option for all schools that are "unique." Ultimately, reformers hope that all schools will qualify for this designation and that teachers will be able to function as professionals in this way and in many others. Although alternative schools are able to create different staffing arrangements for themselves and to create their own agreements with staff about roles and responsibilities, this opportunity to deviate from board staffing rules and contractual work rules is not yet widely available across schools. Consequently, the ways in which these schools have redesigned their work cannot yet be widely emulated.

In theory, school-based management and shared decision making are now required in New York State. In practice, many decisions are constrained by a geological dig of regulations that have accrued since Taylor introduced his management theories in the 1920s. In such environments, creating high-involvement schools will require reinventing policy while redesigning practice.

Finally, incentives for the development of teacher knowledge and skill will be needed to support the kind of informed practice that permeates high-performance schools. Currently, poorly prepared teachers are as readily hired and as well paid as well-trained ones, and there are few incentives for developing greater expertise focused on meeting the needs of students more effectively. The schools described in this chapter provide opportunities for their expert teachers to engage in ongoing professional development and to earn additional stipends, consulting fees, recognition, and additional resources for their schoolwork through the wide-ranging professional tasks they take on and the grants that they write. In the future, compensation systems that recognize knowledge, skill, and needed expertise—such as deep knowledge of subjects (especially multiple fields and high-need fields), special aspects of student learning, guidance and counseling, and other functions of direct relevance to their work—may encourage teachers to continue to improve their skills and to enhance the distributed expertise available within teaching teams. Supports for the development of teacher knowledge and skill, and recognition for demonstrated expertise (see Odden, this volume), should undergird efforts to create high-involvement schools that serve students responsibly and well.

Notes

1. In an NCREST study comparing staffing and resource allocation decisions between small restructured high schools and large comprehensive high schools, we found substantial differences in how staff

are allocated and used. In a typical big school, with an enrollment of about 3300 students, pupil–adult ratios of fourteen to one nonetheless translate into average class sizes of thirty-three to thirty-four and very little planning time for teachers. This is because more than 40 percent of staff are nonteaching personnel: nine assistant principals, nine guidance counselors, twelve secretaries, ten school-based services specialists, and seventeen security guards are employed along with twenty-seven school aides, librarians, and teachers. "Big School" administrators and supervisors have little or no contact with students in a teaching or advising capacity. Their jobs are heavily paperwork oriented and consumed by the tasks of coordinating the otherwise fragmented work of all the other personnel.

2. Co-director Paul Schwarz estimates that a minimum of thirty-six hours per year per graduate are spent in graduation committee meetings. Since the average graduation load is six students per teacher, Senior Institute teachers spend a minimum of 216 hours in graduation committees. It is not unusual for graduation meetings to occur after official school hours, in the evening, or on weekends to accommodate parents and other students.

References

Ancess, J. *An Inquiry High School: Learner-Centered Accountability at the Urban Academy.* New York: National Center for Restructuring Education, Schools, and Teaching, Teachers College, Columbia University, 1995.

Armour-Thomas, E., Clay, C., Domanico, R., Bruno, K., and Allen, B. *An Outlier Study of Elementary and Middle Schools in New York City: Final Report.* New York: New York City Board of Education. 1989.

Bensman, D. *Lives of the Graduates of Central Park East Elementary School: Where Have They Gone? What Did They Really Learn?* New York: National Center for Restructuring Education, Schools, and Teaching, Teachers College, Columbia University, 1994.

Bensman, D. *Learning to Think Well: Central Park East Secondary School Graduates Reflect on their High School and College Experiences.* New York: National Center for Restructuring Education, Schools, and Teaching, Teachers College, Columbia University, 1995.

Benveniste, G. *Professionalizing the Organization: Reducing Bureaucracy to Enhance Effectiveness.* San Francisco: Jossey-Bass, 1987.

Braddock, J. and McPartland, J. *Education of Early Adolescents.* In L. Darling-Hammond (ed.): *Review of Research in Education, Vol. 19.* Washington, D.C. American Educational Research Association, 1993.

Central Park East Secondary School (CPESS). *Senior Institute Handbook.* New York: CPESS, 1990.

Central Park East Secondary School. *A Public High School: Central Park East Secondary School.* New York: CPESS, undated.

Cohen, D. K., McLaughlin, M. W., and Talbert, J. E. *Teaching for Understanding: Challenges for Policy and Practice.* San Francisco: Jossey-Bass, 1993.

Comer, J. P. "Educating Poor Minority Children." *Scientific American,* 1988, *259* (5), 42–48.

Cronbach, L. J. "Beyond the Two Disciplines of Scientific Psychology." *American Psychologist,* 1975, *30* (2), 116–127.

Darling-Hammond, L. "Reframing the School Reform Agenda: Developing Capacity for School Transformation." *Phi Delta Kappan,* 1993, *74* (10), 753–761.

Darling-Hammond, L. *Professional Development Schools: Schools for Developing a Profession.* New York: Teachers College Press, 1994.

Darling-Hammond, L. "Inequality and Access to Knowledge." In James Banks (ed.): *Handbook of Research on Multicultural Education.* New York: Macmillan, 1995.

Darling-Hammond, L. and Ancess, J. *Graduation by Portfolio at Central Park East Secondary School.* New York: National Center for Restructuring Education, Schools, and Teaching, Teachers College, Columbia University, 1994a.

Darling-Hammond, L. and Ancess, J. *Authentic Assessment and School Development.* New York: National Center for Restructuring Education, Schools, and Teaching, Teachers College, Columbia University, 1994b.

Darling-Hammond, L., Ancess, J., and Falk, B. *Authentic Assessment in Action: Studies of Schools and Students at Work.* New York: Teachers College Press, 1995.

Darling-Hammond, L., Ancess, J., MacGregor, K. and Zuckerman, D. *Inching Toward Systemic Reform: The Coalition Campus Schools Project in New York City.* New York: National Center for Restructuring Education, Schools, and Teaching, Teachers College, Columbia University, forthcoming.

Darling-Hammond, L., Snyder, J., Ancess, J., Einbender, L, Goodwin, A. L., and Macdonald, M. B. *Creating Learner-Centered Accountability.* New York: National Center for Restructuring Education, Schools, and Teaching, Teachers College, Columbia University, 1993.

Defazio, A. and Hirschy, P. D. *Integrating Instruction and Assessment.* New York: International High School, 1993.

Elmore, R. et al. *Restructuring Schools: The Next Generation of Educational Reform.* San Francisco: Jossey-Bass, 1990.

Ferguson, R. F. "Paying for Public Education: New Evidence on How and Why Money Matters." *Harvard Journal on Legislation,* Summer 1991, *28* (2), 465–498.

Fine, M. *Chartering Urban School Reform.* New York: National Center for Restructuring Education, Schools, and Teaching, Teachers College, Columbia University, 1994.

Firestone, W. "Redesigning Teacher Salary Systems for Education Reform." *American Educational Research Journal,* 1994, *31*(3), 549–574.

Fowler, W. J. "What Do We Know About School Size? What Should We Know?" Paper presented at the annual meeting of the American Educational Research Association, San Francisco, Calif., April 1992.

Garbarino, J. "The Human Ecology of School Crime: A Case for Small Schools." In E. Wenk (ed.): *School Crime.* Davis, Calif.: National Council on Crime and Delinquency, 1978, pp. 122–133.

Gardner, H. *The Unschooled Mind: How Students Learn and How Schools Should Teach.* New York: Basic Books, 1991.

Gottfredson, G. D. and Daiger, D. C. *Disruption in 600 Schools.* Baltimore: The Johns Hopkins University, Center for Social Organization of Schools, 1979.

Green, G. and Stevens, W. "What Research Says About Small Schools." *Rural Educators,* 1988, *10* (1), 9–14.

Hackman, J. R. and Oldham, G. R. *Work Redesign.* Reading, Mass.: Addison-Wesley, 1973.

Haller, E. J. "High School Size and Student Indiscipline: Another Aspect of the School Consolidation Issue?" *Educational Evaluation and Policy Analysis,* 1992a, *14* (2), 145–156.

Haller, E. J. "Small Schools and Higher-Order Thinking Skills." Paper presented at the annual meeting of the American Educational Research Association. San Francisco, 1992b.

Haller, E. J. "Small Schools and Higher-Order Thinking Skills." *Journal of Research in Rural Education,* 1993, *9* (2), 66–73.

Howley, C. B. "Synthesis of the Effects of School and District Size: What Research Says About Achievement in Small Schools and School Districts." *Journal of Rural and Small Schools,* 1989, *4* (1), 2–12.

Howley, C. B. and Huang, G. "Extracurricular Participation and Achievement: School Size as Possible Mediator of SES Influence Among Individual Students." *Resources in Education,* January 1992.

Jacobson, D. *Productivity and Job Quality in Services: A Case Study of Human Resource Innovation in High School.* New York: Institute of Education and the Economy, Teachers College, Columbia University, 1994.

Kornhaber, M. and Gardner, H. *Varieties of Excellence: Identifying and Assessing Children's Talents.* New York: National Center for Restructuring Education, Schools, and Teaching, 1993.

Lawler, E. E. *High-Involvement Management*. San Francisco: Jossey Bass, 1986.

Lawler, E. E. *The Ultimate Advantage: Creating the High-Involvement Organization*. San Francisco: Jossey-Bass, 1992.

Lee, V., Bryk, A., and Smith, M. "The Organization of Effective Secondary Schools." In L. Darling-Hammond (ed.): *Review of Research in Education, Vol. 19.* Washington, D.C. American Educational Research Association, 1993.

Lieberman, A. *The Work of Restructuring Schools: Building from the Ground Up.* New York: Teachers College Press, 1995.

Lieberman, A., Darling-Hammond, L., and Zuckerman, D. *Early Lessons in School Restructuring.* New York: National Center for Restructuring Education, Schools, and Teaching, Teachers College, Columbia University, 1991.

Lindsay, P. "The Effect of High School Size on Student Participation, Satisfaction, and Attendance." *Educational Evaluation and Policy Analysis*, 1982, *4*, 57–65.

Lindsay, P. "High School Size, Participation in Activities, and Young Adult Social Participation: Some Enduring Effects of Schooling." *Educational Evaluation and Policy Analysis*, 1984, *6* (1), 73–83.

McDonald, J. *Planning Backwards from Exhibitions. In Graduation by Exhibition: Assessing Genuine Achievement.* Alexandria, Va.: Association for Supervision and Curriculum Development, 1993.

Meier, D. *The Power of Their Ideas.* Boston: Beacon, 1995.

Mohrman, S. A., Lawler, E. E., and Mohrman, A. M. "Applying Employee Involvement in Schools." *Educational Evaluation and Policy Analysis*, 1992, *14* (4), 347–360.

Mohrman, S. A. and Wohlstetter, P. *School-Based Management: Organizing for High Performance.* San Francisco: Jossey-Bass, 1994.

National Institute of Education (NIE). *Violent Schools–Safe Schools: The Safe School Study Report to Congress.* Washington, D.C.: NIE, 1977.

New York State Council on Curriculum and Assessment. *Learning-Centered Curriculum and Assessment for New York State.* Albany: New York State Education Department, 1994.

Odden, A. and Odden, E. "Applying the High Involvement Framework to Local Management of Schools in Victoria, Australia." Paper presented at the annual meeting of the American Educational Research Association, New Orleans, 1994.

Ogbu, J. "Understanding Cultural Diversity and Learning." *Educational Researcher,* 1992, *21* (8), 5–14.

Pittman, R. and Haughwout, P. "Influence of High School Size on Dropout Rate." *Educational Evaluation and Policy Analysis*, 1987, *9*, 337–343.

Resnick, L. *Education and Learning to Think.* Washington, D.C.: National Academy Press, 1987.

Rosenholtz, S. *Teachers' Workplace: The Social Organization of Schools.* New York: Longman, 1989.

Schlechty, P. *Schools for the 21st Century.* San Francisco: Jossey-Bass, 1990.

Senge, P. M. *The Fifth Discipline: The Art and Practice of the Learning Organization.* New York: Doubleday, 1990.

Snyder, J., Lieberman, A., Macdonald, M. B., Goodwin, A. L. *Makers of Meaning in a Learning-Centered School: A Case Study of Central Park East 1 Elementary School.* New York: National Center for Restructuring Education, Schools, and Teaching, Teachers College, Columbia University, 1992.

Sizer, T. *Horace's School: Redesigning the American High School.* Boston: Houghton Mifflin, 1992.

Wehlage, G., Rutter, R. A., Smith, G. A., Lesko, N., and Fernandez, R. R. *Reducing the Risk: Schools as Communities of Support.* Philadelphia: Falmer Press, 1989.

Wohlstetter, P., Smyer, R., and Mohrman, S. A. "New Boundaries for School-Based Management: The High Involvement Model." *Educational Evaluation and Policy Analysis,* 1994, *16* (3), 268–286.

Part Three

Going to Scale

Chapter Six

Standards as Incentives for Instructional Reform

Brian Rowan

In the past decade, educational policy makers have turned increasingly to "standards" as an instrument of instructional reform in schools (Fuhrman, 1994; Smith and O'Day, 1990). By standards, I mean *institutionalized* rules or criteria that are used to judge the adequacy or quality of educational processes, products, or personnel.[1] In general, three types of educational standards can be defined:

- *Student standards* describe the desirable outcomes of schooling in terms of what students should know and be able to do. Today, ambitious, new student standards are being defined in the numerous curriculum frameworks and assessment instruments developed by state departments of education, national subject-area associations, and other education groups.
- *Teacher standards* identify the required knowledge, skills, and abilities teachers need to practice the occupation of teaching. Today's new teacher standards are being developed in the various tests, assessments, and educational requirements used in teacher licensing and certification.
- *School standards* are used to judge the adequacy of school programs. Historically, such standards have been established by accreditation agencies and state law, but more recently, a new approach to setting school standards has appeared in congressional debates about "opportunity to learn" standards for schools (Porter, 1993).

In theory, the new educational standards being formulated by agencies of social control in education are designed to provide local educators with sophisticated forms of instructional guidance that will improve instruction in classrooms (Cohen and Spillane, 1992). Thus, today's educational standards are intended to establish ambitious, new learning goals for students, to define the knowledge and skills that teachers need to provide instruction consistent with these goals, and to make explicit the kinds of organizational environments that support ambitious instructional reforms. In today's policy environment, there is much hope that such new standards will lead to instructional reform. But there is also much uncertainty. As new standards are developed and institutionalized, will classroom activities necessarily come to focus on newly defined learning goals? will teachers really begin to acquire the knowledge and skills needed to teach toward these goals effectively? and will schools begin to reorganize in ways that support rather than impede new forms of instruction?

Most observers agree that the educational standards now being developed are an important step forward in the current educational reform agenda. But there is little consensus about whether these new standards can promote *real* change in schools. Skeptics note that previous attempts to change instruction along the lines envisioned in current reform initiatives met with little success in the past (see, for example, Cuban, 1984). Moreover, the current standards-setting movement has gained momentum despite the absence of persuasive empirical evidence demonstrating that educational standards can have pervasive effects on classroom activities (Cohen and Spillane, 1992). As a result, we do not yet know if a standards-setting movement like the one we are currently experiencing can lead to lasting instructional reforms or whether such a movement will result in the same limited successes that occurred during previous efforts to reform instruction in American schools.

Teachers as the Key to Instructional Reform

In this paper, I examine the promises and pitfalls of the current standards-setting movement by speculating about the effects of educational standards on teachers. My focus on teachers is deliberate. Under current configurations of instructional management, teachers in American schools have a great deal of autonomy in their choice of instructional goals and methods (Meyer and Rowan, 1978; Rowan, 1990). As a result, there is much classroom-to-classroom variation in the instructional activities undertaken by teachers and in the outcomes produced in American schools (Stevenson and Baker, 1991; Hanushek, 1971; Porter, 1989; Raudenbush, Rowan, and Cheong, 1993). In the American context, in fact, teachers appear to be the ultimate arbiters of instructional reform since their choices and activities determine how policies developed at higher levels of the educational system get implemented at the point of service delivery (Berman and McLaughlin, 1978).

Because teachers hold the key to instructional reform in American schools, I use an approach to policy analysis known as "backward mapping" (Elmore, 1979) to examine the potential effects of new educational standards on classroom instruction. Using this approach, I first develop a list of factors known to affect teachers' instructional activities and then ask whether educational standards can change these factors in ways that promote desired teaching behaviors. From the standpoint of backward mapping, two questions are central to my analysis: (1) What factors control the instructional performances of teachers? and (2) Is there any reason to expect that new educational standards can shape these factors in ways that promote desired instructional practices?

Background

In order to answer these questions, I review research on the determinants of employee performance found in the literature on organizational and industrial psychology. This research identifies three global factors that affect the performance of employees in all kinds of organizations, including schools. These factors are an employee's motivation to perform a job, the job-relevant skills or abilities that the employee brings to the job, and the situation in which the employee performs the job.

Equation 6.1 summarizes these global ideas about job performance in terms of a simple model:

$$P_j = F(M_j, A_j, S_j) \qquad (6.1)$$

where P stands for employee performance (usually measured in terms of some outcome), M stands for employee motivation, A stands for employee ability, and S stands for the situation in which the employee performs the job. The subscript $_j$ denotes that the equation refers only to performance, motivation, abilities, and situations relevant to the performance of a particular job.

In the following sections, I ask whether this general model can be applied to the analysis of teaching in classrooms and whether educational standards can be expected to affect the various components of this formula. Can a teacher's performance in a classroom be seen as a function of that teacher's motivation, abilities, and the situation in which he or she teaches? And will newly developed educational standards affect teachers' motivation, abilities, and job situations in ways that promote desired instructional activities in schools? Before answering these questions, however, I discuss the general model of employee performance in greater detail.

A General Model of Employee Performance

Several points about the general model of employee performance expressed in Equation 6.1 are worth noting. First, behavioral scientists frequently assume that the functional form of this model is multiplicative. For example, job performance is often seen to result from an interaction between motivation and ability (that is, $P_j = M_j * A_j$). In this specification, neither high levels of motivation nor high levels of skill are sufficient to produce high performance. Instead, employees must be both highly motivated *and* highly skilled to perform well. Thus, highly motivated employees will produce low job performance when they lack the required skills for a job, and highly skilled employees will produce low job performance when they are unmotivated. A multiplicative specification of Equation 6.1 also suggests that the effects of motivation and ability on job performance vary depending on the situations in which individuals work (that is, $P_j = M_j * A_j * S_j$). For example, the job performance of highly motivated and skilled employees can be limited by the absence of necessary tools or materials. Finally, researchers assume that job situations affect motivation and abilities directly (that is, $M_j = f[S_j]; A_j = f[S_j]$). For example, workers often use different skills or have different levels of motivation depending on the situations in which they work. The overall point is that job performance results from a complex set of relationships among motivation, ability, and situation.

How Organizations Manage Performance

The literature on employee performance not only specifies a set of global factors that affect job performance, it also describes a set of organizational conditions known to affect these factors. From this perspective, the literature on employee performance in organizations can be seen as an exercise in backward mapping. Researchers first give attention to describing the factors that affect employee performance and then attempt to design organizational policies that affect these factors.

In general, three strategies of performance management have been developed in the literature on job performance: output standards, job selection and training, and technical improvements.

Output Standards

First, employee performance can be improved by the development of output standards. For example, research repeatedly demonstrates that individuals who are assigned specific and difficult performance goals outperform individuals who are given vague ("do your best") goals. The process of setting explicit output goals for employees is assumed to affect performance outcomes through its effects on employee motivation. Explicit outcome goals direct employee attention and effort toward specific targets, allow employees to think more clearly about task strategies, and encourage task persistence. As a result, goal-setting for employees is widely acknowledged as an effective means of performance management in business and industry (Locke and Latham, 1984).

Job Selection and Training

A second strategy of performance management seeks to improve employee skills and abilities. Often, this approach involves setting skill standards as criteria for employment, but organizations also offer incentives for active employees to acquire new skills, especially when technologies require flexible job assignments or are evolving rapidly. Research demonstrates that attempts to select or change employee skills result in improved job performance only when the skills that serve as the focus of the intervention are job relevant (Smith and George, 1992). Although this sounds obvious, the wisdom of selecting for or training employees in job-relevant skills has escaped the attention of many employers. In fact, research demonstrates that many employee selection methods often screen employees on criteria that have little relationship to job performance and that many training programs are focused on global skills that have less effect on situated performance than training in job-specific skills (Smith and George, 1992).

Technical Improvements

A third strategy seeks to improve employee performance by changing the situations in which employees work. Frequently, this process involves changing the tools or technology used by workers, but it can also occur through changes in other working conditions. Often, organizations establish benchmarks or standards against which an organization's technical processes are judged. They then engage in a process of continuous improvement to achieve these standards. Sometimes the process of continuous improvement is managed by developing suggestion boxes, quality improvement circles, or gain sharing programs that encourage employees to contribute new ideas for technical improvement (Morhman, Lawler, and Morhman, 1992). Research suggests that such strategies can have powerful effects on employee performance, but only if accompanied by organizational changes that provide employees with the information and authority needed to make effective decisions about organizational improvement (Morhman and others, 1992).

Applying General Models of Performance Management to Schools

Can these general ideas about employee performance be applied to the management of teaching in schools?

A Model of Teaching Performance

I believe there are interesting parallels between the general model of employee performance just discussed and models of teaching performance developed in research on teaching. When the outcome of teaching is seen as student achievement, research suggests that teaching outcomes *are* affected by the three global factors listed in Equation 6.1. Consider, for example, the effects of teacher "ability" on student achievement. In early research on teaching, this construct was often measured by the level of education or academic degree obtained by teachers, but these broad measures were never found to have much affect on student achievement. On the other hand, more job-relevant measures, such as the verbal ability of teachers, have been found to affect student achievement (Hanushek, 1971). More recently, educational researchers have begun to define even more job-specific measures of teaching ability, including teachers' knowledge of the subject matter they are teaching and knowledge of how to teach these subjects (see, for example, Shulman, 1987). To date, the few available studies that examine the effects of these job-specific abilities on student achievement confirm the general model of performance discussed earlier. For example, job-specific aspects of teacher knowledge (such as the number of course credits taken in the subject taught by a teacher), as well as the specific ways in which teachers teach particular curricula, do appear to have effects on student achievement (see, for example, Hafner, 1994; Monk, 1994).

There is also a literature describing the effects of teacher motivation on student achievement. This literature is still in its infancy, especially compared to the extensive literature on motivation and performance developed in industrial and organizational psychology. In this broader literature, task motivation has been examined from a variety of theoretical perspectives. Early work discussed employee motivation in terms of needs and dispositions, but more recent work focuses on a variety of cognitive processes in motivation. In particular, cognitive theorists assume that task motivation is affected by the goals employees are attempting to achieve, the expectations employees have of mounting appropriate performances and successfully reaching their goals, the value employees expect to receive from achieving goals, and a host of attributions employees make about their own abilities and the causal forces affecting their performance. Cognitive theorists also suggest that there is a reciprocal relationship between task motivation and employee performance. In reflecting on past performance, workers often alter their expectations for future success and change their attributions about the causes of prior performance. These reflective processes, in turn, sometimes change the kinds of skills or abilities employees use in future performances or lead employees to alter the situations in which they work.

Research on teaching has generally failed to study these motivational complexities in great detail. However, there is some evidence of a link between teacher motivation and student achievement. For example, many studies demonstrate that teacher expectations for success with particular students affect student achievement. These findings can be viewed as a demonstration of the kinds of expectancy effects discussed in general theories of employee motivation and as evidence that expectancy theories can be applied to teaching. There is also some evidence that teachers' sense of efficacy affects teaching performance although the measures used in research on teaching often do not closely correspond to the construct of efficacy developed in the broader literature on motivation (for a review, see Guskey and Passaro, 1994). The larger point, however, is that initial evidence supports the idea that teacher motivation (as discussed in the larger literature on expectancy, self-efficacy, and attributions) is related to student achievement.

Finally, educational researchers are beginning to develop an understanding of how the situations in which teachers work affect teaching performance. Here too the findings tend to be consistent with the general literature on employee performance. For example, research on school effectiveness undertaken by economists repeatedly demonstrates that the effects of teacher knowledge and verbal ability on student achievement vary across classroom contexts (see, for example, Summers and Wolfe, 1977; Hanushek, 1971; Monk, 1994), thus confirming the idea that situational variables interact with ability to produce performance. There is also evidence that the situations in which teachers work exercise direct effects on teacher motivation and ability. For example, teachers' sense of efficacy appears to be affected by the situation in which teachers work, with teachers in low track classes and those teaching lower socioeconomic students having a lower sense of efficacy (Ashton and Webb, 1986; Raudenbush, Rowan, and Cheong, 1992).

Similarly, the kinds of skills and abilities teachers use in teaching appear to be conditioned by the situations in which they work, with teachers altering their teaching strategies according to the types of students and classes that they are teaching (Raudenbush, Rowan, and Cheong, 1993). Thus, teaching performance appears to be affected in complex ways by the situations in which teachers work (for a review, see Talbert, McLaughlin, and Rowan, 1993).

Performance Management in Schools

It is also the case that educational administrators use strategies of performance management similar to those found in business and industry. For example, many school systems have developed sophisticated strategies of instructional goal-setting over the past decade. Beginning in the 1960s and 1970s, state education agencies and large, urban school districts began this process by implementing programs of achievement testing that set outcome standards for students. By the 1980s, many of these assessment systems had become quite advanced. They specified grade-level achievement objectives, assessed the extent to which students in various schools (and sometimes classrooms) achieved these objectives, and encouraged school employees to use data from these systems to set targets for school improvement and teacher performance.

School systems have also developed elaborate systems to manage the skills and abilities of teachers. In the early days of public education, skill standards for teachers were developed and administered locally and often involved the administration of various tests to teachers (see, for example, Tyack, 1974). By the middle of the twentieth century, however, elaborate certification systems had emerged. In these systems, skill standards for teachers were defined largely in terms of educational requirements and various legal definitions of teaching competence. During this same period, local school systems developed procedures for teacher evaluation and training. As a result, in the 1990s, a variety of skill standards for teachers are in place. Teacher tests and educational requirements are used in teacher licensing, and more specific skill standards are defined in the evaluation systems used by local school systems. There are also well-defined programs of inservice education for teachers that are designed to upgrade the skills of teachers in specific content areas and to train teachers in specific strategies of teaching.

Finally, criteria for judging the quality of school programs are also in place in education. Traditionally, school standards have been developed by regional accrediting agencies and state legislatures and have specified minimum requirements for school funding, facilities, staffing, and curriculum. In earlier periods, such standards were often seen as benchmarks of quality schooling, but more recently, accreditation procedures have been seen as a way to encourage self-study and innovation, with savvy educational administrators using the accreditation process to encourage teachers to make suggestions for school improvement that go beyond minimum standards and aim for achieving standards of "best practice." More recently, state education agencies and some large school districts have begun to design programs with similar aims. For example, a variety of school recognition programs (and some new forms of school accreditation) have been developed to encourage schools to strive for best practice. Typically, these programs provide incentives for schools to develop concrete plans for improvement. In some programs, schools that achieve specified goals receive modest financial awards. Such programs are similar in many ways to the continuous improvement strategies used in business and industry.

The Effects of Standards on Teacher Performance

To this point, I have argued that a general model of employee performance can be applied to the case of teaching and that school systems manage performance using strategies similar to those used in business and industry. However, today's schools are almost universally seen as organizations in need of improved performance, and this raises an interesting question: if schools are using proven strategies of performance management, why are they not getting the results policy makers desire?

In this section, I describe a set of conditions that I believe must be present if standards-based management is to have desirable effects on teachers. Educational standards, I argue, will achieve the desired effects on teaching performance only when these standards (1) have value to teachers, (2) are based on an empirically valid theory of employee performance, and (3) overcome various problems of measurement. If these conditions are met, I believe educational standards have a good chance of promoting lasting change in teaching practices. But as I also discuss, designing a system of educational standards that meets these three criteria presents formidable challenges to educational policy makers in the United States.

Standards Must Be Valued

An initial problem for those who advocate standards-based management is how to motivate employees to meet standards. Basic theories of motivation predict that employees will try to meet standards only if they think such actions will lead to something they value. Thus, an important question for those who seek to implement standards-based management in schools is how educational policy makers can make conformity to educational standards have value to teachers. Put differently, we can ask what the incentive is for a given teacher to achieve to a given educational standard.

Personal Value

Many schools appear to rely on the personal or intrinsic value that teachers assign to various standards. Consider, for example, the attitudes of American teachers toward standards of student achievement. Research demonstrates that teachers in the United States have great freedom in choosing learning goals for students, even in school systems that have developed elaborate curricular guides and grade-level expectations for student learning (for a review, see Rowan, 1990). But elaborate and formalized student standards often fail to be meaningful to teachers for two reasons. First, the outcomes described in such standards often are not those that teachers personally value. In addition, school systems rarely reward or punish teachers based on achievement of these standards (Floden et al., 1988). As a result, many of the elaborate goal-setting strategies used in American education have only a modest effect on instructional practices.

A similar result occurs in the area of teacher standards. Rules about teacher certification *are* enforced in American education, and the skills and abilities acquired through conformity to these standards do have a loose relationship to teaching performance in classrooms. However, skills and abilities that are much more closely related to teaching performance, for example, the amount a teacher learns about the subject matter he or she teaches, or the particular methods a teacher uses in teaching a subject, are today left largely to the discretion of individual teachers. As a result, teachers frequently report having their own, unique styles of teaching, and the choice of instructional strategy used in classrooms becomes mostly a private matter—a choice made on the basis of personal experience and taste rather than on the basis of public and established standards of teaching (Little, 1982).

School administrators and teachers also have considerable latitude in designing the school as a workplace. Minimum standards of school organization can be found in accreditation rules and the like, but research shows that the aspects of organizational design regulated by these rules have little effect on student learning. On the other hand, aspects of school organization and climate that do exercise effects on students—such as teaming arrangements, collaborative cultures, rules for student discipline, and other school climate factors—are left to the discretion of school personnel. As a result, the presence or absence of these school characteristics is largely determined by the unique and often serendipitous mixture of personnel at a particular site (Rowan, Raudenbush, and Kang, 1991).

Standard-setting activities will not have uniform effects on teaching performance when student, teacher, and school standards are allowed to be valued differently by different teachers, especially if the teaching force is diverse in terms of educational preferences, as appears to be the case in the United States. When teachers have different values and are given autonomy, they will emphasize different instructional outcomes, use different methods, and work within different organizational arrangements. Thus, in the United States, it appears that schools and school systems often have standards—even highly elaborate ones. But in the absence of formal sanctions reinforcing these standards, the value of these standards tends to vary according to the personal preferences of individual teachers. As a result, institutionalized standards rarely produce uniform effects across the full range of schools and teachers.

Consequences for Students

In recent years, education policy makers have recognized this problem and taken steps to correct it. One way policy makers have done this is to develop high stakes tests for students. In high-stakes testing, students are sanctioned for performance. Available evidence suggests that sanctions for students also affect teaching performance in large part because teachers almost uniformly feel an obligation to their students and value their success (see Cohen, this volume). As a result, high-stakes testing apparently promotes fairly predictable responses from teachers. Teachers whose students take high-stakes tests begin to teach toward the tests, and this alters not only the allocations of instructional time to academic content made by teachers, but also the kinds of instructional methods that teachers use. At the same time, however, many teachers report that these adaptations conflict with their personal values, and this raises the possibility that any positive benefits of high-stakes testing will be offset by negative effects on teacher motivation (for a review, see Rowan, 1990).

Pay

An alternative strategy of performance management involves offering monetary incentives to teachers who meet new educational standards. Of course, the value of monetary incentives will vary across teachers, but there is every reason to expect that monetary incentives will motivate a large number of teachers to achieve various standards. As evidence, consider teachers' responses to the monetary incentives for pursuing graduate degrees found in most teacher salary scales. The vast majority of teachers in the United States have pursued advanced degrees, and they have done so even though the training received in such degree programs is widely perceived by teachers to be irrelevant to job performance. In the future, I expect that policy makers in education will continue to experiment with salary incentives in order to give value to new educational standards. For example, Firestone (1994) has discussed a variety of ways that pay scales can be revamped to encourage teachers to acquire new job skills (see Odden et al., this volume), and I have already remarked on the trend toward using monetary incentives to encourage teachers to work toward the achievement of well-specified school improvement goals.

Cultural Controls

Although monetary incentives can be used to motivate teachers to work to standards, policy makers need not rely solely on pecuniary incentives. Teachers will also be motivated to conform to the normative standards of various groups in which they hold membership. When these norms are consistent with the standards developed by policy makers, one can expect policy makers' standards to have value for teachers.

The importance of group norms in shaping employee performance was first noted by the human relations school of industrial psychology, which found that standards of work set by informal workgroups often had a greater effect on employee performance than did standards set by formal organizational policies. More recently, sociologists have extended this line of work by also examining standards of work developed by professional workgroups in organizations (see, for example, Friedson, 1984). In educational organizations, teachers sometimes form into tightly knit workgroups that develop professional standards of work, and these standards can exert substantial pressures for conformity on teachers (Talbert, 1991). However, the organizational structure of American schools places formidable obstacles in the way of creating these kinds of groups (Little, 1982). The cellular structure of American schools, the lack of common planning times for teachers, and the specialization of the American teaching make group formation difficult and limit the amount of time group members can spend with one another.

Sociologists have also looked beyond the local workgroup to study the influence of norms and values institutionalized by powerful groups and agencies in society. Research in the field of organizational sociology suggests that these norms and values can have profound effects on worker performance and workplace organization (Meyer and Rowan, 1977). In education, for example, schools and teachers routinely conform to standards set by state and professional agencies (for example, accreditation standards, certification standards). However, research also shows that state and professional agencies have a very difficult time building consensus around standards in the areas of instruction and curriculum in the United States (Rowan, 1982). In fact, curricular standards, beliefs about effective teaching practices, and theories of effective schooling appear to be in a constant state of flux in the American educational system, as recent debates about new educational standards demonstrate.

The Congruence of Values

One final point about the value of educational standards to teachers requires attention. In this section, I have argued that educational standards affect teaching performance only when they are valued by teachers. I have also argued that standards acquire value from a variety of sources. An important question for this paper is whether policy makers can rely on a single source of value to motivate conformity to standards or whether all sources of value must be congruent for standards to have an effect on teaching performance.

In many nations of the world, the value attached to educational standards is reinforced by many different sources. Strong professional communities and societal regulations enforce standards that are consistent and that have considerable legitimacy in the eyes of teachers. Moreover, these standards are reinforced by high-stakes testing systems and by standards for teacher advancement and remuneration. The United States lacks this kind of tightly coupled educational system, and as a result, different groups in the U.S. educational system often attach different value to the same educational standard. Thus, education standards developed by state authorities are often at odds with the valued standards of teachers and their local professional communities, and all these, in turn, are unrelated to teachers' prospects for professional advancement and remuneration. We know very little about how teachers cope with these inconsistencies, but it makes sense to assume that an educational system in which the multiple sources of value are congruent will produce more conformity to a standard than will systems that lack value congruence.

Standards Must Be Based on a Valid Theory of Performance

Even if educational standards are valued by teachers, they may fail to produce desired teaching performances unless they are also grounded in a valid theory of teaching performance. In my view, a valid theory of teaching performance will have two characteristics: it will be systemic (Smith and O'Day, 1990), and it will take into account the complex processes by which motivation, ability, and situational constraints interact to produce teaching outcomes. Put differently, teaching outcomes are shaped by complex interactions among three factors: the goals that teachers are pursuing, the specific skills and abilities they use to reach these goals, and the situations in which they find themselves (for further discussion of the inherent complexity of teaching, see Cohen, this volume). Accordingly, if educational policy makers want to produce a particular type of teaching performance, they must attempt to revise three types of standards simultaneously: outcome standards that orient teachers to specific learning goals, skill standards that motivate teachers to acquire the specific skills needed to produce these outcomes, and organizational standards that encourage teachers and other school employees to restructure work situations in ways that enhance performance.

Unfortunately, patterns of standards-based management developed in American education have rarely been systemic. For example, recent efforts have been made to develop new standards for student achievement in American education, standards that stress deep conceptual understanding and higher-order thinking by students. These standards have gained widespread endorsement by state agencies and professional associations and are even valued by many teachers. However, many policy makers appear to believe that these outcome standards can be implemented without attention to the simultaneous development of corresponding standards for teacher training. For example, policy makers sometimes argue that central authorities can formulate outcome goals while the selection of means to these goals can be left to the discretion of local educators.

I believe this kind of "partial" approach to standard setting will fail to produce the effects on teaching performance desired by policy makers. For example, in the situation just described, new standards for student achievement are given incentive value (for teachers and students alike), but teachers receive little training in the methods of instruction or content knowledge needed to be effective in achieving these goals. Under these conditions, some teachers might nevertheless learn and use teaching strategies that are relevant and appropriate to the attainment of new standards of achievement, but many others will not. Moreover, under these conditions, it is likely that those teachers who are lucky enough to learn and use relevant teaching strategies will experience increased success and heightened motivation. But those teachers who lack relevant knowledge or skills will experience modest success at best, and if these teachers experience performance failures, their expectations for success and feelings of personal efficacy will begin to decline, leading to declines in task motivation and commitment to achieving the new outcome standards.

One can enumerate many other partial systems of performance management in American education. For example, a school system might invest in training programs that educate teachers about how to teach for conceptual understanding and higher-order thinking but fail to develop corresponding student standards that motivate teachers to teach toward these goals. In this setting, teachers would probably use their newly acquired skills in some settings, for example, in teaching high track classes, but not in other settings, for example, in teaching low track classes. Alternatively, we can imagine a school system in which outcome and skill standards are both present and aligned, but attention has not been given to changing the situation in which teachers work. This, in fact, is the situation discussed in the literature on school restructuring, which suggests that teachers cannot teach toward, much less achieve, ambitious student outcomes without fundamental changes in the way schools are currently organized (Sizer, 1984).

We can also imagine (even observe) systems of performance management in which various types of standards are present but "misaligned." For example, employment and training standards in a school system might encourage teachers to acquire constructivist teaching strategies that help students develop deep, conceptual understanding of academic subjects. But the outcome standards in this same system might focus attention on basic skills outcomes. Alternatively, a school system might adopt a new set of student standards focused on higher-order thinking and conceptual understanding but continue to evaluate teachers using observational instruments that reward direct instruction in basic skills. Misaligned standards can result from an incremental approach to change, in which standards in one area are reformed while others remain unchanged. But misaligned standards can also result from invalid theories of performance. For example, policy makers can hold a faulty theory of teacher performance and design a system of educational standards consistent with this faulty theory.

We know very little about how teachers respond to inconsistencies in performance standards, but I suspect inconsistencies in standards are one reason teachers enjoy the privacy of their classrooms. Behind closed doors, teachers can choose their standards and fashion logical theories of action. But when misaligned standards become public, and when teachers are held accountable for conformity to these standards, we can expect teachers to suffer morale problems, to resist and complain, or to resort to cheating. As a result, a commitment to standards-based management requires careful attention to the construction of a system of educational standards based on an empirically valid theory of teacher performance. This kind of system, I argue, is the only one that has the potential to encourage and achieve the effects on teaching desired by policy makers.

Measurement Procedures Must Be Valid

Even well-developed and logical systems of educational standards will fail to achieve the desired effects on teaching performance, however, if attention is not also paid to problems of performance measurement. There is an adage in organizational psychology to the effect that "you get what you measure," and this adage applies in education as it does in other settings. When the rewards of achieving to a standard are allocated on the basis of measured performance, employees seek to score well on measured criteria, even if these criteria lack validity (Lawler, 1976). Thus, any system of performance management requires careful attention to issues of measurement if it is to produce the desired employee behaviors.

Measurement problems have plagued performance assessment in education for years (see, for example, Cohen, this volume) although steps are now being taken to resolve these problems. For example, over the years, standardized tests of student achievement have tended to assess students' knowledge of basic skills using formats that fail to measure students' actual understanding of relevant concepts or their ability to perform complex tasks in authentic situations. Such measures were acceptable when student standards stressed basic skills achievement, but new and different achievement tests are needed in light of the new student standards now being developed (Wolf, Bixby, Glenn, and Gardner, 1991). Fortunately, progress is being made in this regard (for a discussion, see Murnane, this volume) although it will be some time before standards-based systems of performance management in American education widely reflect these new developments in student testing.

Similar problems plague assessment efforts in the area of teacher standards. For example, teacher evaluation procedures developed at the local level are widely perceived as inadequate. In the typical evaluation procedure, poorly trained observers assess teacher performance infrequently using assessment instruments that do not measure aspects of teacher activity known to be correlated to student achievement. In addition, local teacher evaluations often fail to assess teaching skills that have served as the focus of local staff development and training programs and are thus inconsistent with evolving skill standards (Wise et al., 1985). State-level efforts in teacher evaluation have also been plagued by measurement problems. For example, early career ladder and merit pay initiatives that were designed to encourage teachers to acquire and demonstrate new skills often relied on inadequate measures of teacher performance, and these measurement problems tended to decrease the amount of support these initiatives received from teachers. Today, great strides are being taken to develop measurement procedures that reflect more sophisticated theories of teaching performance (for a review, see Haertel, 1991). At present, however, the vast majority of states and local school systems lack these kinds of measures and thus are not in a position to assess whether teachers possess the relevant skills and abilities needed to teach toward new student standards.

Failures of measurement can have perverse effects on employees, especially in systems where standards are valued and theories of performance are well articulated. To the extent that performance criteria result in important rewards or punishments, employees seek to score well on measured criteria. If these measured criteria are invalid reflections of what is truly desired, pressures to cheat in performance assessments increase, and a process of goal displacement occurs in which employees strive to score well on invalid measures rather than meet the legitimate and valid goals of the system. As a result, problems of measurement are especially important to the implementation of new standards in education since measurement decisions have the potential to shape the implementation activities of teachers.

Questions About Standards-Based Management in American Education

To this point, I have argued that standards-based reforms in American education will succeed in producing desired effects on teaching performance only to the extent that policy makers develop a coherent *system* of educational standards, make sure these standards have value to teachers, and use appropriate assessments to measure the attainment of these standards. I have also argued that standards-based management has existed for years in American education, but that education policy makers need to replace the current hodgepodge of standards with a more logical and coherent approach to standards setting. But this raises two interesting questions: is it possible to create a coherent system of educational standards in the United States, and, if so, is such a move desirable?

Toward a Coherent System of Educational Standards

A strong case can be made that the lack of coherent educational standards in the United States results from the nation's tradition of decentralized educational governance, which delegates authority for educational decision making to fifty state legislatures and thousands of local school boards. In theory, such a system accommodates the diverse educational preferences of a socially heterogeneous nation and is therefore preferable to more centralized forms of educational governance. However, diverse educational preferences and decentralized educational governance in the United States also present significant challenges to those who want to develop a coherent system of educational standards to manage local schools.

Successful models of standards-based management in education almost always occur in nations that are more socially homogeneous than the United States and that have more centralized forms of educational governance. In these nations, the formal institutions governing education (legislatures, professional agencies, and administrative authorities) tend to be more integrated and aligned than in the United States (Meyer, 1983). In the United States, attempts to produce an integrated system of educational standards is proving to be quite difficult. The federal government cannot mandate the adoption of educational standards and instead must rely on more indirect methods to encourage state and local systems to adopt new standards. These indirect methods have included making grants to state and local systems to help these units develop new standards and the establishment of sanctions (like the withdrawal of federal aid) that encourage units to develop appropriate standards. In the United States, these centralizing initiatives have been controversial. The standards now being developed with federal support are viewed with deep skepticism by conservative political forces, and the entire federal approach to standards-based management is being called into question by the Republican-controlled U.S. House of Representatives.

Given these problems with federal initiatives, one might expect American states to have a better chance at developing coherent systems of educational standards. American states vary considerably in terms of educational governance arrangements, and some states with traditions of state activism in education (for example, California) appear to be making progress in the development of coherent systems of educational standards. But whereas some states have begun the process of developing coherent systems of educational standards, other states, with less activist histories of educational governance, have achieved much less and are experiencing setbacks. In Michigan, for example, conservative political forces have gained control over the State Board of Education and have voiced significant opposition to the development of state curricular standards. Moreover, these same political forces are mounting opposition to the entire edifice of teacher certification and associated standards of teacher licensing. In this environment, state-level efforts to develop a coherent system of educational standards face significant challenges.

Given the problems in many states, we might look to local school systems to develop coherent systems of educational standards. Local education units tend to have more socially homogeneous constituencies than state systems, and this just might give these units a greater likelihood of forging a political consensus around a set of educational standards than either state or federal education agencies. However, real questions can be raised about the capacity of local school systems to develop coherent standards along the lines discussed in this paper. Successful efforts at standards-based management require sustained and potentially costly managerial reforms, and to date, most local school systems have lacked the human and financial resources required to succeed at these reforms. More important, even if local school systems do manage to acquire the resources needed for systemic reform, these systems will still be lodged within a larger network of professional and regulatory agencies that may have developed a competing set of standards. As a result, teachers within local school systems might still have to balance adherence to local standards against allegiance to the norms and values espoused by other agencies.

The larger point is this. Successful approaches to standards-based management in education are easier to describe than to implement. In particular, the peculiar nature of the American educational system raises fundamental questions about the feasibility of relying on a coherent set of institutionalized standards to promote educational reform. Clearly, policy makers in the United States cannot simply mimic the patterns of standards-based management found in other national systems of education since the institutions of educational governance in these countries differ greatly from our own. In the 1990s, many different approaches to the development of educational standards are being taken by the federal government, by different states, and in different local systems. But the success of these various strategies remains very much in doubt. Thus, an interesting question emerges: what configurations of policy instruments and forms of educational governance are needed to develop a coherent system of educational standards in the United States?

The Unanticipated Consequences of Standards-Based Management

Even if it is possible to develop a coherent system of educational standards in the United States, such a development might be undesirable. In particular, there is a real chance that standards-based management in education will reinforce the already prevalent trend toward increased organizational differentiation and specialization in American education. Should this occur, any benefits accruing from standards-based management might be outweighed by the potentially negative effects of organizational differentiation and specialization in schooling. For example, many organizational models of school effectiveness now trumpet the benefits of less differentiated, and more "communal," forms of school organization, arguing that this form of educational organization is associated with higher student achievement (Bryk and Driscoll, 1988; Lee, Bryk, and Smith, 1993; Sizer, 1984).

A potential problem with standards-based management lies in its reliance on specialization and differentiation, especially modes of implementation that follow the lead of management practices in business and industry. For example, in business and industry, criteria for employee performance are highly job specific in order to be valid. Performance outcomes are well defined, and the kinds of skills and abilities used by employees to achieve these goals, as well as the situations in which employees work, are closely aligned to these performance goals. To a considerable extent, similarly specific theories of teaching performance are now emerging in the United States. For example, generic models of effective teaching are increasingly being replaced by curriculum-specific models of effective teaching (Reynolds, 1992).

These highly specific theories of teaching are also reflected in new educational standards. For example, new student standards are curriculum specific and come with associated recommendations about how to teach toward particular curricular objectives. Moreover, new teacher standards are highly specialized, as exemplified by the numerous, specialized credentials developed by the National Board for Professional Teaching Standards. The tendency to develop such highly specific standards, it should be noted, reflects the very best in recent research on learning and teaching, which has increasingly developed highly specific theories of learning and teaching. Apparently, the more we know about how students learn particular kinds of academic content, and the more we develop specific approaches to teaching this content, the more powerful our theories of teaching performance become and the better able we are to affect student learning. But if education policy makers begin to act on these highly specific theories, educational goals may become increasingly specified, and the teaching force may become increasingly specialized.

There are two reasons to worry about this increased differentiation and specialization. First, organization theory demonstrates that increased differentiation and specialization create heightened demands for coordination in organizations, demands that are often met through increased bureaucratic controls. In education, however, bureaucratic controls may be ill-suited to the management of teaching (Bidwell, 1965). For example, organization theorists have long argued that complex and uncertain tasks like teaching are best managed by "organic" forms of management characterized by supportive patterns of leadership, network forms of coordination, and participatory forms of decision making (Rowan, 1990; Rowan, Raudenbush, and Cheong, 1993). This pattern of management not only resolves technical problems of performance more adequately than bureaucratic forms under conditions of task complexity, but also tends to promote higher levels of employee commitment to goals and increased task motivation (Raudenbush, Rowan, and Cheong, 1992; Raudenbush, Rowan, and Cheong, 1993). As a result, educational administrators and policy makers who advocate standards-based management in schools need to think carefully about how to handle the increased demands of coordination that arise as school tasks become more differentiated and as school staffs become more specialized. If such specialization results in highly bureaucratic forms of management, the implementation of standards-based management might lead to unanticipated, negative consequences for employee performance.

In addition, a tendency toward differentiation and specialization in education also might promote forms of instructional organization in schools that promote alienation and disengagement among students (Newmann, 1981; Bryk and Driscoll, 1988). For example, research on school effectiveness demonstrates that students benefit from close and supportive relationships with teachers, but such relationships are difficult to establish when schools are organized into a complex division of academic labor (like the departmentalized high school). As a result, many educational reformers call for semidepartmentalized and team forms of instruction in high schools and for self-contained classrooms at earlier grade levels (Lipsitz, 1984; Lee and Smith, 1993). Such organizational forms reduce the numbers of students that teachers see each day and provide limited opportunities for teachers and students to develop the kinds of close and supportive relationships that motivate students to persist in schooling. In this light, the tendency for systems of educational standards to promote increased differentiation and specialization should be carefully examined, for if this tendency exacerbates the already prevalent tendency for schools to become complex and differentiated, the consequences for student alienation, particularly among younger school children, might be negative.

One might argue that the dangers of specialization and differentiation in the standards-setting movement can be diminished by setting more general standards. Thus, standards could be phrased in terms of broad goals (for example, problem solving) rather than in terms of more specific goals. However, as standards become broad, the alignment of specific outcomes, skills, and situations necessarily becomes weaker and the effects of standards-setting on job performance can be expected to diminish. Thus, a tradeoff emerges. Policy makers must set highly specific standards in order to best affect teacher performance, but the setting of such standards unleashes countervailing pressures toward academic differentiation and specialization that have the potential to decrease the motivation and performance of both teachers and students.

Conclusion

Having considered the potential effects of educational standards on teaching performance, I return to the question asked at the beginning of this paper. Is there reason to believe that a standards-setting movement can lead to desirable effects on teaching performance in American education? The analysis presented here suggests a mixed answer to this question. A well-developed system of educational standards has the potential to produce many desirable effects on teaching, but questions remain about whether a coherent system of educational standards can be developed in the United States and whether such a system would have drawbacks as well as benefits.

The analysis presented here also suggests that we need more

knowledge before we can answer these questions. For example, I doubt whether the current body of research on teaching is sufficiently developed to serve as a guideline for the development of coherent educational standards. Certainly, this body of research is beginning to provide sophisticated models of the relationship between particular teaching skills and student outcomes in particular areas of the school curriculum. But much less is known about the effects of teacher motivation and teaching situations on teaching performance. As a result, I believe research on teaching needs to broaden its focus. Attention should still be paid to issues of teaching technique, but there should also be more research on the strategic thinking and motivation of teachers, and how these affect the application of teaching techniques in particular school situations (Talbert, McLaughlin, and Rowan, 1993). Only when we understand how teaching ability, motivation, and situations interact to produce teaching outcomes will we have a truly complete understanding of the nature of teaching performance in schools. Moreover, a sound model of teaching performance is the first step in building a sound system of educational standards to guide instruction in classrooms.

We also need better research on the nature and consequences of different patterns of educational standards in American education. The arguments developed in this paper suggest that in the United States, educational standards originate from many different and uncoordinated sources. As a result, I have argued that the typical teacher in the United States works within a context of multiple and often inconsistent standards. This situation raises two interesting questions for research. First, we need to know more about how teachers handle such inconsistencies. If educational standards originate from multiple sources, how do teachers respond when these sources send inconsistent messages? Second, we need to carefully examine alternative strategies for bringing educational standards in line with one another. Can coherent systems of educational standards be developed at the national level, and, if so, what kinds of strategies can be used by the federal government, professional associations, and other standardizing agencies to promote cooperation and the development of coherent standards? What is the likelihood that American states, with their different patterns of educational governance, can produce coherent systems of educational standards? And how are state actions affected by developments at the national level and local capacity for systemic change? In the absence of sound knowledge about these issues, today's standards-setting movement might easily reproduce the situation we are currently in, where multiple standardizing agencies produce uncoordinated and potentially inconsistent standards that leave teachers with the ultimate responsibility for formulating sound theories of teaching performance.

Finally, we need more knowledge about the potential disadvantages of standards-based management. As one example, I have suggested that a well-developed and coherent system of educational standards has the potential to reinforce the already prevalent tendency for American educational organizations to become increasingly differentiated and specialized. What is needed is some first-hand experience with educational organizations that are deeply engaged in standards-based management, whether these organizations are in the United States or in other nations. How is the division of academic labor organized in school systems using standards-based management? And how are these systems coordinated? Does standards-based management necessarily lead to increased specialization and bureaucratization, or can it coexist with the more communal and less differentiated forms of organization that recent research on schooling suggests produce higher levels of student and teacher performance? Only time and experience can tell us whether there are real costs involved in the implementation of standards-based management and whether these costs exceed the benefits that one expects from the implementation of a coherent system of educational standards in American schools.

Note

1. By defining standards in this way, I mean to focus attention on managerial "standards" embedded in the rules and regulations of bureaucratic and professional agencies that exercise social controls in the education industry (for example, state departments of education, school district offices, and professional agencies). *Institutionalized* standards are an increasingly important feature of the current education system, but they are not the only type of standard that can be discussed. Standards can also exist in a more informal sense in belief or

vision statements of various social groups. This latter type of standard functions less as a rule or criterion imposed by social control agencies on local schools or educators than as an idealized statement about what excellent teaching, learning, and schooling *might* look like. Such informal standards serve more as rallying points in calls for education reform than as institutionalized rules or criteria used to judge the adequacy of particular educational processes, products, or personnel. The two types of standards are related, however, especially when an informal "standard" that initially functions as a rallying point for reform comes to be institutionalized as a set of bureaucratic rules or criteria by social control agencies in education. For good discussions of the processes by which informal standards come to be translated into institutionalized rules, see Zald (1978) and Rowan (1982).

References

Ashton, P. and Webb, R. *Making a Difference: Teachers' Sense of Efficacy and Student Achievement.* New York: Longman, 1986.

Berman, P. and McLaughlin, M. *Federal Programs Supporting Educational Change, Vol. VIII: Implementing and Sustaining Innovations.* Santa Monica, Calif.: Rand Corporation, 1978.

Bidwell, C. "The School as a Formal Organization." In J.G. March (ed.): *Handbook of Organizations.* New York: Rand McNally, 1965.

Bryk, A. S. and Driscoll, M. *The High School as Community: Contextual Influences and Consequences for Students and Teachers.* Madison, Wis.: National Center for Effective Secondary Schools, 1988.

Cohen, D. K. and Spillane, J. "Policy and Practice: The Relations Between Governance and Instruction. In Gerald Grant (ed.): *Review of Research in Education.* Washington, D.C.: American Educational Research Association, 1992.

Cuban, L. *How Teachers Taught: Constancy and Change in American Classrooms, 1890–1980.* New York: Longman, 1984.

Elmore, R. F. "Backward Mapping: Implementation Research and Policy Decisions." *Political Science Quarterly,* 1979, *94,* 639–662.

Elmore, R. F. "Teaching, Learning, and School Organization: Principles of Practice and the Regularities of Schooling." *Educational Administration Quarterly,* in press.

Firestone, W. "Redesigning Teacher Salary Systems for Education Reform." *American Educational Research Journal,* 1994, *31* (3), 549–574.

Floden, R. et al. "Instructional Leadership at the District Level: A Closer Look at Autonomy and Control." *Educational Administration Quarterly,* 1988, *24* (4), 96–124.

Friedson, E. "The Changing Nature of Professional Work." *Annual Review of Sociology,* 1984, *10,* 1–20.

Fuhrman, S. "The Politics of Coherence." In S. Fuhrman (ed.): *Designing Coherent Education Policy: Improving the System.* San Francisco: Jossey-Bass, 1994.

Guskey, T. R. and Passaro, P. D. "Teacher Efficacy: A Study of Construct Dimensions." *American Educational Research Journal,* 1994, *31* (3), 627–643.

Haertel, E. H. "New Forms of Teacher Assessment." In G. Grant (ed.): *Review of Research in Education.* Washington, D.C.: American Educational Research Association, 1991.

Hafner, A. L. "Teaching Method Scales and Mathematics Class Achievement: What Works with Different Outcomes?" *American Educational Research Journal,* 1994, *30,* 71–94.

Hanushek, E. "Teacher Characteristics and Gains in Student Achievement: Estimation Using Micro-Data." *American Economic Review,* 1971, *61* (2), 280–289.

Lawler, E. E. "Control Systems in Organizations." In M. Dunnette (ed.): *Handbook of Industrial and Organizational Psychology.* New York: Rand McNally, 1976.

Lee, V. E., Bryk, A. S, and Smith J. B. "The Effects of High School Organization on Teachers and Students." In L. Darling-Hammond (ed.): *Review of Research in Education.* Washington, D.C.: American Educational Research Association, 1993.

Lee, V. E. and Smith, J. B. "Effects of School Restructuring on the Achievement and Engagement of Middle Grades Students." *Sociology of Education,* 1993, *66,* 164–187.

Lipsitz, J. *Successful Schools for Young Adolescents.* New Brunswick, N.J.: Transaction Books, 1984.

Little, J. W. "Norms of Collegiality and Experimentation: Workplace Conditions of School Success." *American Educational Research Journal,* 1982, *19,* 325–340.

Locke, E. A. and Latham, G. P. *Goal-Setting: A Motivational Technique that Works.* Englewood Cliffs, N.J.: Prentice-Hall, 1984.

Meyer, J. W. "Centralization of Funding and Control in Educational Governance." In J. W. Meyer and W. R. Scott: *Organizational Environments: Ritual and Rationality.* Beverly Hills: Sage, 1983.

Meyer, J. W. and Rowan, B. "Institutionalized Organizations: Formal Structure as Myth and Ceremony." *American Journal of Sociology,* 1977, *83,* 340–363.

Meyer, J. W. and Rowan, B. "The Structure of Educational Organizations." In M. W. Meyer et al.: *Environments and Organizations.* San Francisco: Jossey Bass, 1978.

Mohrman, S. A., Lawler, E. E. III, and Mohrman, A. M. Jr. "Applying Employee Involvement in Schools." *Educational Evaluation and Policy Analysis,* Winter 1992, *14*(4), 31–57.

Monk, D. "Subject Area Preparation of Secondary Mathematics and Science Teachers and Student Achievement." *Economics of Education Review,* 1994, *13,* 125–145.

Newmann, F. M. "Reducing Student Alienation in High Schools." *Harvard Educational Review,* 1981, *51,* 546–564.

Porter, A. C. "A Curriculum Out of Balance: The Case of Elementary School Mathematics." *Educational Researcher,* 1989, *18,* 9–15.

Porter, A. C. "School Delivery Standards." *Educational Researcher,* 1993, *22,* 24–30.

Raudenbush, S. W., Rowan, B., and Cheong, Y. F. "Contextual Effects on the Self-Perceived Efficacy of High School Teachers." *Sociology of Education,* 1992, *65,* 150–167.

Raudenbush, S. W., Rowan, B., and Cheong, Y. F. "Higher Order Instructional Goals in Secondary Schools: Class, Teacher, and School Influences." *American Educational Research Journal,* 1993, *30,* 523–554.

Reynolds, A. "What Is Competent Beginning Teaching? A Review of the Literature." *Review of Educational Research,* 1992, *62,* 1–35.

Rowan, B. "Organizational Structure and the Institutional Environment: The Case of Public Schools." *Administrative Science Quarterly,* 1982, *27,* 259–279.

Rowan, B. "Commitment and Control: Alternative Strategies for the Organizational Design of Schools." In C. Cazden (ed.): *Review of Research in Education.* Washington, D.C.: American Educational Research Association, 1990.

Rowan, B., Raudenbush, S. W., and Kang, S. J. "Organizational Design in High Schools: A Multilevel Analysis." *American Journal of Education,* 1991, *99,* 238–266.

Rowan, B., Raudenbush, S. W. and Cheong, Y. F. "Teaching as a Non-routine Task: Implications for the Management of Schools." *Educational Administration Quarterly,* 1993, *29,* 479–500.

Shulman, L. S. "Knowledge and Teaching: Foundations of the New Reform." *Harvard Educational Review,* 1987, *57,* 1–12.

Sizer, T. *Horace's Compromise.* Boston: Houghton Mifflin, 1984.

Smith, M. and George, D. "Selection Methods." In C. L. Cooper and I. T. Robertson (eds.): *International Review of Industrial and Organizational Psychology,* 1992, *7,* 55–98.

Smith, M. S. and O'Day, J. A. "Systemic School Reform." In S. Fuhrman and B. Malen (eds.): *The Politics of Curriculum and Testing.* Bristol Pa.: Falmer Press, 1990.

Stevenson, D. and Baker, D. "State Control of the Curriculum and Classroom Instruction." *Sociology of Education*, 1991, *64*, 1–10.

Summers, A. S. and Wolfe, B. L. "Do Schools Make a Difference?" *American Economic Review*, 1977, *67*, 639–653.

Talbert, J. E. *Boundaries of Teachers' Professional Communities in High Schools. Report #P91–130*. Stanford, Calif.: Center for Research on the Context of Secondary School Teaching, 1991.

Talbert, J. E., McLaughlin, M. W., and Rowan, B. "Understanding Context Effects on Secondary School Teaching. *Teachers College Record*, 1993, *95*, 45–68.

Tyack, D. B. *The One Best System: A History of American Urban Education*. Cambridge, Mass.: Harvard University Press, 1974.

Wise, A. et al. "Teacher Evaluation: A Study of Exemplary Practices." *Elementary School Journal*, 1985, *86*, 61–121.

Wolf, D. et al. "To Use Their Minds Well: Investigating New Forms of Student Assessment." In G. Grant (ed.): *Review of Research in Education*. Washington, D.C.: American Educational Research Association, 1991.

Zald, M. "The Social Control of Industries." *Social Forces*, 1978, *57*, 79–102.

Chapter Seven

Incentives, School Organization, and Teacher Compensation[1]

Allan Odden

Teacher compensation seems always to be a policy target for education incentives, either consciously or unconsciously. Many policy makers and practitioners at the local, state, and federal level would like to pay teachers differently, that is, in a way that provided incentives for improving practice as well as student performance. Nevertheless, teacher compensation structures have remained relatively constant for many decades. In most districts, teachers are paid according to a single salary schedule that provides salary increases for education units, degrees, and years of teaching experience. Teachers see themselves as being treated fairly by this compensation structure (disregarding dissatisfaction with actual dollar amounts). Indeed, the single salary schedule has brought uniformity of pay to elementary and secondary, male and female, and minority and nonminority teachers (Protsik, 1994).

In recent years, there have been unsuccessful attempts to reform teacher pay practices. One failure of the 1980s was the effort to graft merit pay mechanisms onto the teacher pay structure. Although touted by the 1983 *Nation At Risk* report (National Commission on Excellence in Education), merit pay was tried by a few states and districts, but failed in nearly every instance (Cornett and Gaines, 1992). A second failure was the tepid adoption of career ladder programs, which were created to alter the flat career structure of teaching. Although somewhat less controversial than merit pay, career ladder plans also fell short of their promise (Freiberg and Knight, 1991; Schlechty, 1989).

But efforts to change teacher compensation are not just a recent phenomenon. Throughout the twentieth century, there have been periodic attempts to change teacher pay usually through variations of merit pay programs that attempted to base pay, or a pay bonus, on student or teacher performance. But nearly all these efforts also failed (Johnson, 1986; Murnane and Cohen, 1986). One reason these attempts failed is that they treated compensation as a set of practices that were relatively independent of the larger educational context. But organizations and compensation are inextricably linked.

In order for compensation to serve as an incentive that reinforces broader organizational goals, the norms of the compensation structure must be aligned with the norms of the school organization (Kelley, 1995; Lawler, 1981). One reason the landscape of teacher compensation reform is littered with the relics of old reforms is that past reform strategies failed to make these connections. Performance bonuses, at the heart of most past attempts to alter teacher compensation, simply are not compatible with a bureaucratically organized and managed system. Yes, individual merit is at odds with the collegial character of effective schools (Rosenholtz, 1985, 1989). But more important, in bureaucracies, the organizational form of most schools, supervisors, managers, and executives are responsible for performance; workers—teachers— are responsible only for doing their job. A performance bonus for workers in this type of organization—teachers in education— simply does not make sense.

Fundamental changes in teacher compensation practices, thus, should reinforce rather than lead fundamental change in how education is organized and are best considered an adjunct of overall education system change. Indeed, past changes in teacher compensation have followed just such fundamental changes in the nature of the overall education system. As the next section shows, moreover, organizational change in the education system also tends to follow and reflect change in the broader society and economy (see also Odden and Odden, 1995).

Teacher Compensation Change: 1820 to 1950[2]

The single salary schedule only recently has been the structure for teacher compensation. Prior to this approach to pay, teacher compensation was provided on a different basis and actually evolved through three major restructurings over the period from roughly 1820 to 1950. Each evolution occurred when the education system itself underwent a major change, in part induced by broader changes in the economy and society of the time. The three salary systems can be characterized as "boarding 'round," position-based compensation, and the single salary schedule (Protsik, 1994).

Boarding 'Round

For most of the nineteenth century, public education was provided primarily in one-room, rural schools. The economy was agrarian; over three-fourths of the population lived on farms. There was no "education system"; indeed, there were no "state education systems." Rural schools might have been public, but they were independently organized and managed. School time was interrupted for planting, cultivation, and harvest of crops. Few children attended school all day, or all year.

Education was required by only a small percentage of the population; the needed education, moreover, was mainly mastery of the simple basic skills—reading, 'riting, and 'rithmetic. There was no teaching profession. Teaching was generally not seen as a career. For males, teaching was seen as a means for earning supplementary income. For females, teaching was seen as a transition job from the parent's home to the husband's home. There were low qualifications for teachers, who were mostly female. There were three primary requirements for the job of teacher: mastery of the 3 R's, moral character, and good appearance.

Teacher pay "fit" this education structure. Most teachers "boarded 'round" on a weekly basis, from one house to another in the community. There was a small amount of cash pay, but the largest component of compensation was room and board. The advantages of this system were that it was cheap, it reflected the largely noncash character of the economy, and it provided for direct control of behavior. Being able to "supervise" teachers while they lived in one's home gave the community strong insurance that teachers were of high moral character—there was little opportunity to do anything that might not be considered moral. The disadvantages were that it helped maintain instability in the teaching ranks, both through the lack of professionalism and low pay, and drove most men away from teaching toward other endeavors that provided a way to support a family.

Although such a teacher compensation structure seems outlandish from the perspective of the late 1990s, the key point to remember is that this system of compensation fit the economy and organization of education and schools at that time. Changes evolved not because of some innate problem with this approach to compensation, of which there were many, but because of larger changes in the economy, particularly the shift from an agrarian to an industrial economy that began around 1880.

Position-Based Compensation

As the economy began evolving from an agrarian to an industrial base, and away from the rural farm and toward the city factory, the nature of the education system also began to change. First, the country raised their expectations of the schools. More children were expected to learn more, an education refrain echoed today. Children started to attend schools for longer and more sustained periods since they were less and less needed for or allowed to work in the factories of the city. Education became more salient for more individuals in the society, particularly those moving into managerial positions in the new industrial economy.

States began to create "state systems" of education, with common rules, regulations, and requirements for both school accreditation and teacher licensure. There was a consolidation of the millions of formerly independent, small public schools into larger school sites and larger school systems. These larger units began to be run by "education experts," in both the administrative and teaching ranks. Standards for becoming a teacher were raised; teacher certification laws required greater education and expertise for earning a teacher license. As a result, it became more expensive—in time and financial outlay for training—to enter teaching. Predictably, these changes led to demands for higher

wages and a compensation system that was cash and not "in kind."
Boarding 'round simply did not work as a compensation strategy
for paying teachers in large urban school districts, who also were
better trained, functioned in a cash economy, and wanted to live
on their own.

As a result, a revolution in teacher compensation occurred.
First, teachers began to be paid in cash on a salary basis. Second,
salaries were set for different positions in the increasingly bureaucratically organized school systems. Different pay levels were set for
elementary, middle, and high school teachers, as well as for administrators. Unfortunately, within any position, lower salaries also
were provided for women and minorities, a major inequity that
would be the focus of the next round of change.

From the widely disparate pay in the boarding 'round approach
to compensation, this system provided pay uniformity across
schools within city and even rural school systems. The pay differences by level of school reflected differences in education requirements for earning a teaching license; elementary teachers needed
only two years of post-high-school education in a "normal school,"
whereas high school teachers generally needed a full, four-year
bachelor's degree. Higher pay for administrators also reflected the
additional training for the new breed of educational managers.
The differential by gender reflected the societal norm of having
the male be the family bread winner, and unfortunately, the differential by race reflected discrimination against minorities sanctioned by society and the law.

The Single Salary Schedule

But the built-in inequities in the position-based teacher compensation structure—against minorities, women, and elementary
teachers—destined the structure for future alteration. As opposition to overt discrimination against racial minorities, females, and
education levels began to emerge even in the first part of the twentieth century and as the compensation structure developed for the
bureaucracy of the emerging industrial economy, the position-
based teacher salary schedule, which sanctioned discriminatory
treatment and differential pay for workers doing essentially the
same work, began to change—once again from the force of societal changes outside education per se.

The single salary schedule was the structure that emerged; it paid all teachers the same, regardless of level of school taught, gender, or race. In 1921, Denver, Colorado, and Des Moines, Iowa, became the first cities to implement a single salary schedule, and by 1950, nearly all urban districts had a single salary schedule as the form of teacher compensation. As the 1960s dawned and teacher unions began negotiating salary contracts for all teachers in districts, the single salary structure—which treated all teachers fairly, that is, without discrimination—received further support.

Several aspects of this compensation structure, often not recognized, should be mentioned. First, it eliminated all the overt discrimination in the previous salary structure. With a stroke of the pen, pay differentiation on the basis of gender, race, and education level was expunged from teacher pay schedules. Second, unlike most other salary structures for jobs in a bureaucracy that provided for pay increments on the basis of just years of experience, the single salary schedule provided pay increments also for education units beyond the bachelor's degree. This was politically important because although the single salary schedule included incentives for elementary and middle school teachers to earn a bachelor's degree, the units portion of the new salary schedule provided incentives for high school teachers, who had been required to have a bachelor's degree, to continue to expand their education as well as their professional expertise.

Third, the single salary schedule did not pay all teachers the same. Salaries varied. Teachers with more years of experience had higher salaries. Teachers with more education units had higher salaries. Teachers with master's degrees earned higher salaries. The structure even paid more for additional jobs; coaches earned a salary supplement, advisers of clubs and other cocurricular activities often earned a salary increment. But fourth and critical to the success of the single salary schedule, the bases for paying teachers different amounts—years of experience, education units, and different jobs— were objective, measurable, and not subject to administrative whim.

In short, although the single salary schedule eliminated the overt discrimination in the previous approach to teacher compensation, it did not, as popular rhetoric often implies, pay teachers the same. It paid teachers different amounts, but on the basis of objective measures, on which everyone could agree and which could not be contaminated by administrative or other system ineptitude.

This history identifies the major developmental stages of changes in teacher compensation, but actual salary practices in the country's thousands of school districts did not neatly follow this sequence. Urban districts began switching to the position-based structure long before many rural districts. It took thirty years for most districts to adopt the single salary schedule. And even though the single salary schedule is the dominant structure in most districts today, it too varies significantly with each district having different numbers of steps and columns and different requirements for moving across them.

Although the single salary schedule has lasted for more than fifty years—eighty years in some districts—and has many advantages (Conley and Odden, 1995), the ferment in teacher compensation during the past decades suggests that change once again might be required. If the change forces of the past are a clue to the present, transformation in the broader economy and the organization of work could portend fundamental transformation in the education system, which would then imply that change in teacher compensation should follow.

And indeed such change is affecting the country. The next section shows how changes in school organization have attempted to evolve over the past fifty years and suggests how compensation systems could have but did not change to reflect those evolutions. The following section describes more current changes in the broader economy and workplace, including alterations in pay systems, and discusses how the current education reform movement parallels these change forces outside education. The remainder of the chapter then describes the compensation implications of several education reform strategies, two of which are discussed in other chapters in this book (see Chapters 4 and 5).

Teacher Expertise as a Basis for Teacher Compensation

Compensation theory counsels policy makers on the importance of matching pay practices to the strategic needs of organizations. Although the compensation structure might not be the lead instrument for organizational change, it clearly can be designed to function as an incentive that reinforces the goals, norms, values, human resources policies and workers' roles in any organizational change that a system—either in the private or public sector—could adopt. The compensation theory literature is filled with not only these general recommendations but also suggestions for particular compensation systems that would be appropriate for different types of organization and management approaches (Lawler, 1981, 1990; Schuster and Zingheim, 1992).

Kelley (1995) has recently applied this type of organization-compensation analysis to education in the twentieth century. In an intriguing article, she described six different organizational models of schooling, from one that would fit the scientific management of the early portion of the twentieth century to the virtual school that could become part of the information economy, and for each she discussed their emphasis on organizational goals, teachers' roles, organization and management, and human resources policy. From these emphases, she then identified the type of compensation structure that would have been appropriate for each school model, in terms of the emphasis on beginning pay, seniority pay, skill-based pay, and team and organizational performance-based pay.

The article shows that in many ways the single salary schedule was appropriate for the bureaucratic organization of schools at the beginning of the century. The teachers' job was to teach a basic skills curriculum to all students. The skills needed for licensure were deemed sufficient for this task. Administrators and district leaders were responsible for district goals and management of resources. Thus, teachers were expected to implement a set curriculum under the supervision of an administrative hierarchy. Payment for years of experience was appropriate for this view of teachers. Payment for increasing the number of education units was appropriate because, originally, this was designed as an incentive for elementary teachers to earn a bachelor's degree. Since secondary teachers generally already had a bachelor's degree, the ability to earn higher salary for earning more education credits was seen as a parity incentive. Unfortunately, over time, the types of education units became disconnected with teachers' work, often providing extra salary for units that had little to do with teaching, such as preparing teachers to leave teaching for administrative positions.

Of the many fascinating findings in the paper for evolutions of school organizations after the initial bureaucracy, two are especially important for this chapter. First, the single salary schedule started to become disconnected with the hierarchical organizational form of school during the effective schools movement in the 1970s. Second, this disconnection widened in the 1980s as the education system began to change the overall curriculum to one of higher standards, and it was further exacerbated by the high-standards and high-involvement components of the 1990s education reform movement discussed later.

In all instances, there were three major, and quite similar, disconnections: a rising and expanding focus on the professional expertise needed by effective teachers, the increasing roles for teachers in school management and operations, and a growing focus on results and school outcomes. The focus on professional teacher expertise, beyond just the initial set of skills to enter teaching, began with the effective schools movement. The effective schools movement entailed developing among all teachers a generic set of pedagogical skills required to teach the basic skills (Cohen, 1983); this focus on teacher professional expertise was relatively new within education reform, which had hitherto emphasized only entry-level skills. Although teacher evaluation systems in some school districts were altered to focus on effective teaching expertise, no compensation reinforcement was provided.

The emphasis on teacher professional expertise continued into the 1980s and 1990s. The content-driven reforms of the 1980s, begun in California with changes in its curriculum frameworks (Guthrie, Kirst, and Odden, 1989) and accelerated through publication of national mathematics standards by the National Council of Teachers of Mathematics (1989), required that teachers not only learn extensive new subject matter content but also new, content-related pedagogical strategies to teach the content successfully to all students [see, for example, the entire issue of *Educational Evaluation and Policy Analysis*, 1990, *12* (3)].

Finally, the high-standards and high-involvement reforms of the 1990s not only required this curriculum and instructional knowledge of teachers, but also required a wide variety of additional expertise in order to engage successfully in the site-based management of schools. The single salary schedule was only loosely coupled to these very specific and complex skill requirements, assuming that experience and education units represented the requisite skills and knowledge.

With hindsight, it is possible to identify changes in compensation that could have buttressed these changes in school organization, teacher roles, and education goals. Salary incentives for teachers to develop the new skills and competencies required for the effective teaching for the 1980s or the new curriculum standards of the 1990s would have been possible. Additional incentives for developing the expertise needed to engage effectively in site-based management also would have been appropriate. Incentives for producing improvement in results, on a school or group but not individual teacher basis, also would have been supportive. Clearly, designing appropriate measures of individual competencies or school performance as well as designing a sound performance reward system would have been critical to the success of such innovations in teacher pay. But aside from those important design issues, the point here is that they could have been substantively justified, but they simply were inappropriate for the bureaucratically managed school of the 1950s.

In this light, restructuring in the private sector—which has included not only changes in goals, organization, and management of the workplace, but also fundamental changes in the compensation structure, including skill-based pay structure (Jenkins, Ledford, Gupta, and Doty, 1992) and group performance awards (Lawler, 1990)—could provide insight into how education could make progress on the compensation front.

Current Changes in Workplace Organization and Compensation

Dramatic changes are occurring in the broader economy today with parallel changes beginning to occur within education as well. Both, moreover, could presage change in compensation. The country's economy is undergoing change from an industrial- to an information-based system (Johnston, 1987; Osterman, 1994). As part of this evolution, changes are occurring in the organization of the workplace and in the manner in which employees are being paid. One dimension of this change, induced largely by the internationalization of the economy, is that companies are faced with pressures to improve quality, in a short time frame and often at lower costs (Lawler, 1992). Incidentally, government agencies are facing similar pressures (Osborne and Gaebler, 1992).

Although companies' responses are many and vary dramatically, there are several characteristics to the approaches being taken, many of which have similarities in current education reform. The first is an intense focus on quality or results. This is not just an emphasis on profits, either short term or long term. It is an emphasis on the quality of the service provided or product made, with the requirement that the quality must improve in quantum, not marginal, amounts. The goal is to dramatically improve quality and thus organizational performance by large amounts.

Second, companies are learning that such large increases in performance cannot be attained by improvements made within a hierarchically organized and managed system (Galbraith and Lawler, 1993; Lawler, 1992; Mohrman, 1994). As a result, many companies decide they need to restructure and reorganize to produce this new, higher level of performance. In this process, they decentralize both their organizational structure and their management systems. Increasingly, they create multifunctional work teams and give them power, authority, and autonomy to accomplish organizational goals. They also hold these teams accountable for results (Barzelay, 1992; Katzenbach and Smith, 1993; Lawler, 1986, 1992; Mohrman, 1994; Mohrman, Lawler, and Mohrman, 1992). Galbraith and Lawler (1993) have termed the overall approach, which has many dimensions but for which self-managed work teams are key, the new logic of how to organize for high performance. Odden and Odden (1995) show how these principles can be applied to education.

Third, in order to function well, teams generally recruit and develop multiple-skilled team members. The skills generally include deep expertise in the technical requirements for the tasks the team must perform, but also expertise in many additional functional areas, as well as expertise in the business skills needed to engage in self-management. New and ongoing investments in training members of the work teams—teachers in education—accompany this new focus on worker knowledge and skill.

Finally, many companies implementing decentralized approaches to management and organization also have designed new ways of compensating members of the work teams. They have learned the importance of matching pay practices to the strategic needs of their organizations (Kelley, 1995; Lawler, 1981, 1990; Lawler and

Jenkins, 1992; Schuster and Zingheim, 1992). These lessons include creating pay practices that enhance the core competencies on which organizations base their strategies. These core notions include higher performance, multiple skills and competencies, and self-management.

As a result, concepts such as skill-based pay, pay for knowledge, pay for professional expertise, collective rewards for adding value to performance, and gain-sharing characterize new compensation strategies that have been developed and used successfully in organizations outside the schools (Jenkins, Ledford, Gupta, and Doty, 1992; Lawler, 1990; Ledford, 1991; Schuster and Zingheim, 1992). In these new systems, individuals are not paid on the basis of seniority for just the job they have been hired to do because in fact they perform many jobs. They are paid on the basis of the skills and competencies they develop that enable them to perform many job tasks as members of work teams. Further, work team members often have a portion of pay that depends on the results of the team's effort in terms of organization performance. In these systems, job-based pay, seniority-based pay, and individual merit and incentive pay are out, and skill-based pay and team-based performance awards are in. In short, compensation has been changed to align itself, and the individuals in the work team, to the strategic directions and goals of the organization.

Current education reforms reflect many of these changes in the nonschool portion of the nation's economy. For example, since about 1986, with publication of the National Governors' Association (1986) *Time for Results* report, education reform has had a strong results orientation. Though not universally accepted, the results focus was reinforced by the national education goals that emerged from the 1989 Education Summit called by President George Bush, and was undergirded by the 1994 Goals 2000: Educate America Act, which was enacted in a bipartisan manner during the presidential administration of Bill Clinton and codified the national goals into federal education policy.

Current education reform also is struggling with designing the appropriate governance and management system for a results-driven education system. There have been proposals to restructure local school boards (Danzberger, Kirst, and Usdan, 1992), to decentralize education management to school sites (Committee for Economic Development, 1994), and to move to a school-based financing system (Odden, 1994). Although the bulk of site-based management strategies have been poorly and insufficiently designed (Summers and Johnson, 1994; Wohlstetter and Odden, 1992), emerging research is providing information on how both design and implementation could be improved (Mohrman and Wohlstetter, 1994; Odden and Wohlstetter, 1995; Odden, Wohlstetter, and Odden, 1995; Robertson, Wohlstetter, and Mohrman, 1995; Wohlstetter, Smyer, and Mohrman, 1994).

The multiple skill nature of the workforce and changes in compensation have not yet had as explicit parallels in the education reform agenda. Although the Coalition of Essential Schools argues for a multiple-skilled teacher workforce—essentially trading in all high school administrative and nonteaching professional staff for teachers skilled in at least two content areas as well as counseling, deaning, and other functional areas—this notion has not become a central part of either the mainstream of education reform or approaches to site-based management. Although the failed attempts to alter compensation discussed earlier reflect the ferment in compensation and the angst surrounding the current structure, explicit movements to change the nature of teacher compensation, as is occurring in many private sector organizations, is only beginning to occur in education (Cornett and Gaines, 1992).

A related phenomenon, however, has become part of education reform and could well be the trigger for more significant movement on the teacher compensation front—namely, the effort to license beginning teachers and then certify more advanced teachers on the basis of measures of professional expertise, that is, what teachers know and are able to do [Darling-Hammond, Wise, and Klein, 1995; Interstate New Teacher Assessment and Support Consortia (INTASC), 1992; National Board for Professional Teaching Standards (NBPTS), 1994; Wise and Darling-Hammond, 1987; Wise and Leibbrand, 1993]. These initiatives seek to professionalize teaching by upgrading standards for earning a beginning teaching license, which would include not only tests of knowledge about content, how students learn, and effective pedagogical practice, but also rigorous assessments of classroom practice and expertise for each individual seeking a license. With a similar assessment design, the National Board for Professional Teaching Standards would then determine whether individual teachers had developed a more advanced array of teacher knowledge, skill, competency, and classroom practice sufficient to earn Board Certification. By the end of the 1994–1995 school year, some states and local districts will provide salary increments for teachers who are certified by the National Board for Professional Teaching Standards; this policy will represent an element of skill-based pay for teachers.

As the full coterie of Board Certificates at all education levels is developed over the next five years, and as states move to license teachers on the basis of a beginning set of knowledge and skills, the country will have mechanisms that could be adapted to identify and measure several levels of teacher professional competence according to a set of written standards and a rigorous assessment system. These mechanisms, moreover, should reflect a professional approach to assessing teacher practice; the mechanisms encourage the development of advanced practice, and the processes of assessment include interaction over professional practice with local teacher teams and school faculties, then with different networks of teachers outside the home school, and, finally, with a broader, national community of expert teachers. Since the single salary schedule now allows for differential pay according to objective measures, a skill-based dimension to teacher compensation could draw on these new mechanisms to measure teacher expertise and use these measures as the basis for providing salary increments to teachers.

In sum, significant changes are occurring in the economy, in the organization and management of the workplace, and in compensation practices in organizations outside education. Within education, there are strong parallels to all these changes, although some components are not as well developed yet, and changes in compensation are only in the beginning stages. Nevertheless, the linkages between organization and compensation that are developing outside education appear to be relevant to education as well, especially the shift to a skill-based pay approach (Firestone, 1994). Care needs to be taken in adapting any of these noneducation initiatives to school settings, particularly given the co-production of education achievement discussed by Cohen in this volume. With this caution in mind, the next sections describe three different approaches to improving schools (two of which are discussed in Chapters 4 and 5 in this volume) and the compensation changes that would be consistent with them.

Motivation for Higher School Performance

Mohrman and Lawler's chapter (Chapter 4) describes generally how school organization and management can be altered to motivate teachers to become centrally and psychologically involved in reconceptualizing schools and thus designing new strategies—both instructional and organizational—that can be deployed to produce much higher levels of student performance. Based on expectancy theory, they discuss a range of organizational designs, characterized by an increasing degree of organizational change and teacher involvement, that can be used to produce increasing improvements in the performance of an organization, in this case, schools.

Three major features of their argument can be highlighted, all of them leading to potential change in teacher compensation. First, their argument focuses on the involvement of teachers, the key professionals in schools, in producing hikes in organizational results. Their purpose is to engage teachers in the issue of school-wide performance. Both intrinsic and extrinsic incentives can be designed to foster this engagement.

Second, the degree and span of teacher involvement increases as the expected degree of improvement in organizational results rises. Modest improvements might only require quality circles or suggestion involvement. The next level of improvement might entail redesigning jobs or redesigning unit, team, or house strategies. But quantum improvements in performance, such as teaching nearly all students to high standards, would require the highest level of teacher involvement and a concern with the performance of the entire school. The focus of such high involvement would entail redesigning the entire school organization, the curriculum and instruction program, the human resources strategies, the management systems, and the organizational culture and norms, which include an intense focus on results. Skills to engage in these broader tasks go far beyond curriculum and pedagogy.

Third, Mohrman and Lawler note that an important element of organizational redesign includes an altered compensation structure, which is any organization's—including a school's—formal, extrinsic reward system.

Based on contingency theory and findings from other knowledge production organizations, Mohrman and Lawler argue that broad and deep involvement of teachers in these many aspects of schools far beyond their own classrooms would likely provide substantial intrinsic rewards. The high-involvement model would provide teachers with power over the budget and the recruitment and selection of individuals to be part of the school faculty; it also would provide substantial professional development and a wide array of new information from fiscal data to student achievement data as well as community and parent satisfaction. In other organizations, the authors note, these factors function as substantial intrinsic incentives. The best teachers also are motivated by these factors (Hart, 1995).

Mohrman and Lawler also state that such a high level of teacher involvement in redesigning the school would require a range of new professional expertise that included new skills in curriculum and instruction, but also skills in management and in other functional areas usually staffed by supervisors and administrators such as professional development, curriculum development, and student counseling. Implicit in their argument is a different staffing of schools, much like the pattern in the schools described in Linda Darling-Hammond's chapter in this volume (Chapter 5), in which teachers are the primary staff and engage in multiple roles, with teaching being the core role.

A redesigned compensation system that provided incentives through a skill-based pay structure for teachers to develop the expertise to engage professionally in these multiple roles would function as an extrinsic reward for the skill needs of the new, higher-performance school. Further, a schoolwide faculty or within-school house or team performance award could also become a formal, extrinsic incentive that would reinforce the results focus of the school and the school's need to produce high levels of student performance. Put differently, a redesigned teacher compensation system that consisted of skill-based pay for curriculum, instruction, functional, and management skills, and school and team awards for increases in school performance (primarily student achievement) would align the formal, extrinsic rewards and incentives of the school with the intrinsic rewards and incentives that flowed from high involvement, organizational restructuring, and job redesign.

Restructured Schools in New York City

The restructured, learner center schools described by Linda Darling-Hammond in this volume reflect many of the general suggestions provided by Mohrman and Lawler, and can function as a specific example of how a revised teacher compensation system could undergird a successful strategy to boost school performance. The schools Darling-Hammond describes have been successful over a six- to ten-year period in producing high student achievement results, including thinking, problem solving, communication, and writing.

These schools reflect the high-involvement model (Mohrman, 1994; Odden and Wohlstetter, 1995; Wohlstetter, Smyer, and Mohrman, 1994) for decentralized management and organization, and the strategies for motivating teachers to produce high results discussed in Mohrman and Lawler's chapter. Schools have budget and personnel *power* and have dispersed power within the school through a variety of houses and teams and other small teacher decision-making groups; many of these teams, moreover, are cross-functional, thus engaging teachers in job tasks usually provided either by professional staff within schools or at the central office. The schools have an intense focus on developing a wide variety of *professional expertise* from curriculum and instruction, to cross-functional tasks and team-based decision making. The schools also have developed numerous *information* dissemination and sharing channels, both horizontally and vertically. However, although the schools have developed a variety of extrinsic and intrinsic incentives, so that they have some dimensions of the *rewards* component of the high-involvement model, they have not altered the formal, extrinsic reward: teacher salaries.

It is clear that these schools require a wide range of complex expertise from the teachers in order to function effectively. Teachers need deep knowledge of curriculum content and related pedagogy; further, because the schools use an integrated, multidisciplinary curriculum approach, most teachers also need a strong knowledge of content and pedagogy in a second subject area. Incentives for teachers to develop and use these skills could be incorporated into a revised compensation system that:

- Started teachers at a beginning salary that was competitive but provided a pay increase when they met the standards of practice required for a beginning professional in the school
- Provided pay increments for teachers who developed expertise in a second, and even third, subject area so that they could be flexibly used in the multidisciplinary approach of the school
- Provided additional pay increments for teachers who advanced their professional expertise by working toward higher than beginning standards of professional practice
- Provided a further salary increase for teachers who, over the long term, earned Board Certification from the National Board for Professional Teaching Standards

In other words, the teacher compensation structure could be altered or replaced with a skill-based structure that provided direct incentives for creating the curriculum and instructional expertise needed by all teachers. Such a compensation approach also would reinforce school investment of funds and teacher investment of time and effort in the extensive professional development that is embedded in all operations of these schools.

In addition, since the school is staffed by teachers who not only provide the instructional program, but also engage in team-based management of school operations and provide a variety of functional services such as curriculum development, professional development, student counseling, parent outreach, marketing, and recruiting, a skill-based pay structure could be expanded with a series of skill blocks for these management and decision-making tasks and these multifunctional tasks. Although the exact form of such a skill-based system could vary across each school, Mohrman, Mohrman and Odden (forthcoming) provide the outlines of one type of generic structure.

A school performance bonus, either for salary supplements for faculty or for school improvement, could also potentially enhance the operations and effectiveness of these schools. Although outside recognition of the success of these schools currently is a form of extrinsic rewards teachers now receive, a school performance bonus would have to be carefully designed in order to not diminish the intrinsic and extrinsic rewards currently operating for both teachers and students as well as to provide an additional incentive for the focus on student achievement results that currently is a norm of these schools' cultures.

Systemic Reform[3]

Systemic education reform is a broadly based, state and district strategy that seeks to link bottom-up school change, reflective of the general suggestions made by Mohrman and Lawler and the specific example of Darling-Hammond's learner-centered schools, with externally or professional set standards and assessment of results (Smith and O'Day, 1991). Systemic reform envisions fundamental change in education and how it is organized; it seeks to provide a policy context that will motivate teachers to design and implement many versions of high-performance schools. The goal is literally to raise the performance of all children to a level attained only by the top 10 percent today—a quantum improvement in performance.

More specifically, systemic education reform includes expectations that all students will perform at high levels, implementation of high-quality curriculum standards (see, for example, National Council of Teachers of Mathematics, 1989) coupled with new and revised instructional materials, use of new forms of performance assessment linked to the curriculum standards, substantially expanded professional development along with dramatically revised preservice teacher training (Little, 1993), and restructured management, governance, and school finance policy (Mohrman and Wohlstetter, 1994; Odden, 1994; Wohlstetter, Smyer, and Mohrman, 1994). In short, systemic educational reform requires (1) that teachers develop a new array of professional knowledge and skills to teach a thinking-oriented curriculum, (2) a dramatic change in the organization and management of schools that also requires new teacher expertise, and (3) focused attention on school performance and student achievement results.

Again, a redesigned compensation structure could reinforce these core dimensions of systemic reform. First, a compensation structure aligned with systemic reform could provide incentives— salary increments—for developing the knowledge and skills needed to teach new curriculum standards. Research [see, for example, Ball, Cohen, Peterson, and Wilson, (1994)] shows that although there is strong, positive local teacher response to new ambitious curriculum frameworks, teachers generally lack the knowledge and skills to implement them. This curriculum requires deeper and more conceptual understandings of content, an array of new pedagogical strategies that focus on concept development and problem solving, and a set of new sophisticated assessment expertise. Creating this new professional expertise will require substantial investment of time and energy in professional development, an element also part of systemic reform. Although enhancement of professional expertise could be reward enough for many to engage in this process (McLaughlin and Yee, 1988), a change in the compensation structure to stimulate this engagement and to reward those who develop and use such new knowledge could also be warranted.

A compensation structure aligned with systemic reform could also provide incentives to engage in effective school-based management (SBM). Engaging teachers in the management and decision processes of the schools requires yet another array of expertise. Including this expertise in a skill-based compensation structure would connect such new organization and management strategies to the compensation system. Further, we are beginning to learn more about how to design effective SBM programs. Although many efforts at decentralized management have had little success (Wohlstetter and Odden, 1992), the high-involvement management framework has been useful in distinguishing more from less effective programs; the more power, knowledge, and information are part of SBM strategies, the better they work (Odden and Odden, 1994; Odden and Wohlstetter, 1995; Robertson, Wohlstetter, and Mohrman, 1995; Wohlstetter, Smyer, and Mohrman, 1994). Changes in compensation could further strengthen these efforts, as they have in other organizations (Jenkins, Ledford, Gupta, and Doty, 1992; Lawler, 1986, 1992).

Finally, a compensation structure aligned with systemic reform could also provide rewards—incentives—for schools and faculties that produce *improvements* in educational results. Focusing on results is a central aspect of systemic reform. Although student outcomes are a complex result of individual differences and educational experiences, they also derive from educational experiences in schools. Compensation practices can focus attention on results by tying them, at least in some small but significant way, to rewards. Keep in mind that the focus would be on school performance in terms of results and not individual teacher performance. Collective awards for organization performance have been used successfully in many organizations (Lawler, 1992; Schuster and Zingheim, 1992) and offer potential for education (Richards, Fishbein, and Melville, 1993).

Summary and Research Recommendations

School organization, incentives, and teacher compensation should be closely linked. Indeed, however structured, compensation is *a,* if not *the,* major, formal extrinsic incentive in any organization, including schools. As this chapter has argued, the incentives embedded in the compensation system function best when they are aligned with the broader goals of the organization and directly reinforce them.

The chapter has argued that since mid-century and particularly for the current era of education reform, school organization and education goals have been changing in ways that could have been substantially fortified by changes in teacher compensation. Teacher compensation could have changed from the single salary schedule invented in the early part of this century, which provided salary increments based on the objective measures of years of experience and education units, to a single salary schedule, which provided salary increments based on direct, sophisticated, and professional measures of teacher knowledge, skill, and competency, and which also included performance awards that would be provided for all school faculties and teams with schools for improving schoolwide performance, with student achievement in academic subjects being the anchor performance indicator.

Such changes in compensation—skill-based pay and collective performance awards—have been developed and tried in a wide variety of nonschool organizations, including nonprofit, human service, and knowledge production organizations. Further, these compensation innovations outside education have helped improve the performance of the organization in which they have been tried, have improved the individual salaries of the individuals on the teams in those organizations, and have improved working conditions because they usually have been part of new management structures that decentralized operations to decision-making teams (Jenkins, Ledford, Gupta, and Doty, 1992; Lawler, 1990). Thus, the time seems to be ripe for redesigning the formal, extrinsic incentive in all schools: teacher compensation. Embarking on this task, though, poses many challenges and at least four categories of substantive, research issues.

Identification and Assessment of Skill Blocks

One of these issues is the nature of skill blocks that could be identified and the type of assessment system needed to determine when each teacher had mastered the competencies in the skill block and could use them successfully in the workplace. The work of the Interstate New Teacher Assessment and Support Consortia (INTASC) (1992), the PRAXIS system (a performance-based system for teacher licensure) of the Educational Testing Service, The Professional Teacher Initiative of the National Council for the Accreditation of Teacher Education, and the National Board for Professional Teaching Standards (1994) can be used to inform both of these issues, but numerous questions remain. An important task in this effort is to determine the type of content knowledge, classroom management, and pedagogical expertise needed by a range of teachers, from beginning to expert. An important hurdle in this effort will be to identify levels of professional practice that are attainable and distinguishable since the tendency is to expect beginning teachers to be as accomplished as experienced teachers (Reynolds, 1995). Another issue is whether each of these three areas of expertise would be emphasized equally at all levels. Since content knowledge is absolutely necessary to teaching subject matter, and is somewhat easier to assess, it might be argued that it could be stressed more at the beginning stages, and assessments of content knowledge could be rapidly developed and used to expand a school system's ability to provide pay increments for such an important teacher skill in the very short term.

A further issue is how skill block mastery in a new skill-based pay system would be assessed. Implicit in the preceding discussion is that many skills and competencies, particularly those related to curriculum and instruction, could be assessed externally according to national or state standards (such as those in INTASC and the NBPTS). Indeed, this is the practice of many professions, particularly those that individuals enter after earning a bachelor's degree (Kelley and Taylor, 1995). But some skill blocks could also be assessed by the local education system or school site, particularly those that pertained to the specific strategies (for example, non-graded elementary classrooms, cooperative learning, and middle school houses) chosen by a site to accomplish ambitious student achievement goals. The array of skill blocks and the mix of external and internal assessment is a large issue on which more information should be collected as districts experiment with such new forms of teacher compensation.

Still another issue is how a skill-based pay system, with several levels of distinguishable knowledge and skills, would be connected with a new licensure system, National Board Certification, tenure, as well as the recertification requirements in many states. It might easily be argued that a skill-based pay structure could be designed to replace the latter two elements in current policy. This could turn tenure into a requirement that teachers reach a level of professional practice beyond that required for licensure or lose their license. It could transform recertification from a credit-taking exercise to a process of demonstrating even higher levels of professional practice. The issue here is whether a new form of teacher compensation is simply an add-on policy to all current structures or potentially a mechanism to replace many related structures.

Performance Awards and Skill and Competency-Based Pay

The design of performance awards would need to be carefully considered, and much work is needed to identify alternative designs that work. Student achievement undoubtedly would be a core aspect of a performance award, but states and districts would need a good test to serve as the basis for such an award because research shows that organizations with such awards produce more of what is in their performance measures and less of what is not (Lawler, 1990). Ensuring that the measure pertained to all students in the school, or in houses or teams, is another issue in order not to have performance awards for individual teachers. How to measure performance, so as to ensure that the incentives function to encourage schools to boost the performance of all students and to do so each year, is another thorny issue that needs to be addressed. The standard that would qualify a school or team of teachers for the award is another issue; setting the standard as some type of rolling, historical average, so that each school is measured against past performance, is probably the most feasible. But designing the specifics is complex and will require careful attention to numerous technical issues. Finally, a stable funding pool for an effective performance award is another nontrivial topic that is critical to such a piece of compensation. The tendency in the past has been to eliminate funding when dollars are scare—a practice that erodes trust in the system and undercuts the incentive force of such a program.

How to sequence skill-based pay with a performance award is an additional topic that should be researched. Since student achievement is co-dependent on both what the teacher does and what the student does—constructivist learning requires significant student engagement, effort, and work—it could be more appropriate to implement the skill-based components of teacher compensation before a performance award (see Cohen, this volume). Some argue, moreover, that a performance award—stakes for teachers—is not appropriate unless consequences for students also are attached to test performance. Undoubtedly, practice on this issue will vary across the 15,000 school districts and 50 states in the country. Analyzing which set of practices produces the best results and why is another important topic on which more information is needed.

Since skill-based pay and group performance awards have usually accompanied decentralized, team, and high-involvement management strategies in nonschool organizations, another important research topic is the interconnections between these two initiatives in education. It could be that an important element of skill-based pay, linked primarily to the curriculum and instructional expertise needed to teach a high-standards curriculum, would provide a substantial boost to education system performance. It also could be that an even broader skill-based pay structure, which also included compensation skill blocks for functional and management skills, would be much more powerful, especially as an accompaniment to more dramatic decentralized management. The linkage between the management and organization system and the teacher compensation structure, as well as the individual and interactive effects on performance, is a further topic that should be analyzed as education moves to design and implement innovations in teacher compensation.

Process of Designing Change

The processes of designing new approaches to pay also matter. Indeed, experience in organizations outside education suggests that the design and implementation process is more important than nearly all the technical issues (Dewey, 1994; Jenkins, Ledford, Gupta, and Doty, 1992). Further, the key aspect of the design process is high involvement of the people affected—teachers in education—in design, implementation, and modification. The implication for education is that teachers, unions, administrators, school boards, and, at the state level, political leaders, will all need to be involved as equal partners in order to design any new compensation structure that can be supported by all parties. How districts and states structure the design and implementation processes could be one of the most important, short-term research priorities (Kelley and Odden, 1995).

A related issue is how the aforementioned proposals for changes in teacher compensation could affect administrator pay, as well as current staffing patterns in schools. If teachers are paid on the basis of knowledge, skill, and collective performance, could not administrators be paid that way as well? If so, what types of skill blocks should form the basis of administrator pay? Further, what types of staffing restructurings are part of decentralized school management, especially in structures that have teachers engaged in much broader school roles, and how is this reflected in new compensation design?

Contextual Influences

Finally, contextual variables that affect any of these issues need to be considered. Questions such as level and changes in resources need to be considered. Are compensation changes easier to make when resources are growing rather than declining? Do high-revenue districts have an advantage over low-revenue districts in designing compensation innovations? Can performance awards work when the funding pool for them is not legally protected, for example, in some kind of a trust fund? Further, does the legality of collective bargaining and the type of decision-making practice matter? Are compensation changes more easily made when a union is involved or when bargaining is not legal? Does joint and collegial decision making pave a better road for teacher compensation innovation, compared with hard-nosed collective bargaining or unilateral administrative decision and policy making? Do urban districts, which have a strong incentive to innovate and improve, provide a better context for engaging in the preceding far-reaching reforms, or are such changes easier in suburban or rural districts, where it might be easier to reach consensus on complex issues?

Conclusion

The time seems to be substantively ripe for reconsidering how teachers (and administrators) are paid. Current education reforms, and higher-performing school organizations, require individuals who have an array of curriculum and instructional skills far beyond those attained for initial licensure, usually also require individuals with skills to engage in a variety of nonteaching functional and managerial tasks in schools, and expect the results to dramatically boost the academic achievement of all students. These goals could be reinforced with a single salary schedule that provided pay increases on the basis of skills, knowledge, and expertise rather than years of experience and educational units, as well as bonuses for school and within school team and house performance improvements. Developing, designing, implementing, and funding such new compensation strategies raise a host of technical, substantive, financial, and political issues, all of which need to be researched over time. But it seems more than appropriate to consider the formal, extrinsic incentive in the education system—compensation—and to reconstitute it so that it reinforces the broader changes in education rather than remains as the largest expenditure of the education dollar with little direct connection with the goals of the education system.

As final comment, the country's two teacher unions are very interested in these issues. Both the American Federation of Teachers and the National Education Association have been working with the Consortium for Policy Research in Education (CPRE) and the author for the past year on these topics. The recent CPRE policy brief on revising teacher compensation (Kelley and Odden, 1995) reflect the range of topics addressed and the possibilities for dramatic change. Although the process of actual design and implementation of new teacher compensation structures will be complex and conducted state by state, and district by district, many new ideas should have general union support. If the change process is inclusive, and teachers and their unions are substantially involved in new design efforts, chances for successfully changing teacher compensation in the future should be high.

Notes

1. This chapter was supported by a grant from the U.S. Department of Education, Office of Educational Research and Improvement to the Consortium for Policy Research in Education, as well as by The Pew Charitable Trusts (both through the Pew Forum on Education Reform and the CPRE Teacher Compensation Project) and the Wisconsin Center for Education Research, School of Education, University of Wisconsin–Madison. The opinions expressed are those of the author and do not necessarily reflect the view of the U.S. Department of Education, the Office of Educational Research and Improvement, the institutional partners of CPRE, the Pew Charitable Trusts, or the Wisconsin Center for Education Research.
2. This section draws heavily on Protsik (1994).
3. This section draws on Mohrman, Mohrman, and Odden (forthcoming).

References

Ball, D. L., Cohen, D. K., Peterson, P. L., and Wilson, S. M. *Understanding State Efforts to Reform Teaching and Learning: Learning from Teachers About Learning to Teach.* Papers presented at the annual meeting of the American Educational Research Association, New Orleans, 1994.

Barzelay, M. *Breaking Through Bureaucracy: A New Way for Managing in Government.* Berkeley: University of California Press, 1992.

Cohen, M. "Instruction, Management and Organizational Issues in Effective Schools." In Odden A. and Webb L. D. (eds.): *School Finance and School Improvement: Linkages for the 1980s.* Cambridge, Mass.: Ballinger, 1983.

Committee for Economic Development. *Putting Learning First: Governing and Managing the Schools for High Achievement.* New York: CED, 1994.

Conley, S. and Odden, A. "Linking Teacher Compensation to Teacher Career Development: A Strategic Examination." *Educational Evaluation and Policy Analysis,* 1995, *17* (2), 253–269.

Cornett, L. N. and Gaines, G. F. *Focusing on Student Outcomes: Roles for Incentive Programs. The 1991 National Survey of Incentive Programs and Teacher Career Ladders.* Atlanta, Ga.: Southern Regional Education Board, 1992.

Danzberger, J. P., Kirst, M. W., and Usdan, M. D. *Governing Public Schools: New Times, New Requirements.* Washington, D.C.: Institute for Educational Leadership, 1992.

Darling-Hammond, L., Wise, A. E., and Klein, S. P. *A License to Teach: Building a Profession for 21st Century Schools.* Boulder, Colo.: Westview Press, 1995.

Dewey, B. J. "Changing to Skill-Based Pay: Disarming the Transition Landmines." *Compensation and Benefits Review,* 1994, *6* (1), 38–43.

Educational Evaluation and Policy Analysis, 1990 *12* (3) (entire issue).

Firestone, W. "Redesigning Teacher Salary Systems for Education Reform." *American Educational Research Journal,* 1994, *31* (3), 549–574.

Freiberg, J. and Knight, S. "Career Ladder Programs as Incentives for Teachers." In Conley S. C. and Cooper, B. S. (eds.): *The School as a Work Environment: Implications for Reform.* Boston: Allyn & Bacon, 1991, pp. 204–220.

Galbraith, J. R. and Lawler E. E., III. *Organizing for the Future. The New Logic for Managing Complex Organizations.* San Francisco: Jossey Bass, 1993.

Guthrie, J. W., Kirst, M. W., and Odden, A. R. *Conditions of Education in California.* Berkeley: University of California, School of Education, Policy Analysis for California Education, 1989.

Hart, A. W. "Work Feature Values of Today's and Tomorrow's Teachers: Work Redesign as an Incentive and School Improvement Policy." *Educational Evaluation and Policy Analysis,* 1995, *16* (4), 458–473.

Interstate New Teacher Assessment and Support Consortia. *Model Standards for Beginning Teacher Licensing and Development: A Resource for State Dialogue.* Washington, D.C.: Council of Chief State School Officers, 1992.

Jenkins, D., Ledford, G., Gupta, N., and Doty, H. *Skill-Based Pay: Practices, Payoffs, Pitfalls and Prescriptions.* American Compensation Association, 1992.

Johnson, S. M. "Incentives for Teachers: What Motivates, What Matters?" *Educational Administration Quarterly,* 1986, *22* (3), 54–79.

Johnston, W. *Workforce 2000.* Indianapolis: Hudson Institute, 1987.

Katzenbach, J. R. and Smith, D. K. *The Wisdom of Teams: Creating the High-Performance Organization.* Boston: Harvard Business School Press, 1993.

Kelley, C. *Teacher Compensation and Organization.* Madison: University of Wisconsin-Madison, Wisconsin Center for Education Research, Consortium for Policy Research in Education—The Finance Center, 1995.

Kelley, C. and Odden, A. *New Ideas for Reinventing Teacher Compensation.* New Brunswick, N.J.: Rutgers University, Eagleton Institute of Politics, Consortium for Policy Research in Education, Finance Brief, 1995.

Kelley, C. and Taylor, C. H. *Compensation and Skill Development in Four Professions and Implications for the Teaching Profession.* Available from the University of Wisconsin–Madison (CPRE), 1995.

Lawler, E. E. and Jenkins, G. D. "Strategic Reward Systems." In Dunnette, M. D. and Hough, L. M. (eds.): *Handbook of Industrial and Organizational Psychology,* 2nd ed., Palo Alto, Calif.: Consulting Psychologists Press, 1992, pp. 1009–1055.

Lawler, E. E., III. *Pay and Organizational Development.* Reading, Mass.: Addison-Wesley, 1981.

Lawler, E. E., III. *High-Involvement Management.* San Francisco: Jossey Bass, 1986.

Lawler, E. E., III. *Strategic Pay.* San Francisco: Jossey-Bass, 1990.

Lawler, E. E., III. *The Ultimate Advantage.* San Francisco: Jossey-Bass, 1992.

Ledford, G. "The Design of Skill-Based Pay Plans." In Rock, M. and Berger, L. (eds.): *Handbook of Compensation.* New York: McGraw-Hill, 1991.

Little, J. W. "Teachers' Professional Development in a Climate of Educational Reform." *Educational Analysis and Policy Analysis,* 1993, *15* (2), 129–152.

McLaughlin, M. and Yee, S. "School as a Place to Have a Career." In Lieberman, A. (ed.): *Building a Professional Culture in Schools* New York: Teachers College Press, 1988, pp. 23–44.

Mohrman, S. A. "High Involvement Management in the Private Sector." In Mohrman, S. A. Wohlstetter, P. (eds.): *School-Based Management: Organizing for High Performance.* San Francisco: Jossey-Bass, 1994, pp. 25–52.

Mohrman, A., Mohrman, S. A., and Odden, A. "Aligning Teacher Compensation with Systemic School Reform: Skill-Based Pay and Group-Based Performance Rewards." *Educational Evaluation and Policy Analysis,* forthcoming.

Mohrman, S. A. and Wohlstetter, P. (eds.): *School-Based Management: Organizing for High Performance.* San Francisco: Jossey-Bass, 1994.

Mohrman, S. A., Lawler E. E., III, and Mohrman, A. M., Jr. "Applying Employee Involvement in Schools." *Education Evaluation and Policy Analysis.* 1992, *14* (4), 347–360.

Murnane, R. J. and Cohen, D. K. "Merit Pay and the Evaluation Problem: Why Some Merit Pay Plans Fail and a Few Survive." *Harvard Educational Review,* 1986, *56* (1), 1–17.

National Board for Professional Teaching Standards. *National Board Certification: Principles of Successful Implementation.* Detroit: National Board for Professional Teaching Standards, 1994.

National Commission on Excellence in Education. *A Nation at Risk: The Imperative for Educational Reform.* Washington, D.C.: U.S. Government Printing Office, 1983.

National Council of Teachers of Mathematics. *Curriculum and Evaluation Standards for School Mathematics.* Reston, Va.: National Council of Teachers of Mathematics, 1989.

National Governors' Association. *Time for Results.* Washington, D.C.: National Governors' Association, 1986.

Odden, A. "Decentralized Management and School Finance." *Theory Into Practice,* 1994, *33* (2), 104–111.

Odden, A. and Odden, E. *Applying the High Involvement Framework to Local Management of Schools in Victoria, Australia.* Paper presented at the annual meeting of the American Educational Research Association, New Orleans, 1994.

Odden, A. and Odden, E. *Educational Leadership for America's Schools.* New York: McGraw-Hill, 1995.

Odden, A., Wohlstetter, P., and Odden, E. "Key Issues in Effective School-Based Management." *School Business Affairs,* 1995, *61* (5), 4–16.

Odden, E. and Wohlstetter, P. "Strategies for Making School Based Management Work." *Educational Leadership,* 1995, *52* (5), 32–36.

Osborne, D. and Gaebler, T. *Reinventing Government.* Reading, Mass.: Addison-Wesley, 1992.

Osterman, P. "How Common Is Workplace Transformation and Who Adapts It?" *Industrial and Labor Relations Review,* 1994, *47* (2), 173–188.

Protsik, J. *History of Teacher Pay and Incentive Reforms.* Paper prepared for the Conference on Teacher Compensation, Washington, D.C., November 2–4, 1994.

Reynolds, A. "The Knowledge Base for Beginning Teachers: Education Professionals' Expectations versus Research Findings on Learning to Teach." *Elementary School Journal,* 1995, *95* (3), 199–221.

Richards, C., Fishbein, D., and Melville, P. "Cooperative Performance Incentives in Education." In Jacobson, S. L. and Berne, R. (eds.): *Reforming Education: The Emerging Systemic Approach.* Thousand Oaks, Calif.: Corwin Press. 1993, pp. 28–47.

Robertson, P. J., Wohlstetter, P., and Mohrman, S. "Generating Curriculum and Instructional Innovations Through School-Based Management." *Educational Administration Quarterly,* 1995, *31* (3), 375–404.

Rosenholtz, S. J. "Effective Schools: Interpreting the Evidence." *American Journal of Education,* 1985, *93* (3), 352–388.

Rosenholtz, S. J. *Teachers' Workplace: The Social Organization of Schools.* New York: Longman, 1989.

Schlechty, P. C. "Career Ladders: A Good Idea Going Awry." In Sergiovanni, T. J. and Moore, J. H. (eds.): *Schooling for Tomorrow: Directing Reforms to Issues That Count.* Boston: Allyn & Bacon, 1989, pp. 356–376.

Schuster, J. R. and Zingheim, P. *The New Pay: Linking Employee and Organizational Performance.* New York: Lexington Books, 1992.

Smith, M. S. and O'Day, J. "Systemic School Reform." In Fuhrman, S. and Malen, B. (eds.): *The Politics of Curriculum and Testing.* Bristol, Pa.: Falmer Press, 1991, pp. 233–267.

Summers, A. A. and Johnson, A. W. *A Review of the Evidence on the Effects of School Based Management Plans.* Presented at the Conference on Improving the Performance of America's Schools: Economic Choices. Board of Science, Technology and Economic Policy, National Research Council, National Academy of Sciences, Washington, D.C., 1994.

Wise, A. and Leibbrand, J. "Accreditation and the Creation of a Profession of Teaching." *Phi Delta Kappan,* 1993, *75* (2), 133–136.

Wise, A. and Darling-Hammond, L. *Licensing Teachers: Design for a Profession.* Santa Monica, Calif.: RAND Corporation, 1987.

Wohlstetter, P. and Odden, A. R. "Rethinking School-Based Management Policy and Research." *Educational Administration Quarterly,* 1992, *28* (4), 529–549.

Wohlstetter, P., Smyer, R., and Mohrman, S. A. "New Boundaries for School-Based Management: The High Involvement Model." *Educational Evaluation and Policy Analysis,* 1994, *16* (3), 268–286.

Chapter Eight

Teaching to New Standards

Richard J. Murnane and Frank Levy

In June 1994, 125 Vermont public school teachers drove to Johnson State College, 40 miles north of Ben and Jerry's ice cream factory, to spend 5 days at "Camp Portfolio." As at most camps, the first day was devoted to orientation. But at Camp Portfolio this did not mean finding out where the swimming pool and volley ball courts were located. Instead, the teachers practiced scoring the mathematics and writing work of Vermont fourth and eighth graders to develop skill in grading with common standards. The thirty fourth-grade teachers scoring the mathematics work of Vermont fourth graders spent the first day evaluating student responses to problems like the Magic Rings described in Exhibit 8.1.

The Magic Rings problem differs from the simple computation problems typically included on tests of American elementary school students' mathematics skills. Instead of requiring only computations, solving the Magic Rings problem requires figuring out what is asked and designing an analysis strategy—a lot to ask of a fourth grader, but much closer to the skills required for success in today's economy than computational speed and accuracy. Not only did the Magic Rings problem differ from conventional tests, the method of scoring it also differed. Instead of determining simply whether the student wrote down the correct answer, the teachers at Camp Portfolio evaluated the quality of the student's work in seven dimensions, four of which concerned problem-solving skills, and the other three, communication skills. In each dimension, the teacher assigned a grade ranging from 1 to 4 based on standards described in the rating scale provided in Table 8.1. Exhibit 8.2 reproduces one of the student responses that the teachers were asked to evaluate.

Exhibit 8.1. Magic Rings Problem.

1994 Vermont Uniform Assessment
Mathematics Part 2: Problem
Grade 4

MAGIC RINGS

It's your birthday. You have just turned 9 years old. Your present is three boxes of magic rings. The instruction book that goes with the rings says:

- You can wear no more than ten rings at a time.

- Once a ring is worn, it loses its power.

Contents: 10 rings	Contents: 10 rings	Contents: 10 rings
Blue Rings	**Green Rings**	**Yellow Rings**
Each blue ring doubles your age.	Each green ring adds 5 years to your age.	Each yellow ring takes 2 years away from your age.

You put some rings on your finger and start to grow at once. Within seconds, the magic works and you are 40 years old. Your two friends, also fourth graders, do the same thing. All of you are now 40 years old.

Which rings are each of you wearing?

Before you begin working, take some time to think about the problem and how you will come up with a solution. Because there are lots of different ways these friends could wear the rings, you won't be able to find all of them in the time allowed. Show as many as you think you need to support your solution.

Show all of your work, including scratch work, and write your complete solution in the response booklet. You can put charts, tables, graphs or drawings on the lined pages or on the dot page.

In your solution be sure to include the following:

- Factors you thought might affect the solution to the problem
- How you solved the problem
- Reasons for decisions you made along the way
- Anything you discovered as you solved the problem
- Accurate, appropriate mathematical language
- Accurate, appropriate representation

Then Check...

- Did I answer the question?
- Will someone who reads my solution know how I solved this problem and the reason for my decisions?

Table 8.1 Fourth-Grade Math Portfolio.

	RATING				Rating
	Level 1	Level 2	Level 3	Level 4	
PS1 Understanding the Problem	. . . didn't understand enough to get started or make progress.	. . . understood enough to solve part of the problem or to get part of a solution.	. . . understood the problem.	. . . identifies special factors that influenced the approach before starting the problem.	
PS2 How You Solved the Problem	. . . approach didn't work.	. . . approach would lead to solving part of the problem.	. . . approach would work for the problem.	. . . approach was efficient or sophisticated.	
PS3 Why - Decisions Along the Way	. . . no reasoning is evident from the work or reasoning is incorrect.	. . . only partly correct reasoning or correct reasoning used for only part of the problem.	. . . didn't clearly explain reasons for decisions, but work suggests correct reasoning used throughout the problem.	. . . clearly explained the reasons for the correct decisions made throughout the problem.	
PS4 So What - Outcomes of Activities	. . . solved the problem and stopped.	. . . solved the problem and made comments about something in the solution.	. . . solved the problem and connected the solution to other math OR described a use for what was learned in the "real world."	. . . solved the problem and made a general rule about the solution or extended the solution to a more complicated situation.	
C1 Mathematical Language	. . . didn't use any math vocabulary, equations, or notations, or used them incorrectly.	. . . used basic math words or basic math notation correctly.	. . . went beyond occasional use of basic math language and used the language correctly.	. . . relied heavily on sophisticated math language to communicate the solution.	
C2 Mathematical Representation	. . . didn't use any graphs, tables, charts, models, diagrams or drawings to communicate the solution.	. . . attempted to use appropriate representation.	. . . used appropriate math representation accurately and appropriately.	. . . used sophisticated graphs, tables, charts, models, diagrams, or drawings to communicate the solution.	
C3 Presentation	. . . response is unclear.	. . . response contains some clear parts.	. . . if others read this response, they would have to fill in some details to understand the solution.	. . . response is well organized and detailed.	

Exhibit 8.2. Student Answer to Magic Rings Problem.

MATHEMATICS: PART 2

Grade 4

Begin working your problem here. Be sure to show all of your work, including scratch work.

I got my answer by first doubling their age twice then I decide I shouln't double that age because it was 36 and if I did I would have been over 40. So I added 5 and that was 41 so I decided to subtract 2 which means using a yellow ring and age After that I added 5 and then got 44 39 Subtacted two and got 42 did that again and got 40 Each child had the Same pattern of rings. They each had 7 rings on their fingers which meant all together they only used 28 rings All together they used 6 blue rings, 6 green rings and 9 yellow rings. You could use this in real life if you had a magic set that had rings and they did a certian thing and you could only →

Continue on next page if needed.

Exhibit 8.2. Student Answer to Magic Rings Problem, Cont'd.

MATHEMATICS: PART 2
(continued)

Be sure to show all of your work, including scratch work.

use so many of them!

Continue on next page if needed.

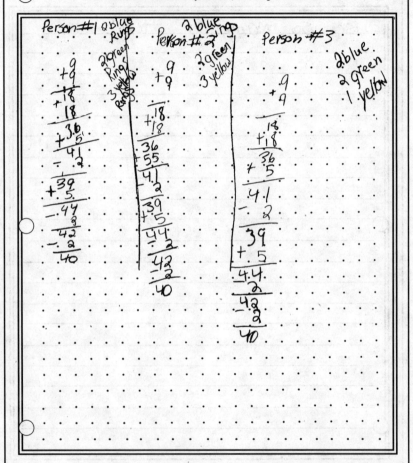

Exhibit 8.2. Student Answer to Magic Rings Problem, Cont'd.

MATHEMATICS: PART 2
(continued)

You may use this page to continue your work or for a table, chart, graph or drawing.
Be sure to show all of your work, including scratch work.

Continue on next page if needed.

After considerable arguing, the fourth-grade teachers agreed with Jill Rosenblum, the leader of the group and one of the committee that had assigned the benchmark grades, on the appropriate scores for the student answer. The response merited a grade of 3 for understanding the problem (PS1), developing an approach (PS2), and showing work that suggested appropriate reasoning for solving the problem (PS3). The grade for "So What" (PS4) was 2, reflecting the judgment that this child demonstrated the ability to make observations. The score was not a 3 because the child, like most Vermont students, had not developed significant skill in forming generalizations from particular problems. The grades for mathematical language (C1) and presentation (C3) were 3, reflecting consistent use of arithmetic terms, inclusion of a running total in the answer, and providing a relatively clear presentation. The grade for mathematical presentation (C2) was 1, reflecting the lack of diagrams, charts, tables, or drawings in the answer. Scoring the quality of presentation reflects the concern of Vermont educators that the state's students not only learn to solve problems, but also learn to communicate their problem-solving strategies clearly.

Throughout the first day at Camp Portfolio, the teachers argued about their evaluations of students' work. Often heated, the discussions focused on what constitutes good communication and problem-solving skills, how first-rate work differs from less adequate work, and what types of problems elicit the best student work. In essence, the discussions were about *standards*.

The last four days of Camp Portfolio were spent scoring the writing and mathematics work in the portfolios submitted by approximately 2000 Vermont fourth- and eighth-grade students chosen randomly from Vermont's 60 supervisory unions (geographic groupings of small school districts; each union has a single superintendent). Each portfolio consisted of five to seven pieces representing the writing or mathematics that a student had worked on during the school year.

Why did the teachers come to Camp Portfolio? They didn't come because it was a vacation—the teachers started scoring at 8:45 A.M. and finished at supper time on the short days and at 9:00 P.M. on the longer days. They didn't come because the accommodations were luxurious—the teachers slept two or three to a room in Spartan-like dormitories and made up their own beds. The $500 each participant received for the five days—not an enormous sum, but a significant supplement to modest Vermont teacher salaries—was an incentive. Most came, however, because it was a chance to talk with colleagues teaching the same subjects, to collect new problems to use in their classrooms, to see the work of other Vermont students, to get new ideas, and to develop more skill in evaluating how their own students' work measured up to the state standards. In the words of Deborah Armitrage, a forty-five-year-old fourth-grade teacher from a rural district in northeast Vermont, "Through the scoring I find my own personal weaknesses in what I am doing with my children. By seeing so many portfolios and listening to Jill (the leader of the fourth grade math scorers) I find lots of avenues that I can bring back to my children." Given the dismal reputation of professional development for teachers, the discussions among teachers at Camp Portfolio were remarkable. They focused on the quality of student work as measured against external standards. The standards concerned the extent to which students had mastered critical elements of the New Basic Skills.

For the Vermont State Department of Education, Camp Portfolio is part of a program to provide Vermont citizens, taxpayers, and businesses with information about the skills of Vermont students. The student scores provide the basis for reports entitled *Vermont Assessment Program: Summary of Assessment Results* and *The Condition of Education in Vermont,* which the Department makes public each fall. The first report describes the quality of Vermont fourth- and eighth-graders' work in seven dimensions for mathematics and five for writing, and compares the scores to those of the previous year.[1] The second report provides information on the mathematics proficiency of fourth and eighth graders in each supervisory union—information that parents, taxpayers, and businesses can use in evaluating the adequacy of public education.

This chapter is very much about incentives, especially about the incentives that portfolio assessments provide for individual teachers to alter their teaching practices. The chapter also touches on incentives for students—a topic emphasized by Arthur Powell (Chapter 2) and by David Cohen (Chapter 3) in this volume.

This chapter is also about the tension between using a single assessment system both to promote instructional improvement *and* to promote accountability. We show how Vermont educators struggled with this tension, which is present in every state educational reform effort. The chapter also illustrates the tension between designing an assessment system that provides incentives for, say, fourth-grade mathematics teachers in different schools to learn from each other and an assessment system that provides incentives for teachers in the same school to work together to develop a comprehensive educational program. The importance of incentives for teachers in the same school to work together is emphasized in the chapters in this volume by Linda Darling-Hammond (Chapter 5) and by Susan Mohrman and Edward Lawler (Chapter 4).

Finally, this chapter illustrates several themes described in Brian Rowan's chapter (Chapter 6) about standards. One of these themes is the importance of developing standards that are congruent with teachers' values, and a second is the importance of providing teachers with opportunities to develop the skills needed to teach to new standards.

How Portfolio Assessment Came to Vermont

Until the late 1980s, no chronicler of educational reform would have devoted much attention to Vermont. Local control has always been important in the state, and each of Vermont's 279 school districts values its independence. The State Department of Education, located on two floors of the modest-sized State Office Building across from the State Capitol, historically has not been a potent force pushing for changes in local educational practices—especially when contrasted to New York, with its century-long tradition of an activist State Department of Education.

During the 1980s, the situation in Vermont began to change. Madeline Kunin, the reform-minded governor, convinced the legislature to double the amount of aid the state provided to local school districts. The need to defend the tax increase led legislators to ask, what is the money buying? The governor's response was that the money would buy better education.

Ross Brewer, the Director of Planning and Policy Development for the State Department of Education from 1983 to 1993, played a key role in developing the portfolio assessment system. A jovial ex-academic who decided that staying in Vermont provided a better life than academic tenure elsewhere, Brewer described his position as the best job in state government—even though his hair turned prematurely grey during his years in state government. He described the need to develop an accountability system: "Madeline would say [to educators], 'we're going to give you lots more, but then we're going to come back to you and ask you what we got for our money.' So . . . the Governor was very interested in pointing out to people that accountability was going to be part of this."

In 1987, Richard P. Mills became the Vermont State Commissioner of Education. Tall and thin, with an M.B.A. and a doctorate in Education from Columbia, Mills moved to Vermont from New Jersey, where he had served as Governor Thomas Kean's liaison to other states on educational reform issues.

Deeply committed to improving education in Vermont, Mills knew that the mandate to develop an accountability system was both an opportunity and a danger. The opportunity came from the potential to affect teaching and learning. From his previous work in educational policy, Mills knew that the states and the federal government had tried a variety of strategies to improve the nation's schools, including new curricula, compensatory education, training for teachers, team teaching, open classrooms—the list is almost endless. Although many of these reform efforts evoked creative responses from some teachers, none led to widespread, sustained changes in what teachers and children do in classrooms. In fact, it often seems that the day-to-day interactions of teachers and students in classrooms—what ultimately determines what students learn in school—are remarkably insulated from public education policies.

An exception has been accountability systems. Using student scores on prescribed tests to make judgments about the quality of education provided in particular schools or school districts has evoked changes in what happens in classrooms. This is why the legislature's and the governor's mandate that Mills develop an accountability system provided an opportunity to improve the quality of public education in Vermont.

The danger came from the evidence that teachers' responses to the types of tests used in accountability systems to date had not increased the likelihood that students mastered the New Basic Skills. For example, the National Science Board attributes the decline in American students' problem-solving skills during the

1980s to the increased use of minimum competency tests for determining student promotions and eligibility for high school graduation. The testing led teachers to focus instruction on the computational skills that were given great weight on the test, and to neglect problem-solving skills because they received little weight on the tests.[2] Students' computational skills did rise during the 1980s, but these skills are not enough to obtain access to a middle-class job today.

The difficult question for Mills was whether it was possible to design an accountability system that would improve the teaching experienced by Vermont's children. Mills did not know for sure, but he believed that the way to start looking for the answer was to talk with Vermonters concerned with public education. Mills and Ross Brewer spent much of 1988 talking with Vermont educators, parents, and businesspeople in a search for ideas about accountability that could command widespread support. In Brewer's words:

> . . . we knew we needed to have some kind of assessment system in place so that people would know how Vermont kids were doing . . . We spent the summer of '88 having dinner with people . . . we had six dinners around the state, and we invited teachers and principals and superintendents and Board members and journalists and legislators and business people, about 25 people at each dinner, and we asked them, what do you want to know about what kids are doing in schools? What do you want to know about your schools? How do you think we ought to find out about that? And . . . what would you do with the information?

> One of the really funny stories was that at each of these meetings we asked people, do you do standardized testing? And everybody did standardized testing. Now, there's no state testing program so it wasn't the State, they were all local tests, and so we'd ask teachers, well, you do standardized testing, how do you use the information? And they would say, we don't. And so we would say, well then why do you do it? And they'd say, because the principal makes us. So then we turn to the principal or two or three principals at this meeting and say, why do you do standardized testing, why do you make the teachers do it? They say it upsets their classes . . . it doesn't give them information they use. Well, we do it because the superintendent thinks we ought to. So then you turn to the superintendent or two superintendents who are at this meeting

and say, well, let me see, the principal doesn't use the information and the teacher doesn't use the information, so why are you using standardized testing? Well, because the community expects it. So then you turn to a Board member and you say, well, let me see, the superintendent doesn't really use the information, the principal doesn't use the information, the teacher doesn't use the information, everybody's doing standardized testing, why do they do it? Well, we don't know. The superintendent comes in once a year, gives us a half hour report, tells us our kids are above average and that things are okay. So everybody was doing standardized testing, nobody knew why they were doing it. That was one of the things that really came out of these meetings that was really very interesting.

Mills' and Brewer's discussions with Vermonters also made clear that teachers disliked the tests. Because the tests were not closely related to the schools' instructional goals, students' scores did not provide a fair assessment of students' mastery of what they had been taught or of the quality of teaching. Moreover, time spent taking the tests reduced the time available to work on the curriculum.

Mills and Brewer also heard from employers concerns about the skills of the state's high school graduates. Given the very low unemployment rate in the state, employers were sometimes forced to hire graduates who did not write well or did not have good problem-solving skills. Moreover, employers found it difficult to get information from the schools about students' academic performances.

These many conversations with groups concerned about Vermont public education led Mills and Brewer to the conclusion that the state needed new methods of assessing students' skills. As Brewer put it:

> . . . there was just the accumulation of pieces. There was the pressure on the one hand, from the Legislature and the Governor and there was . . . what we learned about standardized testing, plus all the horror stories were coming out about standardized testing . . . about how it affects instruction and narrows the curriculum and so on, and all of that stuff, the Lake Woebegone stuff was beginning to emerge . . . and then there was this stuff that we heard from people. And there was Rick asking us to step back and take another look at . . . the direction that we thought we might go in. So all of those pieces came together to . . . bring us to the point where we decided we would try this portfolio assessment program.

In October 1988, Rick Mills proposed to the State Board of Education the development of a new system of measuring student performance, based in part on portfolios reflecting the work that students did during the school year.[3] The portfolios would be collections of the students' best work. One goal of the system was to respond to the legislator's desire for accountability measures. But this was not the only goal. As Mills explained to the State Board of Education and the legislature, he was determined that portfolio assessment also:

- Avoid the distortions of educational practice that conventional test-based accountability induced.
- Encourage good educational practice and provide a focus for the professional development of educators.
- Encourage local initiative in developing curricula and approaches to teaching.
- Provide a common high standard for all students.
- Encourage greater equity in educational opportunity.[4]

Mills and Brewer made clear to the State Board of Education that the development of new methods of student performance would be an expensive and time-consuming process. As Brewer put it, "there are no smart people to copy on this one." It was a useful investment, they argued, because the new assessments would not only provide better information about the skills of Vermont students; more important, they would be a vehicle for improving public education in the state. The State Board of Education approved the proposal, and initiated five years of intense activity involving large numbers of Vermont educators.

Developing the New Assessment System

Early in the discussions about developing a new assessment system, Rick Mills and Ross Brewer decided it should focus on writing and mathematics. The attraction of writing was that most schools in the state had already introduced "process writing," an approach that emphasized multiple drafts and peer criticism of early drafts. Implementation of the process writing curriculum had necessitated questioning the goals of writing and the appropriate standards for judging writing—both issues critical to the development of new assessment strategies.

Mills and Brewer were also aware that the National Council of Teachers of Mathematics (NCTM) was in the final stages of publishing a report that would describe the mathematical skills American children should have at each grade level, and would provide examples of problems students should be able to solve to demonstrate these skills.[5] The promise of the NCTM "Standards" report would give Vermont educators a framework for determining goals for students' mathematical skills and ways of assessing these skills.

As Brewer described the decision to focus on writing and mathematics:

> . . . the Vermont writing program had been in place a long time. There were a lot of people who were familiar with keeping kids' work in folders in writing. We thought that Vermont kids might actually look pretty good in writing because they had this experience, and that it was important to have some kind of success early in the program . . . on the other hand, we were fairly convinced that if we assessed mathematics in an authentic fashion that performance would be pretty poor, and . . . we wanted to balance a poor performance with a good performance . . . we knew that there would be some kind of help that we could get in terms of developing an authentic mathematics assessment from NCTM. . . . So it was a combination of knowing that there was huge need for improvement and at the same time knowing that at least in this area we could probably find some help.

Initially, Mills suggested that statewide assessments be developed first for students in grades four and eleven, but he changed this on the advice of a panel of employers appointed by the Vermont Business Roundtable to review the portfolio assessment proposal. In his words:

> [The panel] suggested one really significant change. I had proposed that we have a fourth grade assessment and an eleventh grade, I really wanted four, eight, and 11, couldn't afford it, and so I said, well, we'll take a look at the beginning and look at the end . . . their view was that wasn't smart, that we should go four and eight and then phase in to the high school. And I said, [that] makes sense . . . we'll do that, and then [the panel] very clearly let the word get out that [the portfolio assessment plan] was a good idea.

From the beginning, teachers liked Mills's idea that student portfolios would play a central role in the new assessment system. An attraction was that portfolios seemed likely to promote good teaching. The process of building portfolios would promote classroom dialogue about standards for good work. The requirement that portfolios include multiple drafts of writing products would encourage students to revise work and examine whether they were making progress, and why. Portfolio assessment would also provide opportunities for students to evaluate each other's work and develop the facility to describe strengths and weaknesses. Students could explain to peers why they chose particular strategies and defend the value of their approaches. In other words, the goals of portfolios were to help students develop high standards for their work and that of others, to appreciate the value of sticking with particular projects until the products improved, and to develop the facility to work productively in groups. These are all skills of increasing importance in the labor market.

Once the commitment was made to move toward an assessment system in which portfolios of student work would play a major role, a host of practical questions arose. Must the writing portfolios include examples of particular types of writing, for example, letters or essays? Must the mathematics portfolios for a particular grade level include students' solutions to the same problems? What criteria would be used for assessing the quality of students' work in writing and mathematics? What should the scoring system be? Who would do the scoring? Who would have access to the assessment scores—parents? employers? taxpayers? Answers to these and many other questions had to be resolved while developing and implementing the new system of student assessment.

Decisions about how the assessment system would work in practice were complicated by the advice of experts on assessment. They pointed out that the design that would best fulfill one of Vermont's objectives, improving teaching, would be quite different from the design that would provide the most reliable evidence about the skills of the state's students. To stimulate exciting classroom discussions about standards for good writing, teachers should be free to choose topics for writing assignments that interested them and their students. This would produce writing portfolios in which student essays dealt with very different topics. It would be difficult to score these essays in a consistent manner. Having all students write about the same topic would probably result in more reliable scoring, but this would reduce teachers' discretion in organizing instruction.

Recognizing that the new assessment system would be a success only if the state's teachers felt that it contributed to educational improvement, Mills decided to have teachers play a central role in the design of the system. This signaled that promoting good teaching was his first priority, even if this created problems in providing reliable evidence on student performance. This decision reflected adherence to a principle emphasized in the chapters by Rowan and by Mohrman and Lawler, namely, that standards for student performance will enhance school effectiveness only if they are valued by teachers.

In Ross Brewer's words:

> . . . from the very beginning our commitment was, it's got to be teachers who do this because they're the ones who come out of the classroom, and they're the ones who know what the challenges are . . . they were not typical teachers, but they were teachers, and I'm convinced that that's what made the difference. I think that if the [State] Department [of Education] had come or if we had brought experts up from Harvard the thing would have gone right down the tube . . . it wouldn't have had any credibility, and probably wouldn't have resonated with what teachers really needed.

The committees of teachers chosen to design the assessment system faced a near-Herculean task. All were skilled teachers, but none had an extensive background in testing and measurement. As Marge Petit, a tall, lively middle-school teacher who emerged as a leader of the mathematics committee, described the challenge: "We knew about assessment in our classrooms, but we didn't know assessment . . . from a psychometric [perspective]." Despite the daunting nature of the task, the mathematics committee produced an operational plan for an assessment system in time for piloting in the 1991–1992 school year.[6] (A similar development effort produced the assessment system for writing.) The assessment comprised three parts: best pieces of student work, whole portfolios of student work, and student responses to a common mathematics examination administered to all students in a particular grade level in the state. Teachers were asked to include the five to seven best pieces of students' work on puzzles, applications, and investigations. The Teacher's Guide[7] explained that puzzles are tasks that require students to identify and explore approaches to nonroutine problems like the Magic Rings. Applications require students to apply knowledge they already possess. Investigations include explorations and analysis that leads to conclusions. Although teachers were given guides that included examples of each type of task, they were free to choose the tasks that their students worked on for their portfolios.

The goal of the "best pieces" part of the assessment was to assess problem-solving abilities and communication skills. The whole portfolios of student work would provide a picture of the work students did during the school year. The scores on the uniform test would indicate understanding of particular concepts and could link the performance of Vermont students with those of students in other states.

In addition to determining the composition of the assessment, teachers also developed "rubrics"—procedures for scoring student work. Instead of giving each student's best pieces a single grade, the subcommittee concerned with scoring criteria chose a multidimensional scoring system designed to provide detailed information about the strengths and weaknesses of each student's work. Each of the best pieces that a student submitted would be graded in the seven dimensions described in Table 8.1, four of which related to problem solving and three to communications. The grades on a particular dimension would be averaged among the best pieces producing a total of seven grades, one for each dimension. The committee decided not to average scores across dimensions, arguing that this would reduce the quality of the information that the assessment would provide. For example, a student might devise a clever analytic strategy but communicate it poorly. Averaging a high score with a low score would conceal that the student's work had important strengths as well as significant weaknesses.

As the committee's work on developing the mathematics assessment system proceeded, it became clear that the emphasis on problem solving and communication would require significant changes in the practices of most of the state's teachers. Typical instructional strategies—teacher explanations followed by students completing work sheets and completing the exercises in the back of mathematics textbooks—would not develop the problem-solving skills and communications skills that were central in the new assessment system. As Marge Petit described the problem:

> . . . problem-solving in mathematics prior to this was, Dick and Jane went to the store, and they had 10 bucks, and . . . then they bought X and Y and what do you have left? And so there was huge training that had to take place, and so that first summer we started with summer institutes. . . . We tried our best in those summer institutes to model the type of problem-solving that should occur in the classroom, and some of the things we did . . . were good. [But] we knew that the institutes weren't enough and we all knew that what teachers need was consistent help over time.

One of the first people to point out the need for ongoing help was Jill Rosenblum, a young fourth-grade math teacher in Stratford, Vermont, whose school participated in the piloting of the new assessment system:

> I won't say I complained a lot, but I talked a lot about the need for professional development because not only were they, at that time it was they, asking people to change the way they assess students' work, they were also asking for some pretty dramatic changes in instruction. . . . As a pilot teacher I was making a fair amount of noise about that.

Ross Brewer found Jill Rosenblum's complaints compelling and was impressed by her ideas for providing ongoing professional development. He persuaded her to leave her teaching position and to design a system of ongoing professional development to improve the mathematics teaching of the state's fourth- and eighth-grade teachers. In this way, Jill became part of the "they" who were attempting to use portfolio assessment to improve the teaching in Vermont schools.

The system of professional development that Jill and her colleagues designed is based on the idea of a network. Each school is part of one of seventeen networks, and the fourth- and eighth-grade teachers in each network meet for training four times a year. Most networks have four leaders, one for each subject for each of the grades where the assessments are done. The network leaders not only lead the training session, but also provide ongoing support to the teachers in their network. As Jill describes the system:

> I am the trainer's trainer, and the trainers themselves are all classroom teachers, and that was the design, to take classroom practitioners who were having some success, give them more tools to have more success, give them training and professional development, and then they lead a series of local meetings to provide training to their colleagues. So that's what my job is, basically, to train those leaders and to develop the materials that they use to train other teachers.

It is through the network training and the summer institutes that Rick Mills is trying to provide Vermont teachers with the skills to help children do well on the new assessments.

High Stakes or Low Stakes?

A controversial question that surfaced early in discussions about portfolio assessment in Vermont concerned the uses of the scores. At one extreme was the possibility of devising high-stakes consequences, for example, making teachers' salaries or even their jobs depend on the results. At the other extreme was the possibility of not reporting results for particular school districts at all. (In Vermont, most school districts have only one elementary school and one middle school; thus, reporting results by school district means reporting results by school.) Even though there were advocates for each of these polar possibilities, Mills and Brewer rejected both alternatives. They recognized that high-stakes consequences would alienate teachers and jeopardize their most important goal: improving teaching in Vermont's public schools. On the other side, the legislature and the Business Roundtable supported the new assessment system in part because it was billed as promoting accountability. Retaining this support required at least the reporting of information about the performances of students in particular school districts. Moreover, making public district-specific scores would act as a spur to those principals and teachers who would prefer not to implement portfolio assessments.

In searching for a middle ground between high stakes and no stakes, Mills and Brewer proposed that the State Department of Education provide each community with a report describing the distribution of scores for the students in their public schools. The report would begin with a description of the community, its schools, and its students. Information about the community would include household income, educational attainments of adult residents, and property values. School data would include per pupil spending, student–teacher ratios, and the percentage of faculty participating in assessment-related professional development activities. Similarly, student data would include the percentages of students in special education, in compensatory education, and in preschool programs. Every table would include not only information about the community, its schools, or its students, but also the analogous information for the state as a whole. The purpose was to provide readers with a basis for judging how the community compared to the state. For example, residents in a relatively affluent, well-educated community that spent an above-average amount of money on public schools would be primed to expect relatively high scores for students in their schools.[8]

The report would then provide results on the distribution of portfolio assessment scores for the students in the community's public schools. The data would include separate distributions of scores for each of the seven dimensions in which mathematics portfolios were graded and the five dimensions in which writing portfolios were graded. To facilitate comparison, the same information would be provided for the state as a whole, and for a sample of similar communities in the state.

Would the publication of these community reports be a low-stakes or high-stakes use of the assessment scores? Clearly the answer depends on the responses of residents. If they are not interested in the results, the stakes would be low. If their response is to demand dramatic changes in the schools, the stakes could be quite high. In typical Vermont fashion, Mills and Brewer saw their job not as determining what the stakes should be, but as providing local communities with good information about the skills of students and letting the communities decide how to use this information.

Reliability of the Portfolio Scoring

Not only do most school districts in Vermont have only one elementary school, a great many have only one fourth-grade class and one eighth-grade class. Consequently, reporting portfolio scores by school district means reporting the scores of the students who worked with individual teachers. Understandably, this has been a concern for many Vermont teachers. Some teachers fear that students' scores might reflect the grading practices of individual scorers more than they reflected the skills of their students. To allay these fears, Mills agreed that no scores would be reported by school district until there was evidence that the teachers doing the scoring had succeeded in adopting quite uniform grading standards—in technical terms, until interrater reliability was high.

To learn about the reliability of the portfolio scoring, Mills asked the Rand Corporation to conduct an independent review of the Vermont portfolio assessment system and to examine the reliability of scores from teachers' ratings of students' mathematics and writing portfolios. The Rand group found that different teachers scored the same student mathematics and writing portfolios quite differently in the first year of the program. As a result, there was a good chance that differences in students' scores reflected differences in grading practices rather than differences in the quality of students' work.[9]

Several factors contributed to the low reliability of the first year scoring. First, the decision to rate each best mathematics piece in seven dimensions and each best writing piece in five dimensions (as opposed to giving an overall rating) meant that teachers were asked to draw subtle inferences about the weaknesses of individual pieces of work. Although the dimensions differed conceptually, in practice, they often blurred together.

The rapid pace with which the portfolio program was introduced also contributed to the low reliability of the scoring. Most of the professional development activities in preparation for the first year of statewide implementation focused on using portfolios in teaching. While most grade 4 and grade 8 teachers participated in workshops dealing with scoring portfolios, these were held shortly before the statewide scoring in April. This timing provided few opportunities for teachers to argue with colleagues about scoring procedures and to reassess the standards appropriate for assigning particular scores.[10]

Rick Mills recognized the importance of the reliability issue, and agreed not to publish scores pertaining to individual districts until the Rand research showed that the reliabilities had increased. A consequence is that the scores from the initial year of statewide adoption did not contribute to one of the goals of portfolio assessment: to inform parents and taxpayers about the skills of students in local schools.

In the fall of 1992, Rick Mills hired Sue Rigney to be Director of Assessment for the State Department of Education. A transplanted Midwesterner, Sue had an extensive background in student assessment and came to Vermont from Michigan, where she had developed a new mathematics test for use in that state's assessment program. Sue's appointment signaled Rick Mills's recognition that the reliability problem was serious and that changes in the assessment system were needed to make progress toward the goal of providing meaningful information about the academic performance of students in individual school districts.

Acting in part on advice from the Rand analysts, Sue Rigney and her colleagues implemented a number of changes in the assessment system to increase the reliability of the scoring. Although scoring was done at six regional centers by any teachers who volunteered in the first year, they moved the scoring to a single site in the second year to facilitate common training. They changed network training to provide teachers with immediate feedback about the extent to which their scoring of student portfolios matched benchmark scores provided by network leaders. They adjusted the composition of the uniform mathematics test to include a single problem tackled by all Vermont fourth graders (and a different problem for all eighth graders) as well as thirty multiple-choice items drawn from a national test. (The Magic Rings was the common problem in the fourth-grade assessment for 1994.) They told teachers that, contrary to the advice given in the first year, students should not include puzzles in their collections of best mathematics pieces because puzzles were not likely to provide good opportunities for students to display the full range of problem-solving and communication skills included in the scoring system.

Coupled with greater experience in scoring, these changes led to significant improvements in the reliability of the math scoring.[11] The Rand Corporation concluded that the reliability of the mathematics scoring for the second year was sufficiently high to justify reporting information on the math scores for Vermont's sixty supervisory unions. Beginning in January 1994, information on the quality of the mathematics portfolios for fourth and eighth graders in individual supervisory unions has been included in the annual *Condition of Education in Vermont* report.

The progress in improving the reliability of the mathematics scoring was not matched in the writing scoring. For a second year, the reliabilities remained too low to justify reporting scores on writing portfolios for supervisory unions. The state report on writing compared only scores for the state as a whole for the 1992 school year with scores in the previous year.

Rick Mills, Sue Rigney, and the small group overseeing portfolio assessment in Vermont have made progress toward the goal of providing reliable information about the skills of Vermont's students. However, they recognize that the reliability problem remains serious, and much more progress is needed to be able to report reliable information on the portfolio performances of children attending individual schools.

Portfolio Assessment in Franklin Northwest

The Franklin Northwest Supervisory Union is located in the northwestern corner of the state. Primarily agricultural with almost no industrial base, it is one of the lowest-income regions of Vermont and has the lowest per pupil expenditures of any of the state's sixty supervisory unions. The three rooms that constitute the central office are located in the back of a two-story eighty-five-year-old brick building across from the town green in Swanton, Vermont, population 5400. The superintendent's office is reached by walking through the town clerk's office in the front of the building.

Doug Harris, the sandy-haired, hard-driving superintendent of Franklin Northwest, is an enthusiastic supporter of portfolio assessment. Although his reactions to the portfolio initiative and those of the principals and teachers of Franklin Northwest are not shared by all Vermont educators, they do illustrate how portfolio assessment can affect teaching and learning. They also point out some of the issues that arise with its implementation.

For Doug Harris, there is little question that portfolio assessment is changing the way teaching and learning are taking place in the schools of Franklin Northwest:

> I see differences in the kind of work that kids do. I see differences when I walk in a classroom. I see different kinds of things on the wall. I talk to the kids, I walk in a classroom often and I'll go over to a kid and ask them what they're doing, and there's a difference in the way they can talk about what they're doing. I talk to the teachers. Teachers, there's more talk now from teachers about substantive and structural kind of issues than management, logistical kind of issues. Not that those go away, but we spend more time talking about learning, and less time talking about . . . the details . . . not all of it's attributable to the portfolio process for sure, but I think a lot of it is.

One way Doug Harris has supported portfolio assessment is to find money to pay for substitutes so that teachers can attend network training. He also has supported teachers' request that they design and implement their own course on how to use portfolios to improve instruction and assessment. In his words, "[t]eachers created the course, set the goals, set the syllabus, set the evaluation processes. It was all teacher to teacher, the whole thing. I mean that was totally teacher generated, and it was one of the most powerful things we've ever done, maybe for that reason." Harris's actions in supporting teachers' efforts to learn to teach with portfolios reflects a theme running through several papers in this volume—namely, that effective organizational change requires a combination of incentives *and* opportunities to develop the skills needed to respond productively to the incentives.

Highgate Elementary School is one of three schools in the supervisory union with fourth grades. For Brian DuPrat, a young, enthusiastic former high school mathematics teacher who is the principal of Highgate, portfolio assessment is "the Trojan horse of changing instruction." He sees it as primarily responsible for dramatic changes in fourth-grade mathematics instruction:

In fourth grade what's happened is that the assessment process . . .
really stretched the [fourth grade] team to re-examine their teaching of mathematics, and we have quite literally gone from a drill
and practice sort of curriculum to a very hands-on . . . experiential
type of mathematics, much more in alignment with the assessment
practice.

JoAnne Campbell and Faith Johnson are two of the fourth-
grade teachers at Highgate who have worked together to change
the way they teach mathematics. Neither is a rookie. JoAnne,
medium height with short brown hair, has taught elementary
school for twenty years; Faith, tall with long fair hair, has taught for
ten. Both love their jobs and become so excited about the challenges, anxieties, and rewards of teaching with portfolios that they
often finish each other's sentences.

On the network training, JoAnne and Faith remarked:

JoAnne: I've never had an experience where I got to know the
people in my district as much, and we shared an incredible amount of information and experience, and it was
really invaluable.

Faith: We were out of the classroom a lot, that's the downside . . .
the state provides a lot of training, but they take us out
of classrooms to give us that training. So we were gone
two, was it three days a month?. . . . they gave us the
time away from school, but then, you know, you still had
the planning for your classroom to do before you left
and, you know, it, it was a little overwhelming at times.

Both JoAnne and Faith feel that their attempts to prepare their
students for the mathematics assessment has changed their teaching:

JoAnne: You're not just looking at the back of the math book
and doing the basic word problems anymore. You're,
you're constantly looking beyond and looking for more
challenging examples, experiences for the kids to have.
I have to say that in math especially, I work on teaching
the children more strategies for solving different types

of problems, logical reasoning, finding a pattern, working backwards, guess and check, a variety of different
ways to approach problems instead of just reading a
problem, then thinking about how, how you can do it . . .
we work on trying to do a number of different types of
problems that may have patterns in them so kids know
what they're supposed to be looking for—how to use
a table, how to use, make a chart, how to do a good
graph . . . I think those are big changes, big changes . . .
you try everything with the children, get them thinking
in different ways, looking at problems from a different
perspective and, and getting the kids to think about taking math out of the classroom, using it beyond sitting at
a desk . . .

Faith: Or getting them to, to work in groups, to work with
other people. To get along, to work in a cooperative
group with other people to solve a problem. Someone
might have more than one to solve it. . . . Your way is not
always, you know, yours may be right, but there may be
another approach. . . . The portfolios lend . . . [them-
selves] to a lot of cooperative groups.

JoAnne and Faith are enthusiastic about the use of portfolios in
the classroom, but they are less so about their use as part of a
statewide assessment. One concern is about the representativeness
of the three or four children from their classes whose portfolios are
selected for the state-sponsored assessment. As Brian DuPrat
expressed the teachers' worry: "When that list comes from the state
. . . that envelope's torn open and the teachers look at it and just
pray that it's truly representative of their children." In Faith's words,
"it's amazing how they randomly pick so many low level children."

A related concern is that though the scores may reflect a child's
skills at the end of the school year, they do not reflect the progress
the child has made over the school year. As Faith views the problem:

[w]hen you have a portfolio and you put work at the beginning of
the year in and then you work throughout the year with him or her
and then you have the assessment at the end of the year, you can sit
down with that child and say, wow, look what you've done this year,

look at your accomplishments. But I'm afraid the portfolio, when it goes to the state, they don't see that . . . and I find that a little upsetting.

Another concern is that the mathematical skills of the fourth-grade students depend on the instruction they received since starting school, but the assessment is done only in the fourth grade. As Faith sees the issue:

> . . . the first two years . . . we were in this process, they would say to us, this is not an assessment of fourth grade, this is an assessment of K-4 . . . and it's just done at fourth grade . . . We're just collecting the data then. And I said, well, excuse me, but I don't think so because you're not training anyone else how to teach this way, you're only training fourth grade teachers. . . . Fortunately . . . here it's changing. Third grade teachers are teaching problem solving . . . and so kids are coming to us with . . . at least the knowledge of the vocabulary . . . maybe this coming year more than for that . . . but the first two years . . . I think it was an assessment of fourth grade because those kids did not learn these skills, or start being taught these skills, until they walk into my classroom, so you're assessing me. . . . But it's changing. Finally . . . these teachers [in other grades] are getting trained.

Faith's comments reflect a difficult challenge facing schools in Vermont (and in every other state using measures of student performance at particular grade levels as the basis of an accountability system). As Linda Darling-Hammond's paper in this volume emphasizes, the challenge is to create incentives for all teachers in a school to work together to improve student performance.

Portfolio assessment has the potential not only to affect how teachers work, but also how students work. In Marge Petit's words:

> . . . kids became accountable. . . . What I immediately saw in my classroom is that kids in the past who didn't come for extra help, suddenly were showing up at my door and saying, you know, I really didn't get that problem, I really don't understand what I was supposed to do there . . . one of the most important benefits I can think of the whole project . . . has been kids developing perseverance, stick-to-it-iveness.

The papers in this volume by David Cohen and Arthur Powell emphasize the importance of developing stronger incentives for students to work hard in school. An important question in Vermont is whether the planned extension of portfolio assessment to high schools will alter incentives for older students. Not only teachers and students have had to adjust to the implications of portfolio assessment, parents have had to as well. In Brian DuPrat's words:

> . . . initially parents have some concern, some anticipation that, that we're throwing the times tables out the window, or that they're not going to be learning their fractions, or what about long-division the good old-fashioned way with paper and pencil? And we do our best to allay those fears and ensure them, no, this is not new math, we're not teaching new math, that, what you might have had in the '60s and got thoroughly confused with. What we're teaching is real-life mathematics and your children are going to be learning fraction skills and the multiplication facts . . . that is part of our curriculum. Once we get over that hurdle, most parents love the idea.

Faith Johnson found that the emphasis on developing communication skills in the new assessment system has led to questions from some parents:

> I've had parents complain about, if their child's really good in math and . . . a very good problem solver, but not a good communicator, they wonder why I'm pushing so hard for the child to write down what they did and how they solved [the problem] . . . 'Why does he have to write to you and tell you how he did it? He just did it.'

Doug Harris has found that it has not been difficult to sell portfolio assessment to the business community, which reflects in part the efforts he has made to communicate its value to employers:

> One of the clear messages out of the business community is that they want to make sure the kids come to them with marketable skills, and when they talk about marketable skills they are talking about . . . self-confidence, to be able to communicate, they're talking about kids being able to express themselves in writing, they talk about problem-solving. And what the portfolios have done so far . . .

is really elicited a lot of interest because the business community says, yeah, these are the kind of things we care about. Now I can remember . . . doing a portfolio presentation with some of the teachers [in Franklin] and the Board Chair, who's a very successful dairy farmer, has just lots of cows and lots of acres . . . pounding the table and saying, this is exactly what we need.

The reactions of teachers and principals in Franklin Northwest illustrate the potential for portfolio assessment to move teaching toward greater emphasis on the problem-solving and communication skills that are of increasing importance in today's economy. But it would be a mistake to assume that all superintendents are as enthusiastic about portfolio assessment as Doug Harris, or that teachers and principals in other supervisory unions have embraced the new assessment system as avidly as most in Franklin Northwest have. Some see this as yet another fad, and the sensible response is to wait awhile and this will go away.[12]

Yet surveys of teachers and principals indicate that the combination of incentives and professional development brought about by the introduction of portfolio assessment is having an impact on instruction. Teachers report devoting substantially more attention to problem solving and communication in teaching mathematics as a result of the program. They also report students spending more time working in small groups.

In her job as coordinator of the Mathematics Portfolio Network, Jill Rosenblum spends a lot of time talking with teachers and observing how they teach. In her view:

We haven't had what I would call a transformation, but I think that almost every classroom where portfolios have been implemented has seen some change in instruction, and that almost every teacher who's taken any step towards this kind of assessment has changed something about their instruction. . . . I don't see that they never use worksheets anymore . . . that they always elicit good thinking from the students, but I see that they have, at least incrementally, started to change, and to try different things, and to think of themselves in a different role. It's a big change we're asking of these people, particularly in math. It's not something they're comfortable with or used to. It's so different from the way they were taught and the way they were trained in their pre-service training.[13]

The Future of Portfolio Assessment in Vermont

Although portfolio assessment has influenced the work of a great many teachers and students in Vermont schools, many issues still need to be resolved before it becomes an institutionalized part of public education in the state. These issues are relevant not only to Vermont education; they must be faced by every state attempting to develop high standards for student work and to measure progress toward these standards.

A Critical Tension

The tension between the goals of improving instruction and providing reliable data about student performance continues to be a difficult one. Since JoAnne Campbell, Faith Johnson, and many other Vermont teachers embrace the impact that portfolio assessment has had on instruction, but are wary of its use as an accountability system, why not scrap the goal of making portfolios the center of an accountability system and use them solely as a lever for improving instruction? There are three related reasons why pursuit of the dual goals for portfolio assessment may be needed despite the scoring problems. First, taxpayers and employers increasingly want schools to be accountable. It would be much more difficult to retain funding for the network training that teachers find critical to their efforts to incorporate portfolios in their teaching if portfolios were not a central component of an accountability system. Second, the plan to eventually make public school-district-specific scores creates incentives for teachers not enamored with portfolios to learn to use them and to introduce them into their teaching. In other words, the accountability goal may be critical to making progress toward the instructional goal. Finally, if portfolios are not used for accountability purposes, there will be pressure to develop other measures of student skills, such as standardized tests, that will be so used. This will create enormous pressure to abandon portfolio development and to concentrate instruction on helping students do well on the new instruments. As the adage goes, "What you test is what you get." To date, the costs of retaining the dual goals appear manageable. Teachers complain that too much of the network training is focused on improving the reliability of scoring and not enough on using port-folios to improve instruction. Yet the work on scoring reliability has been valuable. As Marge Petit sees it, "the scoring training . . . has been the thing that has really moved the process for the kids. When the teachers understood the standards, they could explain it to the kids." Further, the emphasis in network training has been shifting to greater attention on instructional issues.

The changes made to date to improve the reliability of the scoring have not dramatically compromised the goal of using portfolio assessment to improve instruction. Teachers still choose the portfolio problems they assign to their students. The mathematics rubric still contains seven, very detailed dimensions, and the writing rubric contains five dimensions, and scores are reported for each dimension.

The Rand Corporation has suggested further changes to facilitate progress toward the goal of providing reliable school-district-specific information about student performance in mathematics and writing. These include narrowing the types of problems that teachers assign to students for inclusion in the portfolios that are scored by the state, reducing the number of dimensions in the rubric, and averaging scores across dimensions to produce a "holistic" assessment of a student's work. It remains to be seen whether these changes will be implemented, whether they will improve the reliability of the assessments, and whether they will significantly reduce the power of portfolio assessment to improve teaching.

Portfolio Assessment in High Schools

From the beginning of his thinking about developing an accountability system in Vermont, Rick Mills knew that the high school must ultimately be part of the plan: "We must have some kind of assessment of results at the high school. The Legislature has made that very clear, the State Board has made it very clear." Much less clear is the design of a good high school assessment. Differences in the academic programs that high school students take create questions about the best timing of an assessment and who should be included in the population that is sampled. As Marge Petit described the sampling question: "Do we dip in after kids have finished two years of mathematics? Do we dip in after every kid has finished geometry? What if kids never take geometry?" How these questions are answered could have a major impact on the assessment results.

Perhaps sobered by the challenges of implementing the assessment systems for grades four and eight, the State Department of Education has tackled the design of a high school assessment as a long-term research project. Ray Henderson, a high school mathematics teacher in Franklin Northwest Supervisory Union, and Marge Petit head a small group conducting a pilot study in seventeen high schools of alternative strategies for assessing the mathematics skills of tenth graders. The plan is to learn from the pilot which choices about the design of the assessment have marked impacts on the results.

In anticipation of the introduction of the portfolio assessment to the high school level, Rick Mills enlisted the support of the Vermont Business Roundtable to strengthen the connections between the quality of students' school work and their job prospects. To date, more than 200 Vermont employers have joined the "Performance Counts" initiative, under which they commit themselves to use student portfolios, when they become available, in making hiring decisions.

What will the portfolios of high school students look like? As Doug Harris envisions the system:

> I would like every kid to walk out of here with a portfolio that represents that kid as a communicator, represents him as a problem-solver, represents him as a socially responsible person . . . my dream is, and, you know, we're a resource-poor district, I'd love them to be able to [have] . . . an electronic portfolio. So part of it could be video, part of it might be sound. So that, let's say that you had a kid that was going out to, let's say a kid wanted to go work for a manufacturer. He might be able to really go out and show a videotape of something that he did in a manufacturing setting in school.

Will employers of high school graduates take the time to examine the rich information available in the type of portfolio Doug Harris envisions? Sue Rigney's experiences raise questions:

> My concern and my previous experience in Michigan is that when we had this discussion with employers about portfolios, there was

one camp that understood that this was taking a complex look at an individual, but there's another very large segment of the business community that says, so give me the number, and to use it as a screening device they want a number, a number. And . . . the strength of the portfolio is the richness . . .

Lessons, but Not a Blueprint

Portfolio assessment in Vermont today does not provide a blueprint that other states can follow in measuring students' progress toward mastering critical skills. Not only is the Vermont system different today from how it was in its first year of operation, it will also be different in years ahead as Rick Mills and his colleagues find better ways to balance the twin goals of improving teaching and learning and providing reliable information about student performance. Further, the peculiarities of Vermont demographics—the small size of the state and the relatively high degree of homogeneity of its residents—undoubtedly influenced the process of portfolio development. Each state will need to discover its own process for developing an accountability system.

Although not a blueprint, the brief history of portfolio assessment in Vermont does provide lessons for other states about issues that arise in monitoring the success of the schools in teaching students critical skills. One lesson is the importance of developing an assessment strategy that is consistent with teachers' sense of effective teaching and learning. Many Vermont teachers like JoAnne Campbell and Faith Johnson embrace the changes in their teaching practices that portfolio assessment has encouraged because they believe the changes have improved their teaching. A second lesson is the importance of coupling new assessment strategies with other changes designed to improve teaching performance. For example, the Franklin Northwest contract provides support for extensive professional development. The Moretown teachers' contract provides teachers with four days away from classroom duties to write extensive comments to parents about students' portfolio work and to meet with students and parents to discuss portfolios. In other words, the progress in Vermont toward using portfolios to improve instruction has taken place only because extensive professional development and job redesign aimed at supporting teacher initiatives have accompanied the implementation of the accountability system.

Finally, portfolio assessment in Vermont illustrates the importance of perseverance and learning from mistakes. Marge Petit smiled wistfully as she describes the "Ant in the Well" problem used in training teachers in the first year of portfolio assessment. Though the problem seemed suitable at the time, Marge now sees that it does not provide students with opportunities to display the full range of problem-solving and communications skills evaluated in the scoring system.

Unlike many promising educational innovations, portfolio assessment in Vermont did not die before it had a chance to display its potential for improving teaching and learning. Marge Petit, Jill Rosenblum, and Sue Rigney have had the time to develop better methods of training teachers and to experiment with methods of improving the reliability of the scoring. One reason that educators in Vermont have been able to persevere with a promising innovation in the face of early difficulties is that from the outset Rick Mills made the case to the State Board of Education, the legislature, and the business community that the development of portfolio assessment in Vermont would be a decade-long process. Although long time horizons for accomplishing major changes are part of successful management at successful private sector organizations, they are rare in American public education. All too often promising educational innovations are abandoned before solutions are found to the problems that inevitably accompany significant changes in practice.

A Research Agenda

Vermont is only one of many states struggling to develop accountability systems that will play a key role in educational reform efforts. The Vermont experience raises a number of questions that can fruitfully be explored with cross-state comparisons. In conclusion, we describe two critical research questions.

Stakes

A major issue in the design of an accountability system is the stakes that will be attached to the student scores. Kentucky has chosen quite high stakes: teachers in schools with student test scores better than predicted obtain substantial financial bonuses; teachers in schools with lower than expected student test scores may ultimately lose their jobs. In Vermont, the stakes depend on the responses of local communities. Other states have developed plans with still different stakes. Although the issue of stakes has been controversial in the design of every state plan, little is known about the consequences of different stakes.

Reliability versus Teacher Discretion

In the current Vermont portfolio assessment system, teachers choose the mathematics problems their students work on in developing the seven best pieces that the scorers at Camp Portfolio grade. This freedom to choose problems contributes to teachers' support for portfolio assessment; however, it also contributes to the relatively low interrater reliability of the portfolio scores. Requiring that all students submit solutions to common problems improves the reliability of the scoring; however, it also constrains teachers' freedom to design instruction and may increase resistance to portfolio assessment. More information is needed on the extent to which common problems improve reliability, and the extent to which the requirement of common problems jeopardizes teachers' support for portfolio assessment.

Notes

1. 1993 Vermont State Department of Education, *Vermont Assessment Program Summary of Assessment Results 1992–1993*.
2. National Science Board.
3. Mills and Brewer.
4. As summarized in Koretz and others, July 31, 1992, all these goals are either explicitly stated or implicit in the Mills and Brewer 1988 document.
5. National Council of Teachers of Mathematics.
6. The description of the mathematics assessment system is taken from Koretz and others, July 31, 1992.
7. Vermont Guide of Education, *Vermont Mathematics Portfolio Project: Teacher's Guide*.
8. The Vermont Department of Education distributed for comments a sample assessment report entitled *Dewey, Vermont: Assessment Results*.

9. See Daniel Koretz and others, December 4, 1992.
10. One optimistic sign along the quest for reliable scoring is that teachers did not grade the portfolios of their own students differently from the portfolios of other students. This is important because a central pillar of the Vermont design is that the same assessments should provide parents, employers, and taxpayers with reliable information about student skills and provide teachers with timely diagnostic information about student weaknesses. These two goals are compatible only if teachers adopt the same standards in grading the work of their students and the work of other students.
11. Daniel Koretz and others, December 1993, p. 5. When scores were averaged across dimensions, the correlations between readers' mathematics scores were higher: for fourth-grade scores, .60 in 1992 and .72 in 1993; for eighth-grade scores, .53 in 1992 and .79 in 1993.
12. For a thoughtful discussion of the range of local responses to initiatives by the Vermont State Department of Education, see Susan Follett Lusi, 1994.
13. For an insightful discussion of the difficulties in changing how teachers teach mathematics, see David K. Cohen, 1990.

References

Cohen, D. K. "A Revolution in One Classroom: The Case of Mrs. Oublier." *Educational Evaluation and Policy Analysis*, 1990, *12* (3), 311–329.

Koretz, D., Klein, S., McCaffrey, D., and Stecher, B. *Interim Report: The Reliability of Vermont Portfolio Scores in the 1992–93 School Year*. Rand Corporation, December 1993.

Koretz, D., Stecher, B., and Deibert, E. *The Vermont Portfolio Program: Interim Report on Implementation and Impact, 1991–92 School Year*. Rand Corporation, July 31, 1992.

Koretz, D. et al. *The Reliability of Scores from the 1992 Vermont Portfolio Assessment Program: Interim Report*. Rand Institute on Education and Training, December 4, 1992.

Lusi, S. F. *The Role of State Departments of Education in Promoting and Supporting Complex School Reform*. Doctoral thesis completed at the Kennedy School of Government, Harvard University, May 1994.

Mills, R. P. and Brewer, W. R. "Working Together to Show Results: An Approach to School Accountability for Vermont." Vermont Department of Education, October 18, 1988.

National Council of Teachers of Mathematics. *Curriculum and Evaluation Standards for School Mathematics*. Washington, D.C., 1989.

National Science Board. *Science and Engineering Indicators*. Washington, D.C., 1987.

Vermont Department of Education. *Vermont Mathematics Portfolio Project: Teacher's Guide*. September 1991.

1993 Vermont State Department of Education. *Vermont Assessment Program Summary of Assessment Results 1992–93*. Montpelier, Vt., November 1993.

Chapter Nine

Getting to Scale with Successful Educational Practices[1]

Richard F. Elmore

The Problem of Scale in Educational Reform

Why do good ideas about teaching and learning have so little impact on American educational practice? This question, I will argue, raises a central problem of American education. A significant body of circumstantial evidence points to a deep, systemic incapacity of American schools, and the practitioners who work in them, to incorporate, develop, and extend new ideas about teaching and learning in anything but a small fraction of schools and classrooms. This incapacity, I will argue, is rooted primarily in the incentive structures in which teachers and administrators work. Therefore, solving the problem of scale means substantially changing these incentive structures.

Changing the Core: Students, Teachers, and Knowledge

The problem of scale in educational innovation can be briefly stated as follows: innovations that require large changes in the core of educational practice seldom penetrate more than a small fraction of American schools and classrooms, and seldom last for very long when they do. By the "core" of educational practice, I mean how teachers understand the nature of knowledge and the student's role in learning, how these ideas about knowledge and learning are manifested in teaching and classwork. The core also includes the structural arrangements of schools, such as the physical lay-out of classrooms, student grouping practices, teachers' responsibilities for groups of students, relations among teachers in their work with students, and processes for assessing student learning and communicating it to students, teachers, parents, administrators, and other interested parties.

One can think of schools as generally representing a standard set of solutions to these problems of how to manage the core. Teachers tend to think of knowledge as discrete bits of information about a particular subject and of student learning as the acquisition of this information through processes of repetition, memorization, and regular testing of recall, see, for example, Cohen, 1988 ("Teaching Practice: Plus que ça change"). The teacher, who is generally the center of attention in the classroom, initiates most of the talk and orchestrates most of the interaction in the classroom around brief factual questions, if there is any discussion at all.

Hence, the teacher is the main source of information, defined as discrete facts, and this information is what qualifies as knowledge. Often students are grouped by age, and again within age groups, according to their perceived capabilities to acquire information. The latter is generally accomplished either by within-class ability groups or, at higher grade levels, in "tracks," or clusters of courses comprised of students whom teachers judge to have similar abilities. Individual teachers are typically responsible for one group of students for a fixed period. Seldom working in groups to decide what a given group of students should know or how that knowledge should be taught, teachers are typically solo practitioners operating in a structure that feeds them students and expectations about what students should be taught. Students' work is typically assessed by asking them to repeat information that has been conveyed to them by the teacher in the classroom, usually in the form of worksheets or tests that involve discrete, factual, right-or-wrong answers (Elmore, 1995).

At any given time, there are some number of schools and classrooms that deliberately violate these core patterns. For example, students may initiate a large share of the classroom talk, either in small groups or in teacher-led discussions, often in the context of some problem they are expected to solve. Teachers may ask broad, open-ended questions designed to elicit what students are thinking and how they are thinking rather than to assess whether they have acquired discrete bits of information. Students' work might involve oral or written responses to complex, open-ended questions or problems for which they are expected to provide explanations that reflect not only their acquisition of information but their judgments about what kinds of information are most important or appropriate. Students may be grouped flexibly according to the teacher's judgment about what the most appropriate array of strengths and weaknesses is for a particular task or subject matter. Teachers may share responsibility for larger groups of students across different ages and ability levels and may work cooperatively to design classroom activities that challenge students working at different levels. In other words, students' learning may be assessed using a broad array of tasks, problems, mediums of expression, and formats.

In characterizing these divergences from traditional educational practice, I have deliberately avoided using the jargon of contemporary educational reform—"teaching for understanding," "whole language," "heterogeneous grouping," "team teaching," "cooperative learning," "authentic assessment," and so on. I have done this because I do not want to confuse the problems associated with the implementation of particular innovations with the more general, systemic problem of what happens to practices, by whatever name, that violate or challenge the basic conventions of the core of schooling. The names of these practices change, and the intellectual traditions associated with particular versions of the practices ebb and flow. But the fundamental problem remains: attempts to change the stable patterns of the core of schooling, in the fundamental ways described here, are usually unsuccessful on anything more than a small scale. It is this problem on which I will focus.

Much of what passes for "change" in American schooling is not really about changing the core. Innovations often embody vague intentions of changing the core through modifications that are only weakly related, or not related at all, to the core. American secondary schools, for example, are constantly changing the way they arrange the schedule that students are expected to follow—lengthening and shortening class periods, distributing content in different ways across periods and days, increasing and decreasing class size for certain periods of the day, and so on. These changes are often justified as a way to provide space in the day for teachers to do a kind of teaching they would not otherwise be able to do or to develop a different kind of relationship with students around knowledge.

However, the changes are often not explicitly connected to fundamental changes in the way knowledge is constructed, nor to the division of responsibility between teacher and student, the way students and teachers interact with each other around knowledge, or any of a variety of other stable conditions in the core. Hence, changes in scheduling seldom translate into changes in the fundamental conditions of teaching and learning for students and teachers. Schools, then, might be "changing" all the time—adopting this or that new structure or schedule or textbook series or tracking system—and never change in any fundamental way what teachers and students actually do when they are together in classrooms. I am not interested, except in passing, in changes that are unrelated to the core of schooling, as I have defined it. My focus is on that narrower class of changes that directly challenge the fundamental relationships between student, teacher, and knowledge.

In some instances, such as the high-performance schools described by Linda Darling-Hammond (this volume), a whole school will adopt a dramatically different form of organization, typically by starting from scratch rather than changing an existing school, and that form of organization will connect with teaching practices that are dramatically different from those traditionally associated with the core of schooling. At any given time, there may be several such model schools, or exemplars of good practice, but as a proportion of the total number of schools, they are always a small fraction. In other words, it is possible to dramatically alter organization and practice in schools, but it has to this point never been possible to do it on a large scale.

The closer an innovation gets to the core of schooling, the less likely that innovation is to influence teaching and learning on a large scale. The corollary of this proposition, of course, is that innovations that are distant from the core will be more readily adopted on a large scale. I will later develop some theoretical propositions about why this might be the case.

The problem of scale is a "nested" problem. That is, it exists in similar forms at different levels of the system. New practices may spring up in isolated classrooms, or in clusters of classrooms, within a given school, but never move to most classrooms within that school. Likewise, whole schools may be created from scratch that embody very different forms of practice, but these schools remain a small proportion of all schools within a given district or state. And finally, some local school systems may be more successful than others at spawning classrooms and schools that embody new practices, but these local systems remain a small fraction of the total number of systems.

The problem of scale is not a problem of the general resistance or failure of schools to change. Most schools are, in fact, constantly changing—adopting new curricula, tests, and grouping practices; changing schedules; creating new mechanisms for participation in decision making; adding or subtracting teaching and administrative roles; and myriad other modifications. Within this vortex of change, however, basic conceptions of knowledge, of the teacher's and the student's role in constructing knowledge, and of the role of classroom- and school-level structures in enabling student learning remain relatively static.

Nor is the problem of scale a failure of research or systematic knowledge of what to do. At any given time, there is an abundance of ideas about how to change fundamental relationships in the core of schooling, some growing out of research and demonstration projects, some growing directly out of teaching practice. Many of these ideas are empirically tested, and many are based on relatively coherent theories of student learning. We might wish that these ideas were closer to the language and thought processes of practitioners, and we might hope that they were packaged and delivered better, but there are more ideas circulating about how to change the core processes of schooling than there are schools and classrooms willing to engage them. There are always arguments among researchers and practitioners about which are the most promising ideas, and conflicting evidence on their effects, but the supply of ideas is there. The problem lies then not in the supply of new ideas, but in the demand for them. That is, the primary problem of scale is understanding the conditions under which people working in schools seek new knowledge and actively use it to change the fundamental processes of schooling.

Why Is the Problem of Scale Important to Educational Reform?

Two central ideas of the present period of U.S. educational reform raise fundamental, recurring problems of American education. One problem is captured by that famous, controversial line from *A Nation at Risk,* "a rising tide of mediocrity" (National Council on Excellence in Education, 1983). Among the things that this phrase refers to is the widely shared observation that teaching and learning in American schools and classrooms is, in its most common form, emotionally flat and intellectually undemanding and unengaging. This is a perennial critique of American education, dating back to the first systematic surveys of educational practice in the early twentieth century[2] and confirmed by contemporary evidence. One recent survey of classroom practice characterized the typical classroom this way:

> No matter what the observational perspective, the same picture emerges. The two activities involving the most students were being lectured to and working on written assignments. . . . Students were working alone most of the time, whether individually or in groups. That is, the student listened as one member of a class being lectured, or the student worked individually on a seat assignment. . . .
>
> In effect, then, the modal classroom configurations which we observed looked like this: the teacher explaining or lecturing to total class or a single student, occasionally asking questions requiring factual answers; the teacher, when not lecturing, observing or monitoring students working individually at their desks; students listening or appearing to listen to the teacher and occasionally responding to the teacher's questions; students working individually at their desks on reading or writing assignments; and all with little emotion, from interpersonal warmth to expressions of hostility (Goodlad, 1984, p. 230).

Every school can point to its energetic, engaged, and effective teachers; many students can recall at least one teacher who inspired in them an engagement in learning and a love of knowledge. We regularly honor and deify these pedagogical geniuses. But these exceptions prove the rule. For the most part, we regard inspired and demanding teaching as an individual trait of teachers, much like hair color or shoe size, rather than as a professional

norm, or an expectation that might apply to any teacher by virtue
of his or her occupational status. As long as we treat engaging
teaching as a trait of individual teachers, rather than a norm that
might apply to any teacher, we feel no obligation to ask the
broader systemic question of why more evidence of engaging
teaching does not exist. The answer to this question is obvious for
those who subscribe to the individual trait theory of effective teaching: few teachers are predisposed to teach in interesting ways. Alternatively, other explanations for the prevalence of dull, flat,
unengaging teaching might be that we fail to select and reward
teachers based on their capacity to teach in engaging ways, or that
organizational conditions do not promote and sustain good teaching when it occurs.

The other central idea in the present period of reform is captured by the slogan "all students can learn." What reformers seem
to mean by this idea is that "all" students—or most students—are
capable of mastering challenging academic content at high levels
of understanding, and the fact that many do not is more a testimo-
nial to how they are taught than to whether they are suited for serious academic work. In other words, the slogan is meant to be a
charge to schools to make challenging learning available to a much
broader segment of students than they have in the past. The touchstone for this critique is consistent evidence over the last two
decades or so that American students do reasonably well on lower-
level tests of achievement and cognitive skill but relatively poorly
on tests that require complex reasoning, inference, judgment, and
transfer of knowledge from one type of problem to another (NCES,
1993).

It is hard to imagine a solution to this problem of the distribution of learning among students that does not entail a solution
to the first problem of increasing the frequency of engaging teaching. Clearly, getting more students to learn at higher levels has to
entail some change both in the way students are taught and in the
proportion of teachers who are teaching in ways that cause students to master higher-level skills and knowledge. It is possible, of
course, that some piece of the problem of the distribution of learning can be solved by simply getting more teachers to teach more
challenging content, even in boring and unengaging ways, to a
broader population of students. But, at some level, it seems implau-

sible that large proportions of students presently disengaged from learning academic content at high levels of understanding will suddenly become more engaged in traditional teaching practices in the modal American classroom. Some students are able to overcome the deadening effect of flat, dull, and unengaging teaching through extraordinary ability, motivation, or family pressure. Other students, however, require extraordinary teaching to achieve extraordinary results. The problem of scale, then, can be seen in the context of the current reform debate as a need to change the core of schooling in ways that result in most students receiving engaging instruction in challenging academic content.

This view of educational reform, which focuses on changing fundamental conditions affecting the relationship of student, teacher, and knowledge, might be criticized as being either too narrow or too broad. My point in focusing the analysis wholly on the core of schooling is not to suggest that teaching and learning can be changed in isolation from an understanding of the contextual factors that influence children's lives. Nor is it to suggest that the object of reform should be to substitute one kind of uniformity of teaching practice for another.

Rather, my point is that most educational reforms never reach, much less influence, long-standing patterns of teaching practice and are therefore largely pointless if their intention is to improve student learning. I am interested in what is required before teaching practice can plausibly be expected to shift from its modal patterns toward more engaging and ambitious practices. These practices might be quite diverse. They might involve creative adaptations and responses to the backgrounds, interests, and preferences of students and their families. And they might be wedded in interesting ways to solutions to the multitude of problems that children face outside school. But the fundamental problem I am interested in is why, when schools seem to be constantly changing, teaching practice changes so little on so small a scale.

The Evidence

The central claims of my argument, then, are that the core of schooling—defined as the standard solutions to the problem of how knowledge is defined, how teachers relate to students around knowledge, how teachers relate to other teachers in the course of their daily work, how students are grouped for purposes of instruction, how content is allocated to time, and how students' work is assessed—changes very little, except in a small proportion of schools and classrooms where the changes do not persist for very long. The changes that do tend to "stick" in schools are those that are most distant from the core.

The Progressive Period

To evaluate these claims, one would want to look at examples where reformers had ideas that challenged the core of schooling and where these ideas had time to percolate through the system and influence practice. One such example is the progressive period, perhaps the longest and most intense period of educational reform and ferment in the history of the country, running from roughly the second decade of the twentieth century into the 1940s. What is most interesting about the progressive period, compared to other periods of educational reform, is that its aims included explicit attempts to change pedagogy, coupled with a relatively strong intellectual and practical base. Noted intellectuals— John Dewey in particular—developed ideas about how schools might be different, and these ideas found their way into classrooms and schools. The progressive period had a wide agenda, but one priority was an explicit attempt to change the core of schooling from a teacher-centered, fact-centered, recitation-based pedagogy to a pedagogy based on an understanding of children's thought processes and their capacities to learn and use ideas in the context of real problems of the sort they were likely to face in later life.

In a nutshell, the progressive period produced an enormous amount of innovation, much of it in the core conditions of schooling. This innovation occurred in two broad forms. One was the creation of single schools that exemplified progressive pedagogical practices. The other was attempts to implement progressive pedagogical practices on a large scale in public school systems. In discussing these two trends, I draw upon Lawrence Cremin's *The Transformation of the American School* (1961), which provides a detailed review of progressive education.

The single schools spawned by the progressive movement represented an astonishing range of pedagogical ideas and institutional forms lasting from the early 'teens until the late 1940s. In their seminal review of pedagogical reform in 1915, *Schools of To-Morrow,* John and Evelyn Dewey documented schools such as the Francis Parker School in Chicago and Caroline Pratt's Play School in New York, both exemplars of a single founder's vision. Although these schools varied enormously in the particulars of their curricula, activities, grade and grouping structures, and teaching practices, they shared an aim of breaking the lock of teacher-centered instruction and generating high levels of student engagement through student-initiated inquiry and group activities. Furthermore, these schools drew on a common wellspring of social criticism and prescription, exemplified in John Dewey's *The School and Society* (1899), which focused school reform on "shift(ing) the center of gravity" in education "back to the child. His natural impulses to conversation, to inquiry, to construction, and to expression were . . . seen as natural resources . . . of the educative process" (Cremin, 1961, pp. 118–119). Also included in this vision was the notion that school would be "recalled from isolation to the center of the struggle for a better life" (Cremin, 1961, p. 119).

This dialectic between intellect and practice continued through the 1920s and 1930s with the publication of William Heard Kirkpatrick's *Foundations of Method* (1925), an elaboration of Dewey's thinking about the connection between school and society; Harold Rugg's and Ann Schumaker's *The Child-Centered School* (1928), another interpretive survey of pedagogical practice like *Schools of To-Morrow,* and *The Educational Frontier* (1933), a restatement of progressive theory and philosophy written by a committee of the National Society of College Teachers of Education (Cremin, 1961, pp. 216–229). Individual reformers and major social/educational institutions, such as Teachers College, the University of Chicago, designed and developed schools that exemplified the key tenets of progressive thinking.

One example illustrates the power of this connection between ideas and institutions. In 1915, Abraham Flexner, the father of modern medical education, announced his intention to develop a model school that would do for general education what the Johns Hopkins Medical School had done for medical education. He wrote an essay called *A Modern School* (1916). This blueprint for reform described a school that embodied major changes in curriculum and teaching and that would serve as a laboratory for the scientific study of educational problems. In 1917, Teachers College, in collaboration with Flexner and the General Board of Education, opened the Lincoln School, which became a model and a gathering place for progressive reformers, a major source of new curriculum materials, and a source of many reformers over the next two decades. The school survived until 1948, when it was disbanded in a dispute between its parents' association and the Teachers College administration (Cremin, 1961, pp. 280–291).

The second form of innovation in the progressive period, large-scale reforms of public school systems, drew on the same intellectual base as the founding of individual schools. A notable early example was the Gary, Indiana, school district. The Gary superintendent in 1907 was William Wirt, a former student of John Dewey at the University of Chicago. Wirt initiated the "Gary Plan," which became the leading exemplar of progressive practice on a large scale in the early progressive period. The key elements of the Gary Plan were "vastly extended educational opportunity," in the form of playgrounds, libraries, laboratories, machine shops, and the like; a "platoon system" of grouping, whereby groups of children moved *en masse* between classrooms and common areas, allowing for economies in facilities; a "community" system of school organization, in which skilled tradespeople from the community played a role in teaching students; and a heavily project-focused curriculum (Cremin, 1961, pp. 153–160).

In 1919, Winnetka, Illinois, hired Carleton Washburn, from San Francisco State Normal School, as its superintendent. Washburn launched a reform agenda based on the idea of individually paced instruction, where the "common essentials" in the curriculum were divided into "parcels," and each student advanced through them, with the guidance of teachers, at his or her own pace. As students mastered each parcel, they were examined and moved on to the next. This individualized work was combined with "self-expressive" work, in which students were encouraged to develop ideas and projects on their own, and group projects, in which students worked on issues related to the community life of the school. Over the next decade, the Winnetka plan was imitated by as many as 247 other school districts, but with a crucial modification. Most districts found the practice of tailoring the curriculum to individual students far too complex for their tastes, so they organized students into groups and applied the idea of differential progress to groups. In this way, a progressive reform focused on individualized learning led to the development of what is now called tracking (Cremin, 1961, pp. 295–298).

A number of cities, including Denver and Washington, D.C., undertook massive curriculum reform projects in the late 1920s and early 1930s. These efforts were extraordinarily sophisticated, even by today's relatively rarified standards. Typically, teachers were enlisted to meet in curriculum revision committees during regular school hours, and outside experts were enlisted to work with teachers in reformulating the curriculum and in developing new teaching practices. In Denver, superintendent Jesse Newlon convinced his board to appropriate $35,500 for this process. Denver became a center for teacher-initiated and teacher-developed curriculum, resulting in the development of a monograph series of course syllabi that got wide national circulation. The resulting curriculum changes were sustained in Denver over roughly two decades, when they were abandoned in the face of growing opposition to progressive pedagogy (Cremin, 1961, pp. 299–302; Cuban, 1984, pp. 67–83). In Washington, D.C., superintendent Frank Ballou led a pared-down version of the Denver curriculum revision model, with teacher committees, chaired by administrators, meeting after school, without the support of outside specialists. Despite these constraints, the process reached large numbers of teachers in both black and white schools in the city's segregated system (Cuban, 1984, pp. 83–93).

Larry Cuban concluded in *How Teachers Taught: Constancy and Change in American Classrooms, 1890–1980,* his study of large-scale reforms of curriculum and pedagogy in the late-progressive period, that progressive practices, defined as movement away from teacher-centered and toward student-centered pedagogy, "seldom appeared in more than one-fourth of the classrooms in any district that systematically tried to install these varied elements" (Cuban, 1984, 135). Even in settings where teachers made a conscious effort to incorporate progressive practices, the result was more often than not a hybrid of traditional and progressive, in which the major elements of the traditional core of instruction were largely undisturbed.

The dominant pattern of instruction, allowing for substantial spread of these hybrid progressive practices, remained teacher-centered. Elementary and secondary teachers persisted in teaching from the front of the room, deciding what was to be learned, in what manner, and under what conditions. The primary means of grouping for instruction was the entire class. The major daily classroom activities continued with a teacher telling, explaining, and questioning students while the students listened, answered, read, and wrote. Seatwork or supervised study was an extension of these activities (Cuban, 1984, p. 137).

The fate of the progressive movement has been well documented. As the language of progressivism began to permeate educational talk, if not practice, the movement began to lose its intellectual edge and to drift into a series of empty clichés, the most extreme of which was life adjustment education. Opposition to progressivism, which had been building through the 1920s, came to a crescendo in the 1940s. The movement was increasingly portrayed by a skeptical public and press in terms of its most extreme manifestations—watered-down content, a focus on childrens' psychological adjustment at the expense of learning, and a preoccupation with self-expression rather than learning. Abraham Flexner, looking back on his experiences as a moderate progressive, observed "there is something queer about the genus 'educator'; the loftiest are not immune. I think the cause must lie in their isolation from the rough and tumble contacts with all manner of men. They lose their sense of reality" (Cremin, 1961, p. 160).

The particular structure that educational reform took in the progressive period, though, is deeply rooted in American institutions and persists to this day. First, contrary to much received wisdom, intellectuals found ways to express their ideas about how education could be different in the form of real schools with structures and practices that were radically different from existing schools. There was a direct and vital connection between ideas and practice. This connection persists, in a much diluted form, today. But this connection took the institutional form of single schools, each an isolated island of practice, connected by a loosely defined intellectual agenda that made few demands for conformity, and each a particular, precious, and exotic specimen of a larger genus. So the most vital and direct connections between ideas and practice were deliberately institutionalized as separate, independent entities, incapable of and uninterested in forming replicates of themselves or of pursuing a broader institutional reform agenda.[3] A few exceptions, like the Lincoln School, were deliberately designed to influence educational practice on a larger scale, but the exact means by which that was to happen were quite vague. For the most part, progressive reformers believed that good ideas would travel, of their own volition, into American classrooms and schools.

Second, where public systems did attempt to change pedagogical practice on a large scale, often using techniques that would be considered sophisticated by today's standards, they succeeded in changing practice in only a small fraction of classrooms, and then not necessarily in a sustained way over time. Sometimes—as in the case of Washburn's strategy of individualizing instruction in Winnetka—as the reforms moved from one district to another, they became sinister caricatures of the original. The district-level reforms produced impressive tangible products, mostly in the form of new curriculum materials that would circulate within and outside the originating districts. The connection to classroom practice, however, was weak. Larry Cuban likens this kind of reform to a hurricane at sea: "storm-tossed waves on the ocean surface, turbulent water a fathom down, and calm on the ocean floor" (Cuban, 1984, p. 237).

Third, the very successes of progressive reformers became their biggest liabilities as the inevitable political opposition formed. Rather than persist in Dewey's original agenda of influencing public discourse about the nature of education and its relation to society through open public discussion, debate, and inquiry, the more militant progressives became increasingly like true believers in a particular version of the faith and increasingly isolated from public scrutiny and discourse. The developers of progressive pedagogy became increasingly isolated from the public mainstream and increasingly vulnerable to attack from traditionalists.

The pattern that emerges from the progressive period, then, is one where the intellectual and practical energies of serious reformers tended to turn inward, toward the creation of exemplary settings—classrooms or schools—that embodied their best ideas of practice, producing an impressive and attractive array of isolated examples of what practice *could* look like. At the same time, those actors with an interest in what would now be called systemic change focused on developing the tangible, visible, and material products of reform—plans, processes, curricula, materials—and focused much less, if at all, on the less tangible problem of what might cause a teacher to teach in new ways, if the materials and support were available to do so. These two forces produced the central dilemma of educational reform: we can produce many examples of how educational practice could look differently, but we can produce few, if any, examples of large numbers of teachers engaging in these practices in large-scale institutions designed to deliver education to most children.

Large-Scale Curriculum Development Projects

Another, more recent, body of evidence on these points comes from large-scale curriculum reforms of 1950s and 1960s in the United States funded by the National Science Foundation (NSF). In their fundamental structure, these reforms were quite similar to the progressive reforms although much more tightly focused on content. The central idea of these curriculum reforms was that learning in school should resemble, much more than it usually does, the actual processes by which human beings come to understand their environment, culture, and social settings. That is, if students are studying mathematics, science, or social science, they should actually engage in activities similar to those of serious practitioners of these disciplines and, in the process, discover not only the knowledge of the subject but also the thought processes and methods of inquiry by which that knowledge is constructed. Construction of new curriculum for schools, this view suggested, should proceed by bringing the best research minds in the various subjects, largely drawn from universities, together with teachers who actually teach these subjects to students in school, and to use the expertise of the two groups to devise new conceptions of content and new strategies for teaching it. The earliest of these projects was the Physical Sciences Study Committee's (PSSC) high school physics curriculum, which began in 1956. Another of these was the Biological Sciences Curriculum Study (BSCS), which began in 1958. A third was Man: A Course of Study (MACOS), an ambitious social science curriculum development project, which began in 1959 but received its first substantial funding from the Ford Foundation in 1962 and NSF support for teacher training in 1969 (Elmore, 1993; Marsh, 1964; Grobman, 1969; Dow, 1991). These were among the largest and most ambitious of the curriculum reform projects but by no means the only ones.

From the beginning, these curriculum reformers were clear that they aimed to change the core of American schooling, and their aspirations were not fundamentally different from the early progressives. They envisioned teachers becoming coaches and co-investigators with students into the basic phenomena of the physical, biological, and social sciences. Students' work was to focus heavily on experimentation, inquiry, and study of original sources. The notion of the textbook as the repository of conventional knowledge was to be discarded, and in its place teachers were to use carefully developed course materials and experimental apparatus that were keyed to the big ideas in the areas under study. The object of study was not the assimilation of facts, but learning the methods and concepts of scientific inquiry by doing science in the same way that practitioners of science would do it.

The curriculum development projects grew out of the initiatives of university professors operating from the belief that they could improve the quality of incoming university students by improving the secondary school curriculum. Hence, university professors tended to dominate the curriculum development process, often to the detriment of relations with the teachers and school administrators who were expected to adopt the curricula once they were developed and tested in sample sites. The projects succeeded to varying degrees in engaging actual teachers in the development process, as opposed to simply having teachers field-test lessons that had already been developed. Teachers were engaged in one way or another at the developmental stage in all projects, but were not always co-developers. In PSSC, a few teachers judged to be talented enough to engage the MIT professors involved in the project were part of the development process, but the main involvement of teachers came at the field-testing stage, and their feedback proved to be too voluminous to accommodate systematically in the final product (Marsh, 1964). In MACOS, one school in the Boston area was a summer test site and teachers were engaged in the curriculum project relatively early in the process of development. Later versions of the curriculum were extensively tested and marketed in schools throughout the country (Dow, 1991).

By far the most ambitious and systematic involvement of teachers as co-developers was in BSCS. BSCS was designed to produce three distinct versions of a secondary biology curriculum (biochemical, ecological, and cellular) so that schools and teachers could have a choice of which approach to use. The development process was organized into three distinct teams, each comprising an equal number of university professors and high school biology teachers; each lesson or unit was developed by a pair comprising one professor and one secondary teacher; and each of these units was reviewed and critiqued by another team comprising equal partners. After the curriculum was developed, the teachers who participated in development were drafted to run study groups of teachers using the curriculum units during the school year, and the results of these study groups were fed back into the development process. Interestingly, once the curriculum was developed, NSF abandoned funding for the teacher study groups. NSF's rationale was that the teachers had accomplished their development task, but this cut-off effectively eliminated the potentially most powerful device for changing teaching practice (Grobman, 1969; Elmore, 1993).

Evaluations of the NSF-sponsored curriculum development projects generally conclude that their effects were broad but shallow. Hundreds of thousands of teachers and curriculum directors were trained in summer institutes. Tens of thousands of curriculum units were disseminated. Millions of students were exposed to at least some product or byproduct of the various projects. In a few schools and school systems, teachers and administrators made a concerted effort to transform curriculum and teaching in accord with the new ideas, but in most instances, the results looked like what Cuban (1984) found in his study of progressive teaching practices: a weak, diluted, hybrid form emerged in some settings, in which new curricula were shoe-horned into old practices, and in most secondary classrooms, the curricula had no impact on teaching and learning at all (see, for example, Stake, Easely, et al., 1978; Elmore, 1993). Although the curriculum development projects produced valuable materials that are still a resource to many teachers and definitely shaped peoples' conceptions of the possibilities of secondary science curriculum, their tangible impact on the core of American schooling has been negligible.

Most academic critics agree that the curriculum development projects embodied a naive, discredited, and badly conceived model of how to influence teaching practice. The model, if there was one, was that "good" curriculum and teaching practice was self-explanatory and self-implementing. Once teachers and school administrators recognized the clearly superior ideas embodied in the new curricula, they would simply switch from traditional textbooks to the new materials and change long-standing practices because they would be improving their teaching and improving the chances of their students succeeding in school.

What this model overlooked, however, was the complex process by which local curricula decisions get made, the entrenched and institutionalized political and commercial relationships that support existing textbook-driven curricula, the weak incentives operating on teachers to change their practices in their daily work routines, and the extraordinary costs of making large-scale, long-standing changes of a fundamental kind in how knowledge is constructed in classrooms. In the few instances where advocates for the curriculum development projects appeared to be on the verge of discovering a way to change practice on a large scale—as in the BSCS teacher study groups, for example—they failed to discern the significance of what they were doing because they saw themselves as developers of new ideas about teaching and not as institution-changing actors.

The structural pattern that emerges from the large-scale curriculum development projects is strikingly similar to that of the progressive period. First, the ideas were powerful and engaging, and they found their way into tangible materials and into practice in a few settings. In this sense, the projects were a remarkable achievement in the social organization of knowledge, pulling the country's most sophisticated thinkers into the orbit of public education and putting them at work on the problem of what students should know and be able to do. But, second, the curriculum developers proved to be inept and naive in their grasp of the individual and institutional issues of change associated with their reforms. They assumed that a "good" product would travel into American classrooms on the basis of its merit, without regard to the complex institutional and individual factors that might constrain its ability to do so. Third, their biggest successes were, in a sense, also their biggest failures. Those few teachers who became accomplished teachers of PSSC physics, BSCS biology, or MACOS approaches to social studies served only to confirm what most educators think about talent in the classroom. A few have it, most do not. A few have the extraordinary energy, commitment, and native ability required to change their practice in some fundamental way; most others do not. The existence of exemplars, without some way of capitalizing on their talents, only reinforces the notion that ambitious teaching is an individual trait, not a professional expectation.

What Changes?

Critics of this argument posit that American schools have changed in fundamental ways over the last 100 years and that focusing on the fate of what I have characterized as "good" classroom practice gives a biased picture. To be sure, schools have changed massively over the last century. David Cohen argues, for example, that in the critical period of the early twentieth century, when the secondary school population increased fourfold in three decades, massive institutional changes were necessary to accommodate newly arrived students. Larger, more complex schools, a more differentiated curriculum, and grading and retention practices designed to hold adolescents out of the labor force were just a few of those changes (Powell, Farrar, and Cohen, 1985). Vocational education emerged in the post–World War I era as a mechanism to bind schools more closely to the economy and to provide a more differentiated curriculum for a diverse student body. Kindergartens emerged on a large scale in the 1940s and 1950s, extending the period of life when children are legitimately in school to the earlier years and altering the relationship between the family and school in important ways. The equity-based reforms of the 1960s and 1970s revealed the limits of earlier approaches to equality of opportunity, and new programs addressed the needs of students with disadvantaged backgrounds, students with physical and learning problems, and students whose native language is other than English. In brief, this critique states that we face a much different educational system now than we did in the early decades of the twentieth century, and surely these changes have had a significant impact on how teachers teach and how students learn.

I am inclined to agree with those who take an institutional perspective on educational change (Meyer and Rowan, 1978; March and Olsen, 1989; Cuban, 1990; Tyack and Tobin, 1994; Tyack and Cuban, forthcoming). In brief, this argument states that it is possible, indeed practically imperative, for institutions to learn to change massively in their surface structures while changing little at their core. Institutions use their structures to buffer and assimilate the changing demands of a political and social order that is constantly in flux: they add new programs, they develop highly visible initiatives that respond to prevailing opinions in the community, they open new units in the organization to accommodate new clients, they mobilize and organize public opinion by creating new governance structures. But the gap between these institutional structures and the core patterns of schooling I described at the beginning remains slippery and elusive, and the core patterns of schooling remain relatively stable in the face of often massive changes in the structure around them. Hence, schools legitimize themselves with their various conflicting publics by constantly changing their external structures and processes, but they shield their workers from any fundamental impact of these changes by leaving the core intact—hence, the resilience of practice within the context of constant institutional change.

The Role of Incentives

Nested within this broad framework of institutional and political issues is a more specific problem of incentives that reforms need to crack in order to get at the problem of scale. Institutional structures are represented in the behavior of individuals in part through incentives. The institution and its political context set the values and rewards that individuals respond to within their daily work life. Further, as David Cohen (this volume) cogently argues in his discussion of rewards for teacher performance, incentives have to operate on individual values; that is, what the individual values determines to some degree what the institution can elicit with incentives. For example, if teachers or students do not value student academic performance, do not see the relationship between academic performance and personal objectives, or do not believe it is possible to change student performance, then it is hard to use rewards or penalties to motivate them to action that would improve performance.

Thus, individual acts like the practice of teaching in complex institutional settings emanate both from incentives that operate on the individual and the individual's willingness to recognize and respond to those incentives as legitimate. Individual actions are also a product of the knowledge and the competence that the individual possesses. As Michael Fullan has argued, schools routinely undertake reforms for which they have neither the institutional nor the individual competence, and they resolve this problem by trivializing the reforms, changing the language they use and the superficial structures around the practice, without changing the practice itself (Fullan, 1982; Fullan and Miles, 1992). Individuals are embedded in institutional structures that provide them with incentives to act in certain ways, and they respond to these incentives by testing them against their values and their competence.

One way of thinking about the aforementioned evidence I have outlined here is that it demonstrates a massive failure of schools to harness their institutional incentives to the improvement of practice. I think this failure is rooted not only in the design of the institutions, but also in a deep cultural norm about teaching that I have referred to earlier—namely, that successful teaching is an individual trait rather than a set of learned professional competencies acquired over the course of a career.

Both the progressive reformers and the curriculum reformers of the 1950s and 1960s focused their energies on connecting powerful ideas to practice, developing exemplars of good practice, and attracting true believers. These efforts largely failed—often in very interesting and instructive ways—to translate their ideas into broadscale changes in practice. A very large incentive problem is buried in this strategy, and it is this: reform strategies of this kind rely on the intrinsic motivation of individuals with particular values and competencies, and a particular orientation toward the outside world, to develop and implement reforms in schools.

These intrinsically motivated individuals are typically highly engaged in the world outside their workplace; hence, they come in contact with the opportunities presented by new practices. They usually are willing to invest much of their own time in learning new ways to think about their practice and in the messy and time-consuming work of getting others to cooperate in changing their practice. And perhaps, most important, they see their own practice in a broader social context, and they see certain parts of that social context as having authority over how they practice. Progressive teachers and school-builders, for example, saw themselves as participants in a broad movement for social reform, and they were willing to evaluate their own work in terms of its consistency with the goals of that reform (Tyack and Hansot, 1982). Some teachers who were directly involved in the curriculum reform projects formed an identity as science or math teachers affiliated with professional organizations that had authority and influence over their practice. The problem of incentives is that these individuals are typically a small proportion of the total population of teachers. The demands required by this kind of ambitious, challenging, and time-consuming work seems at best formidable, and at worst hopelessly demanding. Fruedrich Engels once said that the problem with socialism is that it spoils too many good evenings at home. One could say the same about the reform of educational practice.

Ambitious and challenging practice in classrooms thus occurs roughly in proportion to the number of teachers who are intrinsically motivated to question their practice on a fundamental level and look to outside models to improve teaching and learning. The circumstantial evidence suggests that, at the peak of reform periods, this proportion of teachers is roughly 25 percent of the total population, and that it can decline to considerably less than that if the general climate for reform is weak (Cuban, 1984). Our most successful and ambitious strategies of reform, then, embody incentive structures that can mobilize, at most, roughly one-fourth of the total population of teachers.

Given this interpretation of the evidence, then, it is possible to see what the enormous power of a cultural norm can be that describes successful teaching as an individual attribute rather than a body of deliberately acquired professional knowledge and skills. If what a teacher does is based wholly or largely on individual traits, it is highly unlikely that the incentive structures of schools could alter the proportion of teachers willing to engage in ambitious prac- tice, other than changing the composition of the teaching force.

It is also possible to see the perverse incentives buried in typical reform strategies. The first step serious reformers typically take involves gathering up the faithful and concentrating them in one place in order to form a cohesive community of like-minded prac- titioners. In the case of the progressives, reformers started schools that embodied their ideas. In the case of the curriculum reform- ers, projects focused on early adopters of their new curricula as exemplars of success. This strategy immediately isolates the teach- ers who are most likely to change from those who are least likely to embrace reform. This dynamic creates a social barrier between the two, virtually guaranteeing that the former will not grow in number, and the latter will continue to believe that only the excep- tional teacher with exceptional resources in an exceptional envi- ronment can do what exemplary teachers do.

One can see vestiges of this perverse incentive structure in the way current school reform movements are designed. These reforms typically begin with a few teachers in a building and nurture a dis- tinctive identity among those teachers, or construct a new school from scratch and recruit teachers who are highly motivated to join the faculty. Both strategies guarantee the isolation of the small frac- tion of teachers who are willing to engage in change from the ma- jority who find it an intimidating and threatening prospect. And both strategies are likely to instigate conflict between the two groups of teachers that renders the scaling up of this reform highly unlikely.

Without some fundamental change in the incentive structure under which schools and teachers operate, we will continue more or less indefinitely to repeat the experience of the progressives and the curriculum reformers. Like our predecessors, we will design reforms that appeal to the intrinsic values and competencies of a relatively small proportion of the teaching force. We will gather these teachers together in ways that cut them off from contact and connection with those who find ambitious teaching intimidating and infeasible. We will demonstrate that powerful ideas can be har- nessed to changes in practice in a small fraction of settings, but con- tinue to fail in moving those practices beyond the group of teachers who are intrinsically motivated and competent to engage in them.

Working on the Problem of Scale

What might be done to change this self-reinforcing incentive structure? Probably the first step is to acknowledge that social problems of this complexity are not amenable to quick, comprehensive, rational solutions. We learn how to make fundamental changes in patterns of incentives not by engaging in ambitious discontinuous reforms but rather by pushing hard in a few strategic places in the system of relations surrounding the problem and then carefully observing the results. My recommendations will be of this sort.

Furthermore, it seems important to continue to do what has yielded success in the past and to continue to do it with increasing sophistication. I have argued that the most successful part of the progressive and curriculum reform strategies was the creation of powerful connections between big ideas, with large social implications, and the microworld of teaching practice. The progressives succeeded in creating versions of educational reform that both exemplified what progressivism was about and embodied concrete changes in the core of schooling. Likewise, the curriculum reformers succeeded in harnessing the talent of the scientific elite to the challenge of secondary school curriculum and teaching.

This connection between the big ideas and the fine grain of practice in the core of schooling is a fundamental precondition for any change in practice. Capacity to make these connections waxes and wanes and probably depends too heavily on the idiosyncrasies of particular individuals with a particular scientific or ideological ax to grind. One could imagine doing a much better job of institutionalizing the connection between big ideas and teaching practice. Samples might include routine major national curriculum reviews with groups comprising equal numbers of university researchers and school teachers, or a national curriculum renewal agenda that targeted particular parts of teaching and curriculum for renewal on a regular cycle. The more basic point, however, is that preserving the connection between big ideas and teaching practice, embodied in earlier reform strategies, is an essential element in tackling the problem of scale.

With these ideas as context, I offer four main proposals for how to begin to tackle the problem of scale. Each grows out of an earlier line of analysis in this paper, and each embodies an argument about how incentives should be realigned to tackle the problem of scale.

Develop Strong External Normative Structures for Practice

The key flaw in earlier attempts at large-scale reform, I have argued, was to rely almost exclusively on the intrinsic commitment of talented and highly motivated teachers to carry the burden of reform. Coupled with strong cultural norms about good teaching being an individual trait, this strategy virtually guarantees that good practice will stay with those who learn and will not travel to those who are less predisposed to learn. One promising approach, then, is to create strong professional and social normative structures for good teaching practice that are external to individual teachers and their immediate working environment, and to provide a basis for evaluating how many teachers are approximating good practice at what level of competence.

I use the term *external normative structures,* rather than a term like standards, because I think these structures should be very diverse, and they need to be constructed on different bases of authority in order to be useful in influencing teaching practice. The category of external structures could include formal statements of good practice such as content and performance standards developed by professional bodies, such as the National Council of Teachers of Mathematics standards. External structures might also include alternative credentialing systems, such as the National Board for Professional Teaching Standards.

But strong external structures could also include less imposing and more informal ways of communicating norms of good practice. For example, curriculum units designed to demonstrate more advanced forms of practice could be accompanied by videotapes of teachers engaging in these practices, and then disseminated through teacher organizations. These external normative structures can be hooked to internal systems of rewards for teachers: salary increments for staff development related to changes in practice, released time to work on curriculum or performance standards, time to develop curriculum units that embody particular approaches to teaching, or opportunities to engage in demonstration teaching. There is no particular requirement for unanimity, consistency, or "alignment" among these various external structures, only that they embody well-developed notions of what it means for teachers to teach and students to learn at high levels of competency in a given area. The important feature of these structures is not their unanimity or consistency, which is probably illusory anyway, but the fact that the structures are external to the world in which teachers work, they form their ideas about practice, and they carry some form of professional authority.

The existence of external norms is important because it institutionalizes the idea that professionals are responsible for looking outward at challenging conceptions of practice in addition to looking inward at their values and competencies. Good teaching becomes a matter for public debate and disagreement, for serious reflection and discourse, for positive and negative feedback about one's own practices. Over time, as this predisposition to look outward becomes more routinized and ingrained, trait theories of teaching competence should diminish. Teachers would begin increasingly to think of themselves as operating in a web of professional relations that influence their daily decisions rather than as solo practitioners inventing practice out of their personalities, experiences, and assessments of their own strengths and weaknesses. Without some kind of external normative structure, teachers have no incentive to think of their practice as anything other than a bundle of traits. The existence of strong external norms also has the effect of legitimating the proportion of teachers in any system who draw their ideas about teaching from a professional community and who compare themselves against a standard external to their school or community. External norms give visibility and status to those who exemplify them.

Develop Organizational Structures That Intensify and Focus, Rather Than Dissipate and Scatter, Intrinsic Motivation to Engage in Challenging Practice

The good news about existing reform strategies is that they tend to galvanize commitment among the already motivated by concentrating them in small groups of true believers who reinforce each other. The bad news is that these small groups of self-selected reformers apparently seldom influence their peers. This conclusion suggests that structures should, at a minimum, create diversity among the energetic, already committed reformers and the skeptical and timid. But it also suggests that the unit of work in an organization that wants to change its teaching practice should be small enough so that members can exercise real influence over each others' practice. Certain types of structures are more likely than others to intensify and focus norms of good practice—organizations in which face-to-face relationships dominate impersonal, bureaucratic ones; organizations in which people routinely interact around common problems of practice; and organizations that focus on the results of their work for students rather than on the working conditions of professionals. These features can be incorporated into organizations, as well as into the composition of their memberships.

Heather Lewis, an accomplished practitioner of school change with the Center for Collaborative Education in New York City, has argued that we will solve the problem of scaling-up by scaling-down.[3] By this, I think she means that more ambitious teaching practice is more likely to occur in smaller schools where adults are more likely to work collaboratively and to take common responsibility for students. Teachers in schools with a tighter sense of mutual commitment, which arguably comes with smaller size, are more likely to exert influence on each other around norms of good practice than are teachers in anonymous organizations in which bureaucratic controls are the predominant mechanism of influence.

The problem here is that there is so little structural variation in American public education that we have little conception of what kinds of structures would have this intensifying and focusing effect. The first job of structural reform should be to create more variation in structure—more small schools, more schools organized into smaller subunits, more structures that create stronger group norms inside larger schools, more ways of connecting adventurous teachers with their less ambitious and reflective colleagues—but not structures that isolate the true believers from the skeptical and timid. Absent such structures, there will be no connective tissue to bind teachers together in a relationship of mutual obligation and force them to sort out issues of practice. Organizational forms that intensify and focus group norms, without nesting them in some system of external norms of good practice, will simply perpetuate whatever the prevailing conventional wisdom about practice happens to be in a given school.

Create Intentional Processes for Reproduction of Successes

One of the major lessons from past large-scale reforms is their astounding naiveté about how to get their successes to move from one setting to another. The progressives seemed to think that a few good exemplars and a few energetic superintendents pursuing systemwide strategies of reform would ignite a conflagration that would consume all American education. If any social movement had the possibility of doing that, it was the progressive movement since it had, at least initially, a high degree of focus, a steady supply of serious intellectual capital, and an infrastructure of committed reformers. But it did not succeed at influencing more than a small fraction of schools and classrooms. The curriculum reformers thought that good curriculum models would create their own demand, an astoundingly naive idea in retrospect given what we know about the limits within which teachers work, the complex webs of institutional and political relationships that surround curriculum decisions, and the weak incentives for teachers to pay attention to external ideas about teaching practice.

This not so much a failure of a theory of how to reproduce success but the absence of a practical theory that takes account of the institutional complexities that operate on changes in practice. I am skeptical that such a theory will emerge without serious experimentation since I know of no clear a priori basis on which to construct such a theory. I suggest five theories that might serve as the basis for experimentation with processes designed to get exemplary practices to scale.

Incremental Growth

The usual way of thinking about increases in scale in social systems is incremental growth. For example, according to the incremental growth theory, the proportion of teachers teaching in a particular way would increase by some modest constant each year, until the proportion approached 100 percent. This model implies a fixed capacity for training a given number of teachers per year in an organization.

The problems with this model are not difficult to identify. The idea that new practice "takes" after a teacher has been trained is highly suspect. The notion that a fixed number of teachers could be trained to teach in a given way by circulating them through a training experience seems implausible although it is probably the way most training programs are designed. Teaching practice is unlikely to change as a result of exposure to training unless that training also brings with it some kind of external normative structure and a network of social relationships that personalize that structure and supports interaction around problems of practice. So the incremental model, if it is to work, probably needs a different kind of specification, which I will call the cumulative model.

Cumulative Growth

The cumulative model suggests that "getting to scale" is a slower, less linear process than that described by the incremental model. It involves not only creating processes that expose teachers to new practices, but also monitoring the effects of those processes on teaching practice and constructing processes that compensate the weaknesses of the initial effects. Cumulative growth not only adds an increment of practitioners who are exposed to a new practice each year, but also involves a backlog of practitioners, some of whom have responded to training by changing the way they teach, and some of whom have not. This problem requires a more complex solution than simply continuing to provide exposure to new practice at a given rate. It might require, for example, the creation of professional networks to support the practice of teachers who are in the process of changing their practice, connecting the more advanced with the less advanced through some sort of mentoring scheme.

Discontinuous Growth

Another possibility is a sharply increasing, or discontinuous, growth model. This could occur only through a process like a chain letter, in which an initial group of teachers would learn a new kind of practice, and each member of that group would work with another group, and so on, so that the rate of growth would go, for example, from x to 10x, to 100x, to 1000x, and so on.

The same problem applies to this model as applies to the

incremental growth model, but on a larger scale. As the numbers of teachers exposed to new practices goes up, so too does the backlog of teachers for whom the initial exposure was inadequate, eventually reaching the point at which this accumulation of teachers overwhelms the system. It also seems likely that the discontinuous growth model would create serious quality-control problems. As growth accelerates, it becomes more and more difficult to distinguish between teachers who are accomplished practitioners of new ways of teaching and those who are accomplished at making it appear as though they have mastered new ways of teaching.

In all the examples of growth models so far, teachers are operating in a system of relationships that provides training and support, but we have not treated them as members of organizations called schools. In addition to these three models that construct training and support around teachers, two additional models treat teachers as practitioners working in schools.

Unbalanced Growth

One of these models is the unbalanced growth model. It extends and modifies the standard model of innovation in education: collecting true believers in a few settings. Whereas the standard model socially isolates true believers from everyone else, virtually guaranteeing that new practices do not spread, versions of the unbalanced growth model correct for these deficiencies. A version of unbalanced growth might involve concentrating a critical mass of high-performing teachers in a few schools, with an explicit charge to develop each other's capacities to teach in new ways. The growth of new practice would be "unbalanced" initially because some schools would be deliberately constructed to bring like-minded practitioners together to develop their skills. Such schools might be called "pioneer schools" or "leading-edge schools" to communicate that they are designed to serve as places where new practices are developed, nurtured, and taught to an ever-increasing number of practitioners. Over time these schools would deliberately be staffed with larger proportions of less accomplished practitioners and teachers not yet introduced to new models of practice. The competencies developed in the high-performing organizations would then socialize new teachers to the norms of good practice.

The main problem with this model is that it goes against the grain of existing personnel practices in most school systems. Teaching assignments are typically made through a combination of collectively bargained seniority and principal entrepreneurship rather than on the basis of a systematic interest in using schools as places to socialize teachers to new practice. Younger teachers are typically assigned to schools with the largest proportions of difficult-to-teach children and spend their careers working their way into more desirable assignments. Principals who understand and have mastered the assignment system can often use it to gather teachers with whom they prefer to work. In order for the unbalanced growth model to work, a school system would have to devise some deliberate strategy for placing teachers in settings where they would be most likely to develop new skills. Teachers, likewise, would have to be willing to work in settings where they could learn to develop their practice as part of their professional responsibility.

Cell Division, or Reproduction

The other model of growth that treats teachers as practitioners working in schools is the cell division, or reproduction, model. This model works from the analogy of reproductive biology. Rather than trying to change teaching practice by influencing the flow of teachers through schools, as in the unbalanced growth model, the cell division model involves systematically increasing the number and proportion of schools characterized by distinctive pedagogical practices.

The cell division model would work by first creating a number of settings in which exemplary practitioners are concentrated and allowed to develop new approaches to teaching practice. Then, on a more or less predictable schedule, a number of these practitioners are asked to form another school, using the "genetic material" of their own knowledge and understanding to recruit a new cadre of teachers whom they would help educate to a new set of expectations about practice. Over time, one could imagine several such schools would surface with strong communities of teachers invested in particular approaches to teaching.[4]

The reproduction model elicits more systematic thinking about what constitutes evidence of the "spread" of good teaching practice. Given the slipperiness of attempts to replicate successful programs or practices from one setting to another, the idea of getting to scale should not be equated with the exact replication of practices that work in one setting to others. For example, when we reproduce as human beings, children are not identical replicates of the parents; rather, each child is a new human being with a distinctive personality that may bear a family resemblance to the mother and father. Furthermore, we expect children from the same family to differ quite dramatically from each other even though they may share certain traits. The reproduction model broadens notions of evidence by allowing for the dissemination of good teaching practices with "family resemblances" in different settings. It causes us to look at the fundamental process by which practices are chosen for reproduction while others are bypassed or significantly modified. It also prompts us to reproduce family resemblances in such a way as to have a meaningful impact on practice, rather than merely promoting assimilation of symbols that don't go to the core.

These alternative models of growth each embody an explicit practical theory of how to propagate or reproduce practice. They also have a kind of transparent logic that can be understood and adapted by others for use in other settings. More such theories, more documented examples of how they work in use, should help in understanding how to get to scale with successful educational practice.

Create Structures That Promote Learning of New Practices and Incentive Systems That Support Them

Reformers typically make very heroic and unrealistic assumptions about what ordinary human beings can do, and they generalize these assumptions to the population of teachers who they assume will respond in the way they are expected to. About the progressive's view of teachers, Cremin observed:

> From the beginning progressivism cast the teacher in an almost impossible role: [she] was to be an artist of consummate skill, properly knowledgeable in [her] field, meticulously trained in the science of pedagogy, and thoroughly imbued with a burning zeal for social improvement. It need hardly be said that here as elsewhere . . . the gap between the real and the ideal was appalling (1961, p. 168).

Likewise, the curriculum reformers appeared to assume that teachers, given the existence of clearly superior content, would simply use the new curricula and learn what was needed in order to teach differently. Missing from this view is an explicit model of how teachers engage in intentional learning about new ways to teach. As Fullan and Miles (1992) have said, "change involves learning and . . . all change involves coming to understand and to be good at something new." While our knowledge is not deep on this subject, it seems probable that teachers are more likely to learn from direct observation of practice and trial and error in their own classrooms than they are from abstract descriptions of new teaching; that changing teaching practice, even for committed teachers, takes a long time and several cycles of trial and error; that teachers have to feel that there is some compelling reason for them to practice differently, with the best direct evidence being that students learn better when they teach differently; and, that teachers need feedback from sources they trust about whether students are actually learning what they are taught.

These conditions are among those that one would expect to accompany the learning of any new, complicated practice. Yet reform efforts seldom, if ever, incorporate these conditions. Teachers are often tossed head-long into discussion groups to work out the practical implications of a new curriculum, without any explicit help or support with the implementation of that curriculum in the classroom. They are encouraged to develop model lessons as a group activity and then sent back to their classrooms to implement them as solo practitioners. Teachers are seldom asked to judge if this new curriculum translates well into concrete actions in the classroom, nor are they often asked to participate as co-designers of the ideas in the first place. The feedback teachers receive on the effects of their practice usually comes in the form of generalized test scores that have no relationship to the specific objectives of the new practice. In other words, the conditions under which teachers are asked to engage in new practices bear no relationship whatsoever to the conditions necessary for learning to implement new and complex practices with success. Why would anyone want to change his or her practice under such conditions?

A basic prerequisite for tackling the problem of scale, then, is to insist that reforms that purport to change practice embody an explicit theory about how human beings learn to do things differently. Presently, few, if any, well-developed theories meet this requirement although I have sketched out some earlier. Furthermore, these theories have to make sense at the individual level and the organizational level. That is, if you ask teachers to change the way they deal with students and to relate to their colleagues differently, the incentives that operate at the organizational level have to reinforce and promote those behaviors. Encouragement and support, access to special knowledge, time to focus on the requirements of the new task, and time to observe others doing it all suggest ways in which the environment of incentives in the organization comes to reflect the requirements of learning.

These four principles constitute departures from previous strategies of broad-scale reform, and they address fundamental problems of previous strategies. It is unlikely that teachers or schools will respond to the emergence of new practices any differently than they have in the past if those practices are not legitimated by norms that are external to the environment in which they work every day. It is unlikely that teachers who are not intrinsically motivated to engage in hard, uncertain work will learn to do so in large, anonymous organizations that do not intensify personal commitments and responsibilities. It is unlikely that successful practices will spontaneously reproduce themselves just because they are successful in the absence of structures and processes based on explicit theories about how reproduction occurs. And it is unlikely that teachers will be successful at learning new practices if the organizations in which they work do not embody some explicit learning theory in the way they design work and reward people. Each of these principles presents a formidable agenda for research and practice. The magnitude of the task suggests that we should not expect to see immediate large-scale adoption of promising new practices. It also suggests that progress will come from an explicit acknowledgment that the problems of scale are deeply rooted in the incentives and cultural norms of the institutions, and cannot be fixed with simple policy shifts or exhortations from people with money. The issue of getting to scale with successful educational practice requires nothing less than deliberately creating and reproducing alternatives to the existing flawed institutional arrangements and incentives structures.

Notes

1. This paper was prepared for the *CPRE Forum on Incentives and Systemic Reform,* sponsored by CPRE and the Pew Forum. It will also appear in the *Harvard Education Review* (Spring 1996). I am indebted to members of the Forum and to students and colleagues at the Harvard Graduate School of Education for their assistance in developing these ideas.

2. Dewey's own ambivalence about the connection between the exemplary practices developed in laboratory schools and the broader world of practice can be seen in his reflections on the University of Chicago Lab School:

   As it is not the primary function of a laboratory to devise ways and means that can at once be put to practical use, so it is not the primary purpose of this school to devise methods with reference to their direct application in the graded school system. It is the function of some schools to provide better teachers according to present standards; it is the function of others to create new standards and ideals and thus to lead to a gradual change in conditions (quoted in Cremin, 1961, p. 290n).

3. Remarks at Project Atlas Forum on Getting to Scale, April 3, 1995.

4. This is, in fact, the model used by the Central Park East Elementary School in New York City to create two other elementary schools to serve parents and children who could not be accommodated in the original school.

References

Cohen, D. "Teaching Practice: Plus Que ça Change." In P. Jackson (ed.), *Contributing to Educational Change: Perspectives on Research and Practice.* Berkeley, Calif.: McCutchan, 1988, pp. 27–84.

Cremin, L. *The Transformation of the American School.* New York: Knopf, 1961.

Cuban, L. *How Teachers Taught: Constancy and Change in American Classrooms, 1890–1980.* New York: Longman, 1984.

Cuban, L. "Reforming Again, Again, and Again." *Educational Researcher,* January 1990, 3–13.

Dow, P. *Schoolhouse Politics: Less from the Sputnick Era.* Cambridge, Mass.: Harvard University Press, 1991.

Elmore, R. *The Development and Implementation of Large-Scale Curriculum Reforms.* Paper prepared for the American Association for the Advancement of Science. Cambridge, Mass.: Center for Policy Research in Education, Harvard Graduate School of Education, 1993.

Elmore, R. "Teaching, Learning, and School Organization: Principles of Practice and the Regularities of Schooling." *Educational Administration Quarterly*, 1995, *31* (3), 355–374.

Fullan, M. "The Meaning of Education Change." New York: Teacher's College Press, 1982.

Fullan, M. and Miles, M. "Getting Reform Right: What Works and What Doesn't." *Phi Delta Kappan*, June 1992.

Goodlad, J. *A Place Called School*. New York: McGraw-Hill, 1984.

Grobman, A. *The Changing Classroom: The Role of the Biological Sciences Curriculum Study*. New York: Doubleday, 1969.

March, J. and Olsen, J. *Rediscovering Institutions: The Organizational Basis of Politics*. New York: Free Press, 1989.

Marsh, P. *The Physical Sciences Study Committee: A Case History of Nationwide Curriculum Development, 1956–1961*. Doctoral thesis, Graduate School of Education, Harvard University, Cambridge, Mass., 1964.

Meyer, J. and Rowan, B. *The Structure of Educational Organizations*. In Meyer, M. (ed.): *Environments and Organizations*. San Francisco: Jossey-Bass, 1978, pp. 78–109.

National Center for Education Statistics (NCES). "1993 Mathematics Report Card for the Nation and the States: Data from the National and Trial State Assessments." Washington, D.C.: U.S. Department of Education, 1993.

National Council on Excellence in Education. *A Nation at Risk*. Washington, D.C.: U.S. Department of Education, 1983.

Powell, A., Farrar, E., and Cohen, D. *The Shopping Mall High School*. Boston: Houghton Mifflin, 1985.

Tyack, D. and Tobin, W. "The 'Grammar' of Schooling: Why Has It Been So Hard to Change?" *American Educational Research Journal*, 1994, *31*, 453–479.

Tyack, D. and Cuban, L. *Tinkering Toward Utopia: Reflections on a Century of Public School Reform*. Cambridge, Mass.: Harvard University Press, forthcoming.

Tyack, D. and Hansot, E. *Managers of Virtue: Public School Leadership in America, 1820–1980*. New York: Basic Books, 1982.

Chapter Ten

Conclusion: Building a Better System of Incentives

Susan H. Fuhrman

The chapters in this book underscore the complex nature of educational reform. If reform is about changing teaching and learning to focus more on understanding and applying knowledge, then all those involved in the educational enterprise must learn how to promote those goals. Teachers must learn to teach in much more ambitious ways; students must take greater responsibility for their own learning; educators and policy makers must learn how to organize and manage schools and systems to support such improvements in teaching and learning. Not only is educational improvement a matter of "education" for all concerned, but also the learning should take place in a mutually reinforcing way so that various parts of the system support the improvement efforts of other parts. This is what is meant by "systemic reform" as it is used throughout this book.

Increasingly, it appears that policy makers and practitioners are acknowledging the complexity of reform and are planning for the learning that needs to take place if reform is to become reality. For example, the widespread interest in professional development, including the efforts of several states to set aside funds specifically for that purpose, indicates that policy makers are aware of the challenges involved in changing instructional practice.

However, many of the policy interventions to support teacher learning or to improve the capacity of systems to manage and operate schools in a manner consistent with reforms are partial rather than systemic. For example, reformers provide assistance—money, time, technical advice—to teachers and other educators; policy makers fund volunteering schools to reform and make their activities available to others as demonstrations; and, increasingly, reform advocates develop curriculum frameworks, model lessons, and guides to serve as resources for reform. All these approaches focus on supplying knowledge and skills for improvement, but they slight the question of whether educators will seize on the opportunities provided, of whether they are motivated to improve capacity.

Why should teachers, other educators, and policy makers set about the difficult journey of reform and seek the knowledge they need to change their practice? What will move them to do so, especially since the going is likely to be rough and the trip long and tricky? As Brian Rowan argues in his chapter (Chapter 6), many current reforms seem to assume that the promulgation of ambitious standards will, in themselves, inspire teachers to reform—an unproven assertion. When it comes to motivation, policy makers are relying heavily on accountability systems that reward or penalize schools for student performance on the standards. But new accountability systems are difficult to design and raise many technical, implementation, and political issues (Elmore, Abelmann, and Fuhrman, 1995). Other reforms, such as deregulation, choice, and charter schools, set about altering the governance structure in ways that are also assumed to improve motivation, but, at least initially, these reforms tend to attract the already motivated, those already committed to reform and using newfound autonomy to promote it (Witte, forthcoming; Fuhrman and Elmore, 1995).

The contributors to this book argue that motivation for reform is just as complex a topic as the reform movement itself. Incentives are not simply matters of standards and linked accountability, nor are they simply matters of removing barriers so that entrepreneurial types can flex their muscles.

Motivation is a matter of organization and management as well as policy, and it is influenced by the larger context in ways beyond the reach of any of those fields of endeavor. Motivational issues concern all involved, including parents and citizens beyond the reach of traditional educational policy instruments. Motivation is constructed by both the motivator and the motivated; neither can assume an incentive will work the same for all individuals, even those within the same category, like teachers.

The complexity surrounding issues of incentives has several implications for policy and suggests a number of issues for further research. I address these implications in the following sections.

Implications for Policy and Practice

The first policy lesson derived from the preceding chapters is a caution about what can be expected from policy interventions. Many questions of incentives do not concern policy but involve larger issues of culture and norms. A second implication is that any incentive system must, in fact, function as a system in that it attends to the motivations of the range of actors, from students, to teachers, to citizens at large. Third, just as incentives must incorporate the range of targets, they must also use a range of strategies to motivate any one target audience because of the variety of individual tastes and choices within any one group of stakeholders.

Incentives and Society

Policy makers tend to think of incentives as something under their control. The popular use of the term *incentive* to mean a monetary award attached to high levels or to improved student performance, what David Cohen in his chapter (Chapter 3) calls a "performance incentive," reinforces this narrow approach to the topic. However, what motivates students to learn and teachers to teach involves so many strong currents of culture and norms that a program of financial rewards seems a very weak intercession.

As Arthur Powell (Chapter 2) puts it, "Students live within educational incentive zones that are larger than what they experience in classrooms." Family, peers, and media all influence student views of learning and the importance of schooling; so do the employment picture and the values employers and postsecondary institutions attach to doing well in school. None of these influences currently promotes excellent performance; in fact, the general culture sends strongly antiintellectual messages.

Teachers are influenced by external norms as well. Susan Mohrman and Edward Lawler (Chapter 4) speak of the skepticism of teachers, who have seen many waves of reform, about current improvement efforts. As Richard Elmore argues (Chapter 9), the historical failure of ambitious practice to take hold beyond those with the most refined taste for reform signals weak cultural support for challenging approaches to instruction. He proposes the creation of strong normative structures that set professional and social expectations for good teaching practice. But these structures are not necessarily, and probably not desirably, a question of policy; instead, they should be diverse and represent various sources of authority. For example, formal statements by professional associations can make contributions to normative structures.

Pointing out the importance, and in many cases, the overwhelming nature of norms and context does not argue for abandoning policy interventions designed at enhancing motivation. Instead, it argues for acknowledging and attending to the larger context in many different ways, including but not limited to policy. It also argues for approaches to incentives that cast a broad net, assessing the range of possible targets and strategies in a comprehensive fashion so as to identify as many points of intervention as possible, in the hopes that mutually reinforcing messages from diverse sources can overwhelm some of the antiintellectual messages sent by the broader culture. The need for a multifaceted, comprehensive approach also underlies the next two implications for policy.

Incentives and Multiple Stakeholders

The contributors to this book stress the importance of incentives for all stakeholders—students, parents, and policy makers—as well as educators. They also argue for a comprehensive approach that eschews narrow shots at a limited number of grade levels or parts of the system.

Does it make sense to penalize and reward teachers for student performance on an assessment when the students have no reasons to take the assessment seriously? Does it make sense to link incentives to performance only at three grade levels if one wants to motivate schools at every grade level? Designers of accountability systems in a number of states are struggling with such issues. In Kentucky, for example, the KIRIS accountability system includes severe stakes for only one set of stakeholders, educators, and focuses on assessments given primarily in grades four, eight, and eleven. As Richard Murnane and Frank Levy point out (Chapter 8), Vermont's approach to portfolios provides incentives for fourth-grade math teachers in different schools to learn from one another and to improve their practice, but it does not necessarily help teachers in the same elementary school to work together to develop a comprehensive educational program.

The clearest case for broadening the targets of incentives concerns students. A number of the authors contend that any system that excludes them is lopsided. Powell makes the strongest argument, contrasting our system to others that value student achievement much more strongly. His solution is multifaceted but relies strongly on holding students to the achievement of a clear core curriculum. Linda Darling-Hammond's (Chapter 5) solution to the problem of student incentives includes a more personalized school environment where teachers and students come to know each other and care about each other's work over a prolonged period.

The solution to the problem of student incentives is not a simple one, one that might be addressed simply by attaching student stakes to tests that already have stakes for teachers. Since student learning is strongly influenced by out-of-school factors, motivational approaches must consider the investment of parents in their children's education and how the economy and the broader culture reinforce achievement in school. The chapters in this book suggest that policy makers examine their incentive approaches to determine whether they place undue emphasis on one set of actors to the exclusion of others and to explore options for greater balance.

Incentives and Multiple Interpretations

Not only should incentives be conceived as systems that include many different groups of individuals, but they should also be viewed as strategies that will have varied effects within the groups they target. Individuals interpret the same incentive differently; some react as policy makers hoped, some do not. So, if policy makers wish to motivate a particular group, they need a range of strategies that will appeal to diverse individuals.

A number of the authors write about the varied impact of incentives. Cohen explores the relations between professional capability, which is unevenly distributed across teachers and schools, and response to performance incentives. Similarly, Rowan argues that the implementation of outcome standards without attending to teacher variation will mean that some people learn and use appropriate teaching strategies, but some do not. Both the teachers and the students in the schools that Darling-Hammond has studied seem to have great unity of purpose, a common interpretation of the signals coming from the external environment, and consensus about the responsibilities assumed by individuals within the community of the school. This unity is not a natural occurrence; teachers are recruited based on their acceptance of the school's mission and students elect to attend the school, thereby consenting to the school's construction of the incentive structure.

Elmore's analysis focuses centrally on the problem of differential response to incentives. If all teachers were alike in responding to invitations to reform, we would never worry about bringing reform to scale or about how to change the system. It would happen automatically. But that is not the case. We cannot seem to enlist more than 25 percent of classrooms or schools in meaningful instructional reform at any point in time, even in the case of reforms that seem to catch the popular imagination as much as the progressive reforms did. Teachers differ as individuals; not all have the same interest in reform or the same inclination to learn from demonstration models and other primary means of spreading reform ideas. The contexts in which they teach differ. Strategies that fail to attend to these differences are unlikely to lead to widespread reform.

Addressing differential responses requires constructing strategies that are multifaceted and build the notion of variation into their design. We need not only policy instruments that enhance incentives but also nonpolicy strategies, such as activities by professional associations, that reinforce and coordinate with the policy strategies. And within the category of policy interventions, we need to develop packages that include a range of approaches addressed at the same goal. Depending on how important the goal is, policy makers might construct a bundle of policies, ranging from removing barriers to changing to monetary inducements to instituting negative consequences or sanctions. Those most inclined to respond positively need little incentive beyond the creation of an opportunity; those least inclined may need a threat or punishment.

Implications for Research

The principles for policy design that are suggested by the chapters in this book provide general guidance for the development of incentive systems. More specific guidance requires more refined understandings of how incentives work in varied situations. Research on incentives should take at least three directions to build a knowledge base sufficient to inform future policy design. First, we must analyze the assumptions underlying current incentives; normative theories, no matter how logical, must be tested empirically. Second, if we are interested in systemic improvement, we must study incentives as they interact with one another in a variety of settings; individual policies cannot be studied in isolation. Third, many of the proposals for enhancing incentives cannot be examined in practice since they do not yet exist in sufficient frequency or scope; action and comparative research are required.

Incentives and Assumed Effects

Much current policy designed to enhance incentives assumes a great deal about how the strategies actually work and how targets are likely to respond. Since schooling is exceptionally bureaucratic, it is assumed that rules and procedures impede creativity. Proponents of deregulation argue that once barriers are removed, educators will embark on multiple innovations designed to improve schooling. Virtually every state is undertaking some form of deregulation, and some are proposing to essentially eliminate their education codes based on this argument. Similarly, designers of incentive rewards believe that teachers will work that much harder to improve student scores if they get bonuses as a result (Clotfelter and Ladd, 1995). But as we have seen, targets are a diverse group, and any policy intervention produces some distribution of response rather than a uniform reaction. Further, the context and historical experience influences response so that incentives may work very differently in different situations.

Research shows that the assumptions underlying popular incentives are not necessarily borne out. Not all schools take advantage of deregulation, and many that do undertake changes that would have been possible in the past (Fuhrman and Elmore, 1992; Fuhrman and Elmore, 1995). Rewards do not necessarily have much salience to teachers; in Kentucky, for example, teachers did not really expect the state to come through with the first rewards under the new accountability system, and many paid much more attention to potential sanctions than to hypothetical rewards. The rewards were actually distributed in the spring of 1995, however, and from this point forward, teachers' reactions may change (Elmore, Abelmann, and Fuhrman, 1995).

A number of authors in this volume propose studies of existing incentives to understand how they actually work in varied situations. Rowan urges studies of standards-based reforms as they develop and play out in classrooms. Can states, districts, and schools develop coherent standards? How do teachers handle inconsistencies among different standards? Murnane and Levy suggest further research on accountability and the use of new assessments in that context. How do different constructions of portfolios, such as varied use of common problems, affect their reliability? As Cohen points out, we know very little about the actual operation of performance incentive rewards. How feasible are they in terms of costs and other administrative issues? Can such systems incorporate assessments that encourage complex student performance? How does variation in the capacity for school improvement influence the development and effects of such rewards?

Incentives and Interactions

No policy intervention operates in isolation. Each new policy exerts its effects in arenas already awash in other influences—those that emanate from existing policies, from the dispositions and skills of the implementors, or from the broader socioeconomic and demographic context. Although all policies are affected by this "busyness" (Cohen, 1982), perhaps the problem of interaction is most acute for policies explicitly designed to motivate. Incentives are intended to capture attention, enough attention to affect the beliefs about personal efficacy and the relationship between work and outcomes (or expectancies, as discussed in this book by Rowan, Mohrman, and Lawler) that underlie motivation. But capturing attention in the midst of all the other signals facing teachers, students, and other stakeholders is no easy feat.

No research agenda would be complete without examining how varied incentives interact with one another, including incentives aimed at the same target and incentives aimed at different targets within the same system. Darling-Hammond elaborates a mix of intrinsic and extrinsic incentives operating in restructured schools, such as reduced pupil loads and financial support for teacher learning. How do these interact with policies, such as new standards and assessments or new supports for professional development, in various settings, and what approaches to policy design are most compatible with the incentive structures operating within reforming schools? Revamped compensation systems, such as those described by Odden (Chapter 7), may be very supportive of the norms developed by learner-centered schools, but only research will inform us if, and under what conditions, this is so. Cohen, appreciating the mix of influences affecting responses to monetary rewards, suggests that such rewards might be thought of as efforts to tip the balance of influences in the direction of increased attention to student performance. But how would such incentives operate amid other state and local policies and influences? For example, what if multiple assessments of student performance were in place? Would the measures that were part of the performance reward scheme draw all the attention, or would other influential assessments distract from the reward strategy? Would incentives in fact focus students and teachers on performance or pit them against each other because school-based incentives for academic performance would be battling social, economic, and cultural incentives for weak performance?

Examining the interaction of various incentives requires research designs that permit careful examination of the context surrounding incentive approaches. So, for example, if one were interested in monetary rewards or bonuses for school performance, one might contrast gains in student achievement between places that have such rewards and places that do not have bonuses. One might also compare gains across schools and systems operating with different designs to performance rewards. All this could be done from afar, using data and documentation of the incentive schemes provided by the school systems. However, if one wants to understand how and why the incentive actually worked or did not work, and how the surrounding policy and community environments affected the working of the incentive, much more intensive understanding of the sites, including field-based research, would be necessary. It might also be necessary to deliberately introduce incentive designs into various contexts. As I discuss in the following section, many interesting incentive interventions are still on the design drawing board and cannot be studied as naturally occurring events. Other types of research are required.

Incentives and Action or Comparative Research

Many of the ideas for enhancing incentives explored in this book require profound changes in norms or adventurous policy designs; these schemes do not yet exist in this country in sufficient frequency to study productively. If they do exist, there may be so few examples of them that it is not possible to understand how they interact with various contexts. So, for example, a few places have elements of skill-based pay, but so few that it will be hard to examine the functioning of such approaches in various communities and in conjunction with differing policy contexts unless more skill-based pay experiments are deliberately initiated. And if an incentive approach requires changing normative structures, the best way to understand its operation may be to research motivation in other normative contexts, such as other countries.

A number of the authors recommend action research or the deliberate introduction of alternative incentive designs into different policy contexts. Mohrman and Lawler propose experimenting with new forms of school organization, generating and testing models for new information systems, skills and knowledge development approaches, structures and processes for sharing power, and rewards that fit the technology and professional nature of teaching. Elmore argues for creating and researching approaches to reproduction of good practice built around explicit alternative theories of propagation. Odden recommends studies of skill-based pay that assess options for designing skill blocks and measuring and awarding attainment of skills. Given the predominance of the single salary schedule, research on skill-based pay will depend in large measure on deliberately crafted experiments that combine research and policy initiation.

The influences of culture and norms discussed by authors such as Rowan and Powell may need to be examined in a comparative context. How do other societies create incentive structures? How do normative differences influence motivation? For example, Rowan proposes research on educational organizations that are deeply engaged in standards-based management, whether these organizations are here in the United States or elsewhere, where the political and social context makes the development of coherent systems of standards more likely.

Further research should shed light on how motivation might be improved in American schools. It is likely that much of what is learned will reinforce the need for normative and cultural, as well as policy, solutions to the problem of incentives. It is also likely that research will highlight the importance of context since incentives will work differently in different situations. Beyond these general understandings, however, we have much to learn about how to craft and implement strategies that will improve the motivation of various stakeholders and how to combine these strategies so that they reinforce one another in a systemic manner. It is our hope at CPRE that this book contributes to more thorough examinations of incentives and lays the groundwork for developing more informed policy and research agendas.

References

Clotfelter, C. T. and Ladd, H. F. "Picking Winners: Recognition and Reward Programs for Public Schools." In Ladd, H. F. (ed.): *Performance-Based Strategies for Improving Schools*. Washington, D.C.: The Brookings Institution, 1995.

Cohen, D. K. "Policy and Organization: The Impact of State and Federal Educational Policy on School Governance." *Harvard Educational Review,* Special Issue, November 1982.

Elmore, R. F., Abelmann, C. H., and Fuhrman, S. H. "The New Accountability in State Education Reform: From Process to Performance." In Ladd, H. F. (ed.): *Performance-Based Strategies for Improving Schools*. Washington, D. C.: The Brookings Institution, 1995.

Fuhrman, S. H. and Elmore, R. F. "Opportunity-to-Learn Standards and the State Role in Education." *Teachers College Record,* 1995, *96* (3), 432–457.

Fuhrman, S. H. and Elmore, R. F. *Takeover and Deregulation: Working Models of New State and Local Regulatory Relationships.* New Brunswick, N.J.: Consortium for Policy Research in Education, 1992.

Witte, J. F. "Who Benefits?: The Milwaukee Parental Choice Program." In Fuller, B., Orfield, G., and Elmore, R. F. (eds.): *School Choice: The Cultural Logic of Families, the Political Rationality of Institutions.* New York: Teachers College Press, forthcoming.

Index

362 INDEX